D0758678

# Yokomitsu Riichi: Modernist

*Modern Asian Literature Series*

# Yokomitsu Riichi: Modernist

## Dennis Keene

*New York*    *Columbia University Press*    *1980*

The Japan Foundation, through a special grant, has assisted the Press in publishing this volume.

Library of Congress Cataloging in Publication Data

Keene, Dennis, 1934–
Yokomitsu Riichi, modernist.

(Modern Asian literature series)
Includes bibliographical references and index.
1. Yokomitsu, Riichi, 1898–1947—Criticism and interpretation.   2. Modernism (Literature)
I. Title.   II. Series.
PL842.05Z77        895.6′34        79-28532
ISBN 0-231-04938-2

Columbia University Press
New York        Guildford, Surrey

# Contents

# Modern Asian Literature Series

Editorial Board

# Preface

YOKOMITSU RIICHI (1898–1947) occupied a central position in the Japanese literary world during the 1920s and 1930s, and is perhaps the only serious counterpart in modern Japanese prose literature to the experimental, "modernist" writing that existed in Europe during and following the First World War. He is thus normally cited by Japanese critics now as an example of the unfortunate effects Western literature had upon his generation of writers, and he was chosen for an extended, analytical study of this kind since he seems to exemplify in a clear, even extreme, form what Western influence upon modern Japanese literature has been. This "influence," although indiscriminately and widely referred to as being there, has rarely been given any form of precise treatment, and even those accepted specific influences of one writer upon another are normally put forward as pure givens requiring neither explication nor interrogation, but merely the reader's assent. In most forms of literary study the question of influence is a marginal one attracting pedestrian minds that lack the wit to see the important questions at issue: in the case of modern Japanese literature, however, it must be a central one, for there can be little doubt that the whole nature of Japanese literature in this century has been profoundly affected from the West. Since the resulting literature looks so unlike that which has supposedly influenced it, the question then becomes one of what this influence can be considered to be.

An idea of this degree of abstraction can be illuminated only by real examples, so I have attempted to write literary criticism rather than literary history, and this has meant detailed discussion of a few texts. Most of these are available in a volume of my translations published by the University of Tokyo Press under the title of *"Love" and Other Stories of Yokomitsu Riichi*, 1974, a volume which has also been distributed under its own imprint by the Japan Foundation, so that it should be around in various libraries connected with Japanese studies, if not conspicuous in bookshops. However, the work has been written so that it should make sense even without those translations.

Literary criticism is obliged to make value judgments, and since some of those made here may appear harsh to many readers I should explain why, and also why such judgments do not diminish the overall importance of the writings I am discussing. My first interest in this author was aroused in the normal way by coming across works which I admired, but the desire to study him at length was brought about by the realization that here was a major talent which had not produced major works, and that understanding why this should have been so told one not only about other aspects of Japanese literature in this century, but also about the society as a whole, and threw light upon more general literary questions and even upon the much wider subject of cross-cultural relationships and influences.

To follow out the consequences of this basic idea about his work I have been obliged to give a selective account of it; and although I still see this as giving what one can call the central truth of his literature, it is still very much an edited account in which whole areas of his writing have been ignored, and the reader will understand, I trust, that there is more to Yokomitsu, and more to Japanese modernism as a whole, than I have implied here. I have used Yokomitsu as an example of what the introduction of European modernism into Japan in the 1920s meant, and I have mainly stressed what went wrong in that process since that seems to me the principal matter of interest. However, I should be unhappy if the reader interpreted this as meaning that nothing had gone right, or as indicating that Yokomitsu's writings were of little literary value. If that value had not been considerable his work would never have responded to the kind of literary critical treatment it has been given here, but would have been material for a historical or psychological study only. My own opinion is that his writings are at present considerably undervalued by Japanese critics who should know better, but this does not mean I was prepared to lavish praise on works which do not deserve nor need it, having much deeper interest if the truth is told about them. There has been a tendency, understandable enough, in some Western writings on modern Japanese literature, to oversell things from honorable but, I believe, misguided motives. The result is that the interest of the works in question becomes diminished, for the intelligent reader will only be annoyed when he reads the translations of those works, and then alienated into believing that the real work lies totally concealed behind its translation. There are, of course, always good reasons for believing that, but Japanese literature (certainly that of this century) is no less (and no more) available in translation than that of France or Russia, and there are no adequate reasons why one should not speak about it in the way one speaks of other foreign literatures; always assuming, of course, that we already speak about such literatures with care.

A written work presupposes a reader (or even readers), and the form this work has taken has been conditioned by the kind of readers I had in mind—they were expected to have the interests and knowledge one can expect of a normal English-speaking "literary intellectual"; thus I hoped they might have some ability to read French but assumed they would not be able to read Japanese, readers knowing something of Sainte-Beuve and Leavis, but probably nothing of Shimamura Hōgetsu or Kobayashi Hideo. Because they would be reading a book of this nature I imagined they would have some interest in, and acquaintance with, Japanese literary culture, having perhaps read *Genji*, the two Donald Keene anthologies, and a handful of other translations. Even with these limited assumptions I have still leaned in the direction of expecting too little rather than too much, so that readers with almost no knowledge of these things would only very rarely find themselves seriously in the dark. This means that I must request the forbearance of Japanese specialists, particularly as some of the other areas of interest I have assumed may be alien to them.

Quotations from the French have been retained in the original, although English translations have at all times been provided. (I would advise the reader not to read them unless he really has to.) This retention of the original French serves three purposes. First, it provides the reader, by way of a foreign language he knows, with a continual and experienced reminder of the fact that foreign languages exist and that the works being dealt with are, in fact, written in one. It is true there is always the danger of the contrary function being performed by making the Japanese texts seem actually closer than the French ones, rather in the way that some dubbed American films on Japanese television create an unjustified sense of audience involvement, for the American soldiers speak Japanese (although they occasionally ask French girls for no good reason if they speak English), while the "enemy" bark away in unintelligible German. The danger is admitted but, other than give the Japanese quotations in the original, and thus in a language already presupposed as unreadable, there seemed no better way since I wished to keep the Japanese and French quotations distinct from each other. Secondly, the image of the modern writer taken over by the Japanese is much more French than English, and a reminder of this is provided by the French quotations, the stress upon Flaubert, perhaps the principal source of this image both in the West and in Japan, being made for the same reason. Third, stylistic questions make up an important part of this work, and clearly quotations were to be retained in the original as far as feasible.

Every attempt has been made to avoid littering the text with Japanese terms, the exception being the word *Shinkankakuha*, which has been left untranslated, not only because it occupies a central position in this work, but also finally because it defied translation. The "accepted" translation (the Kenkyusha dic-

tionaries, and elsewhere), "Neo-Sensualist Group," is quite unsatisfactory since "Neo" gives the wrong associations and "Sen-
sualist" is a serious error, for the group (in theory certainly) were
actually opposed to the "sensuality" of earlier writers, a point
taken up in chapter 3. "New Sensation Group" would be the literal translation but sounds much too odd for one to consider
seriously using, principally because the word "sensation" carries
implications in English which the word *kankaku* does not have in
Japanese. *Kankaku* means "sensation" in the everyday sense of a
"feeling" (not so much an emotion as a sense of things, something that does not go readily into words like an idea), and at the
period of time in question it had started to be used as the word
whereby to translate the Western philosophical concept of "sense
impression." The literary aim of the group (again theoretically)
was that the world should be presented by sense impressions as
they are directly received and not as they are mediated by the
mind or the emotions or the sensibility. The word *shin* meaning
"new" tended to be used even more widely and indiscriminately
at that time than it is now. It is no more descriptive a usage than
calling a form of literary criticism fashionable during the 1930s
and later "The New Criticism." Rather than worry over its meaning it will be better to regard it merely as a name and not as a
descriptive definition, in the way that one does, or should do,
with "Metaphysical Poetry," and so it is left untranslated here.

This work was originally written as a doctoral dissertation
about twice the length of the form it has taken here. I owe thanks
to Dr. Brian Powell, who supervised it, and also to Mr. Kenneth
Strong, Dr. Janine Yamamoto and Dr. Richard Bowring who read
the original manuscript and made comments upon it. My pro-
foundest thanks, however, must go to Professor Donald Keene
for the continuing interest he has shown in this work, and the efforts he has made to enable me to get it published.

Finally I should point out that most of the scholarly appara-
tus of the original (footnotes, additional notes, lengthy bibliography, and the scrupulous effort to justify and support even quite
minor points) has been disposed of since I could imagine very
few people who would be interested in it. For those very few I

can only refer them to the D. Phil. thesis "Yokomitsu Riichi and the Shinkankakuha" in the Bodleian library, or suggest they write to me personally about anything which they would like to have clarified.

## Note

Japanese names are given in the Japanese order of surname first. Long vowels have been marked with a macron except in the case of a few place names, Tokyo, Kobe, etc., which have been assimilated into the English language.

## Abbreviations

| | |
|---|---|
| *Kawade Collected* | *Yokomitsu Riichi Zenshū.* 12. vols. Tokyo: Kawade Shobō, 1955–56. |
| *Kaizo Collected* | *Yokomitsu Riichi Zenshū.* 23 vols. Tokyo: Kaizōsha, 1948–1951. |
| *Selected* | Yokomitsu Riichi. *Nihon no Bungaku 37.* Tokyo: Chūōkōronsha, 1966. |
| *Love* | *"Love" and Other Stories of Yokomitsu Riichi.* Translated and with an introduction by Dennis Keene. Tokyo: University of Tokyo Press and Japan Foundation, 1974; paperback edition 1979. |

# Yokomitsu Riichi: Modernist

*Modern Asian Literature Series*

I first began by writing poems, then plays, then symbolist novels, then novels of pure description. I then worked on ways of heightening the sense of reality in my writings, then I went back to symbolism again which was my "Shinkankakuha Period." And now I'm back to realism again, where I want to settle down for a bit.

Implicit in this was a changing way of looking at the world, at things. At first objects were seen in a fantasy world, and then I concerned myself with attempting to see them in the normal, everyday way. I gradually lost interest in that, and attempted to see things in personal terms, using the viewpoint of the self as the basis for description. However, that also became uninteresting, so I concentrated on the way the sensations take in the world. While attempting this I got an obsession with structure, with seeing things as a whole, as a form. Yet recently I've got rather tired of that too.

Yokomitsu[1]

# Chapter One: Situation

Ne me parlez pas du réalisme, du naturalisme ou de l'expérimental. J'en suis gorgé. Quelles vides inepties.

Flaubert*[2]

YOKOMITSU RIICHI WAS born in 1898, at a time when Japan's transformation into a modern industrial and military state was beginning, and also when the changeover from the old literary style to the new colloquial one was under way. The year 1898 saw the publication of *Konjiki Yasha* (The Gold Demon) by Ozaki Kōyō, in which the author reverted to the literary style after an experiment two years earlier with the colloquial, almost as an indication that he had no desire to participate in the modern world; but in the same year appeared *Musashino* by Kunikida Doppo, which showed a

*Don't talk to me about realism or naturalism or the experimental. I am sick of all that. What empty, inept words they are.

shift to the colloquial in contrast to the literary style in which he had written in the previous year. It is true that Futabatei Shimei had used a form of the colloquial style ten years earlier, but it was not until Kunikida that the style was written with ease, and it was not fully established as a medium in which a writer could truly extend himself until the example of Shiga Naoya in the second decade of the twentieth century. What in effect happened during the first decade of this century was that the colloquial style became the literary medium at the same time that "Naturalism" became *the* literary movement, and there can be little question that the two were linked together.

There is no intention here of writing a history of modern Japanese literature. Instead what is to be described is the situation in which a writer who was twenty-five years old at the time of the Great Kanto Earthquake would have found himself, and by situation is meant primarily the literary situation, the questions of how one should write, what one should write, and even if one should write at all. These questions became peculiarly acute during the early years of the 1920s, for reasons that were social as well as purely literary. These years saw suicides by two distinguished writers, which seemed to indicate a widespread feeling that literature was played out, that one would be better off as a farmer or a hairdresser, and a consequent move on the part of the majority of writers towards literature as some form of action, either as a method of changing society, the writing of proletarian literature, or as a way of making money, writing popular novels for the new organs of mass communication.

In contrast, what marked earlier generations was their confidence in their role as writers. This is as true of the Naturalist group of writers (Shimazaki Tōson, Tokuda Shūsei, Tayama Katai, all born around 1870) as of the "Shirakaba" group (Shiga Naoya, Mushakōji Saneatsu, Satomi Ton, all born around 1885). By the time the third generation of modern Japanese writers, those born around 1900, had reached maturity, Japanese literature had reached some form of impasse. The Shinkankakuha was an attempt to break out of this.

Now this does of course sound as if literary history is being written (literary movements, literary generations, impasses out of which one breaks), and one reasonably questions the relevance of this kind of concern to the study of literature. For example, the real history of the French novel from 1860 to 1920 is the names of a few novelists, and yet literary history will talk about *le roman de mœurs sociales, le roman artiste, catholique, collectif, lyrique, dramatique, synthétique, naturaliste, à thèse, psychologique, social, romanesque, historique.*[3] What one is being given is the detritus of literary fashion, something of quite marginal interest when put beside the achievement of, say, Proust, and which is not particularly illuminating about that achievement either. In the case of modern Japanese writers, however, there is a degree of self-consciousness about their situation as writers which it would be difficult to find among their (admittedly also self-conscious) European contemporaries, and this is a self-consciousness that seems to have been imposed upon them by their historical situation. The attempt to make some kind of systematic sense out of twentieth-century Japanese literature is not only a concern of professional critics, but was, and still is, a deep concern of the writers who actually create that literature. Also, of course, any writer writes in a historical situation which affects his art: there were possibilities open to Proust that were not open to Flaubert; and yet the value of their work must also depend to a considerable extent upon the way in which they were able to withdraw from that situation. Eventually the historical situation as seen in relationship to their novels becomes certainly a limiting factor, even a part of the meaning of their work; but it seems to be irrelevant to our reasons for wanting to read it. Whereas a writer of an inferior kind, De Goncourt, Barrès, for example, becomes his own historical situation insofar as the meaning of his work is little more than that very situation. It is indeed this fact which underlines the lack of importance of such a writer as a novelist.

Now a modern Western writer can transcend his historical situation because he has a long and living literary tradition upon which to rely, something which a modern Japanese writer does not have. It is not being claimed that there is no literary tradition, since there is indeed a great one, nor is it being claimed that a Japanese writer can get no kind of support from the Japanese literary past, since indeed he can, as Tōson, Yokomitsu, and others have done from the example of Bashō. Yet when a young English poet starts to write he can feel English writers from Shakespeare onward controlling his pen; a young French writer such as Raymond Radiguet can turn to Mme de La Fayette in the way that a young Japanese writer cannot turn to Ihara Saikaku. In the early years of the Meiji era turning to Saikaku was a possibility, and in fact Ozaki Kōyō and others did so, but this was a retreat from the imported idea of the novel as a serious form of literature back to the native tradition of the novel as a form of amusement. One could certainly say that it was a continuation of that tradition rather than a retreat, but, whatever one says, it was still a dead end. It is also true that a later writer like Nagai Kafū dreamed of being a traditional *gesaku* ("fiction") writer, but he was perfectly aware that this was only a form of defeat on his part.

For modern Japanese literature, as for moden Japanese society as a whole, the overwhelming fact is the presence of the West, and principally of the contemporary West. The following is Tayama Katai's description of his own encounter with Western literature:

Three thousand years of insularity, of *Bushidō* and Confucianism, of Buddhism and superstition, of the conflict between duty and human feelings, of humiliating suffering and endurance, of the world of compromise and the little quiet pleasures of social life: and it was into this world that there came the magnificent thunder of Nietzsche, the rebellion of Ibsen, the self of Tolstoy, the dissection of Zola. Of course there is always the question of whether this was correctly understood, of to what degree it was understood, of to what degree it was twisted and contorted by us. Those questions I cannot answer, and yet it was a fact that into a Japanese literature that had only known writers like Chikamatsu and Saikaku this hurricane started to blow.[4]

What is most noticeable about this is its vagueness, as one should expect, and the writer's lack of concern with the question of whether the foreign literature had been misunderstood or not. He is probably justified in this, since the concept of misunderstanding is not a useful one when talking about literary influences between different cultures. If, for example, one considers one of the most fruitful influences in Western literary history, that of Poe upon the French symbolists, this could clearly be called some kind of misunderstanding, and yet to do so would be to trivialize it, which would be of little assistance in the reading of a poet of the stature of Mallarmé. If Mallarmé is considered as having "got Poe wrong," one naturally wonders what form "getting Poe right" would have taken. Again, if one looks at Poe's literary theories, over which it is hard to enthuse, and then wonders how the impressive literary theories of Mallarmé could have anything to do with them, one implies a mechanistic view of literary influence which could not apply to a living man who is seriously engaged every day in the act of writing and in thoughts about that act.

In the case of Tayama Katai we have an account of how he came to write his novel *Futon* (The Bedclothes).[5] He describes how the Western literature that he had read (Tolstoy, Strindberg, Ibsen, Nietzsche) had given him the desire to fight against the world and against himself, and that he had felt an affinity with the hero of Hauptmann's play *Einsame Menschen* (Lonely Lives). It is of some interest here that his sense of affinity is not with the writer Hauptmann but with a character created by that writer. This hero is a man concerned with "modern thought," whose wife is his intellectual inferior. A girl student from Russia shares his interests and she comes to stay in his house. Since their relationship cannot remain on a purely Platonic level, the hero, in despair, drowns himself in the lake. Tayama's *The Bedclothes* is about a middle-aged writer (i.e., himself) and his relationship with a young girl student who lodges in his house, since she also wishes to become a writer. Much of the book is about this girl's relationship with a young student, a relationship she confesses to her "teacher," who all the time desires her for himself. Nothing is done or said, the girl returns to her home in the country, upon which the writer goes upstairs and buries his head in her bedclothes.

The connection with Hauptmann is marginal despite certain obvious plot similarities, and it is so because all that Tayama has really taken from him is a theme, that of breaking with the past and setting out upon a new road, a theme he could have found in practically all the Western writers he read. Tayama, like his hero, set out upon no new road in any practical terms, since he saw his task as a preparation for that departure. The destruction of his old self was to be accomplished by the act of confessing his own moral ugliness. What was to be exposed was that even a respected teacher could have lustful thoughts, and the novel certainly caused a sensation at the time. It is difficult to think much of the book now (as Tayama himself later admitted), but it is generally agreed among Japanese critics that this book, because of its confessional nature, determined the road that Japanese literature was to take.

Tayama took nothing specific from Hauptmann, and the true significance of this anecdote is that when he thinks about literature he immediately thinks about Western literature. It is an all-pervasive idea, indeed a form of reflex rather than an idea, very much in the same way that a modern Japanese man when given the word "music" will, in all probability, think of Beethoven, given the word "art" of Van Gogh, and given the words "beauty contest" of a Western woman. Thus, when Tayama describes how he came to write his novel *Inaka Kyōshi* (The Country Schoolmaster) he says that the original impulse came on hearing of a young man living in the country who died on the same day as the fall of Port Arthur.[6] The contrast fascinated him, this lonely death on Japan's great day of triumph. And yet as he broods upon it what comes first of all into his head is a scene from Turgenev's *Fathers and Sons*.

*The Bedclothes* was published in 1907. This novel, along with Shimazaki Tōson's *Hakai* (The Broken Commandment) published in the previous year, is said to mark the beginning of the "Naturalist" movement which then dominated Japanese letters for about five years, and which of all literary movements is said to have had the deepest influence upon the literature that was to come. The term "Naturalism" is a cause of dispute among Japanese critics, it being claimed, not unreasonably, that the term is a misnomer since Japanese Naturalism is not like its Western counterpart. The following is a representative statement of this point of view:

It is correct to say that Shimamura [et.al.] . . . all these typical Naturalist theorists put forward right from the start ideas that were contrary to Naturalism. They were making a queer, fumbling attempt to preserve Romantic context by the use of Naturalist method. Romanticism in Japan . . . seemed in fact to be dying a natural death, and, since they observed and were disturbed by that process, the central fact of European Naturalism, i.e. that the establishment of the self can only remain upon the level of the dream, and that the pressures of Natural Science must imply the denial of this self, this fact was one that was beyond their concern or comprehension. Romanticism had to go on chugging along under the name of Naturalism. Thus our Naturalists, critics and writers alike, did not attempt to take anything of Naturalism but its methods. It is in this strange union of the content of Romanticism which exalts the self, and the method of Naturalism which denies it, that the special nature of Japanese Naturalism consists.[7]

This has been quoted at some length because it does illustrate attitudes towards modern Japanese literature that are not only widespread, but also unilluminating. Perhaps the most distinctive feature of this is that, despite the persistent scepticism shown towards Japanese Naturalism, the European version is accepted as if it existed as a series of indisputable facts; the assumption being that there is such a thing as European Naturalism, that we know what its aims and achievements were, that the term "Naturalism" not only corresponds to but precisely fits a definite literary reality, and that the Japanese Naturalists misunderstood this because they were concerned with preserving another definite literary reality, Romanticism (although, given the terms of this argument there seems no good reason to assume they understood that either). It will be as well to ignore the worse assumption of this (that words such as "Naturalism" and "Romanticism" can be thrown about with so little circumspection) and concentrate on the assumptions it makes about Naturalism, by which he means the French variety. The main error he makes

is in assuming that the theoretical statements of such Naturalism
(in effect Zola's "Le Roman Expérimental") can be taken at their
face value, and that thus a concern with applying the "methods
of Natural Science" is not only serious (whereas it has indeed
hardly any more serious a function than any propaganda slogan),
but has also actually been put into effect in that literature.

En un mot, nous devons opérer sur les caractères, sur les passions, sur
les faits humains et sociaux, comme le chimiste et le physicien opèrent
sur les corps bruts, comme le physiologiste opère sur les corps vivants.
Le déterminisme domine tout. C'est l'investigation scientifique, c'est le
raisonnement expérimental qui combat une à une les hypothèses des
idéalistes, et qui remplace les romans de pure imagination par les
romans d'observation et d'expérimentation.* 8

These are the "vides inepties" of Flaubert, the ideas that
Angus Wilson justifiably called "peculiarly silly." 9 The concept
of the novel as a scientific experiment which one simply
imagined in one's head is not worthy of serious consideration,
for what possible kind of scientific validity could such experimentation have? One would be like the man in Wittgenstein who
buys additional copies of the morning paper to make sure that
the news in it is true. Of more importance than their theoretical
validity, however, is the relevance of such ideas to Zola's own
novels which, when it does exist, leads principally to excesses
that mar a good deal of his work. Even a truly fruitful idea, that
of documentation, of a concern with the observed facts of reality
(hardly an idea limited to Naturalist novelists) often led him to
believe he had understood things which in fact he had not.

Les documents dont se contente Zola sont souvents bien fantaisistes. Il a
la rage de peindre les milieux de riche bourgeoisie de l'époque im-
périale, de l'aristocratie et de la cour, qu'il n'a point connus, car il était
alors un bien pauvre hère. Il a vu, du trottoir, que les gens de la haute
société allaient en voiture; il court s'informer . . . auprès de carrossiers;

---

*To put it briefly, we must operate upon our characters, upon the passions, upon
human and social facts, as the chemist and the physicist operate upon inorganic
matter and the physiologist upon living bodies. Determinism dominates all. It is
this scientific investigation, this experimental reasoning, which will combat one
by one the hypotheses of the idealists, and will replace novels of pure imagination by those based on observation and experimentation.

et cela nous vaut, en fait de peinture de la vie mondaine, une description de tous les types de voitures en usage sous le second Empire.*[10]

One must also point out that this method has its successes, as in *Germinal*, but this tends to be simply a personal triumph for the writer rather than the result of any application of "scientific method." A novel like *Germinal* succeeds because it fully engages Zola's real vision of the world, that sense of human life being crushed out by circumstances. It is this negative, apocalyptic vision which is the truth of his work: Coupeau's dance of death in *L'Assommoir*, the sound of the miners' picks echoing underground in *Germinal* (apparently meant to be a sound of hope for the future, but in fact producing quite the contrary effect), the train full of drunken soldiers careering out of control into the night in *La Bête humaine*. Thus, when a Japanese critic asks: "Why did Zola's naturalism lead him not to fatalism but to moral activism, not to acquiescence but to participation?"[11] he is making the same form of error as that made by Usui Yoshimi in assuming that the truth of literary works appears in abstract messages drawn out of them, whereas their real truth, in fact, exists in the form of reading experiences they create. The above quoted statement has to be based on the false premise that the last novels of Zola possess the same degree of truth as, say, *Germinal*, although these final novels are literary failures. The fact that Zola should have wanted to write books like that is beside the point (as beside the point as his desire for a scientific method), since his truth as a novelist, that truth which appears in those novels which succeed as literary artifacts, contradicts these later novels. Zola's vision of the world is not connected with the various cheering glimpses of the future that nineteenth-century science had to offer, but with the nightmare prospects it opened. It is

---

*The documents with which Zola was satisfied were often remarkably fanciful. He had this craving to portray the lives and surroundings of the upper middle class of the imperial age, the aristocracy and the court, although he had had no knowledge of any of this at the time since he had still been just a poor nobody. He had seen, from the sidewalk, that people in high society went about in coaches, so he sought his information about them . . . from coachdrivers; and that resulted in a portrayal of social life consisting of a description of every type of carriage in use during the second Empire.

that vision which appears in the works of his that matter, and a literary work is significant, both in terms of literary history as well as those of criticism proper, to the extent that it is good or bad.

French Naturalism is not to be equated therefore with any of the various polemical statements made by Zola or the Goncourt brothers. It is noticeable that Huysmans in a preface written in 1903 to a reissue of *À Rebours* (originally published in 1884) said that the Bible of the movement was not anything by Zola but Flaubert's *L'Éducation sentimentale*, which had performed "l'inoubliable service de situer des personnages réels dans les milieux exacts."* If one is prepared to accept that statement, one can see how difficult it would be to consider French Naturalism as an anti-Romantic movement (particularly if òne were thinking of the two in the terms used by Usui Yoshimi). No matter how much *L'Éducation sentimentale* or *Madame Bovary* may attempt to show the failure of Romantic ideas when brought face to face with the real world, we are never given a critique of those ideas, since they are never replaced by other values but simply regretted. It is much more as if Romanticism and Naturalism were the same set of ideas but with different emphases or, more properly, that they represent a clumsy attempt to define a general tendency in Western culture in the nineteenth century which finally can not be defined in those terms. Consequently when a Naturalist writer like Kunikida Doppo was attracted to Wordsworth, or Shimazaki Tōson considered Rousseau's *Confessions* as the work of literature of most importance to him, or Shimamura Hōgetsu claimed that the founding fathers of Japanese Naturalism were Rousseau and Nietzsche, Turgenev's "resistance to authority" and Tolstoy's "anarchistic thought," they were not being stupid, nor were they getting something wrong. They were in fact getting hold of what nineteenth-century European literature had to offer them.

What nineteenth-century literature had to offer them was, first, the idea of the realistic novel as the dominant literary form. As F. R. Leavis puts it: "In the nineteenth century and later the strength—the poetic and creative strength—of the English lan-

*the unforgettable service of setting real people in exact surroundings

guage goes into prose fiction. In comparison the formal poetry is a marginal affair." [12] Indeed, the Japanese novelist and poet, Satō Haruo, made this very point about the Naturalism of his own country, saying that the dominance of prose—a very prosaic prose compared with what had gone before—was established over poetry. Second, it had a mass of ideas to offer about the relationship of man to society—one has only to look at the names of Rousseau and Nietzsche to see what they were—and the key word for all these ideas would be "nature."

The Japanese word for nature in this sense, *shizen*, has existed for a long time, but in so unused a state that it is best to think of its usage in the Meiji Period and onwards as a translation of the English word. Although it covers most of the implications of that word it is, in fact, made up of two characters meaning "self" and "being" ("things as in themselves they really are"), the first character also occurring in the word for "freedom" (another virtual importation), and in a variety of words meaning "individual," "ego," and so on. One can see how the concern of the Naturalists with the self as opposed to society, rather than with society as in itself it is, has been to a certain extent actually built into the language. Also, given the social conditions in Japan, the idea of the self was the most dramatic one the West had to offer. Thus the reality of one's own life as it truly was, the reality of one's own immediate experiences and impressions, was what these writers came to rely upon.

An example can be seen in Shimamura Hōgetsu's preface to his *Studies in the Modern Arts of Literature*, which is called "Reflections on Naturalism as a Philosophy of Life," from which I shall give a few lengthy quotations.

As one approaches forty and reflects upon the battered condition of one's soul, one hardly bothers with having a philosophy of life. As ever the soul inhabits a desolate, deserted house, and one is concerned with only temporary repairs of the gaps in the floorboards, or with the leaks in the roof. The way I actually live is in the achievement of such momentary respites.

What should one do? How should one pass the days? At the end of each day has something actually been achieved? It seems that this is not necessarily so. The truth is that what sways us in our daily lives is nothing but the old, old and commonplace morality. When one reflects on one's past and present one sees that one has not taken a step beyond it. And yet one certainly does not believe that this morality represents what one loves best or one's highest good.

The idea behind human life is the love of one's self, of one's own life. It is to be able to lead one's own life. It is of course true that in the performance of an act one is perhaps not aware of this, that we are controlled primarily indeed by ideas of good and evil imposed upon us by tradition. And yet this is but a limited morality, a morality which has not opened its eyes. When you awake what presents itself to you is neither god nor buddha, but the self. Thus the self it is that is god or buddha.

However, this is only a construct, something created within the confines of my consciousness, nothing more. Being aware of this does not have to imply that the pattern of my daily life will change. Indeed this very consciousness itself unceasingly provides any amount of insoluble problems. In what, for example, does this self consist? And how far will this reliance on the self take one? What is particularly hard to accept is that this individualist morality to which my intellect assents seems quite unable to give me any sense of glory or of wonder . . . The feeling of holiness, of greatness underlying our actual day-to-day living has vanished, and spread out before us lies a world of uniform greyness. . . .

It is perhaps that this grey world requires a corresponding greyness of the heart, that the main purpose behind human life demands that our days be ones of coldness, fear, brutality. And yet I have never been able to accept this. There is a part of me which will not die that demands the redness of blood, the blue of the sky. No matter how subtle the twists and turns of the mind, always this contradiction remains. There is a part of me that would see the world through religious eyes, and yet at the same time I see life as a matter of expedience, a world, indeed, of prose. Caught thus between two worlds we must lead a life without certainty or peace, a life with perhaps no satisfaction in it for us.

I have no real philosophy of life, but the values of the old faiths have died under the light of the intellect. This intellect I consider a curse, but it is beyond cure. If there would arise some power that could subjugate my intellect, then for the first time I should enter into a happiness within which I should feel secure.

So how could I create some fixed philosophy of life? What is required from me now is that I should confess my confusions and my uncertainties as they are. Therein lies the truth; beyond that is the danger of falsehood. And once I start to think like this am I not then committed to the belief that even those who have philosophies of life are, in fact, in the same situation as myself? This being so, then are we not in all probability due for an age of confessions? To avoid falsehood, to shun ornamentation, to take a close and painful look at one's own private life; and having done so, to speak out in all sincerity! In the world as it now stands is there any other subject which can interest us? This is what I mean by an age of confessions. It may well be that mankind can never go beyond the confession, never surpass it.[13]

I have quoted at such length not only to give the literary program, but also the tone of those writers who are termed Naturalists. The ideas here are certainly linked to Western ones, but they seem to have been genuinely felt (as the above quotations should demonstrate); so much so that one could call this the consistent tone of much of modern Japanese literature. What is peculiarly Japanese about it is the nature of the literary program given, for this concentration upon one's own failures and inadequacies as prime material for confession means that the reality of human life is not to consist of any grasp of or transcendence of our day-to-day situation, but merely in a record of how it bears in upon us and renders us powerless.

The above essay was written in 1910, but already such works as *The Bedclothes* and *The Broken Commandment* had been principally concerned with confession. In *The Bedclothes* the act of writing itself was the confession. In *The Broken Commandment* the novel is concerned with the confession of its hero, a young member of the *eta* outcast class who has hidden his origins, and who in the climax confesses before his students in a scene of memorable melodrama.

The desire to confess will be a strong one in a society where there is a conflict between ideas which value the individual beyond his social role, and the actual structure of the society which denies such ideas. In this case the main function of confession seems to be that of reinforcing, perhaps even creating, a sense of personal identity, giving it shape and validity in a society which imposes strict social roles upon its members. It goes without saying that a man might want to confess for numerous other reasons, but as a form of literature that would satisfy a writer the main motive given above seems to be the right one. A simplification of that order should not be overstressed, however. Although it is a truism about the modern Japanese novel that it consists mainly of authors having a second look at their own lives, one must always remember that this is similarly true of much modern literature in the West, such as that of Joyce, Proust, Lawrence. It is surely not surprising that the realistic novel should have this tendency towards the one reality that the writer feels he can be really sure of, his own experience. Where the tradition of the Japanese "I-novel" differs from any of its counterparts in the West is in its limited idea of what the self is, in the diary-like nature of its literary forms, and in the restrictions imposed by a particular kind of sensibility, a sensibility that tends to shrink in upon itself as the history of the modern Japanese novel progresses.

The subject matter of the typical naturalist novel—e.g., Shimazaki Tōson's *Ie* (The Family), Tayama Katai's *Sei* (Life), Tokuda Shūsei's *Kabi* (Mildew)—is the writer as one burdened with the family system, one who is not free and has little hope of ever being so, for the tone of these novels is consistently and gloomily middle-aged. Yet they succeed as novels because the writers have taken an image from private life which has considerable overtones beyond it. What is being given to us, in words already quoted, is "the humiliating sufferings and endurance, the world of compromise and the little quiet pleasures of social life." The hurricane from the West has not blown through this but only over the top of it; and this is a reality about which one can do nothing except patch up the floor and stop the roof from leaking. What makes Shimazaki Tōson perhaps the most interesting of these writers is that he was the one who felt these pressures the most intensely in his private life. Son of a member of that class which perhaps suffered most under the Restoration (the lower strata of *samurai* who had held important posts under the old regime), carrying the burden of his elder brothers who could not fit into the new age, having ideas about heredity which made him believe he was enslaved by the bad blood of his parents to the sexual mores of the past; his situation offered a rich image of man trying to become free. His writings give little sense of the evasion of wider issues since they always imply them. It is when we read the writings of the next generation that the word "evasion" seems to take on meaning.

The Naturalist movement reached its peak in the years after the Russo-Japanese war; that is, in the final years of the first decade of this century. The "Shirakaba" writers issued the first number of their magazine *Shirakaba* (Silver Birch) in 1910, the year of the High Treason Incident, when a number of anarchist/socialists were sentenced to death for allegedly conspiring to assassinate the Emperor. This event was thought of as important for modern Japanese literature, besides being one which indicated quite clearly in what direction Japan was moving politically. The last decade of the nineteenth century had seen an industrialization which brought about the destruction of cottage industries with a subsequent impoverishment (using this term in its widest meaning) of village life, and the creation of a proletarian labor force whose members were treated (and this is little exaggeration) like slaves. There had also been the beginnings of industrial pollution, protests about which were ignored by the government since heavy industry was essential to the war effort. The success of the Russo-Japanese war meant an intensification of these tendencies, and a consequent resistance to any ideas that were opposed to the ideology of *Kō-Tei-Chū-Shin* ("filial piety, brotherly subordination, loyalty, sincerity"). The final years of the Meiji period thus show a significant rise in censorship. As one example there is the case of Hermann Sudermann's play *Heimat* (Home, but usually referred to as *Magda* after the name of its heroine), which was produced in Tokyo in 1912. The play is about a girl who runs away from home to go on the stage, becomes a celebrated prima donna, returns by chance to her home town, and there has a confrontation with her old-school bourgeois father. During this the father, perceiving the horrifying depths of his daughter's immorality, points a pistol at her, but luckily has a heart failure. The great success of the play in many countries was mainly the result of its providing a fat part for a leading lady, Duse, Sarah Bernhardt, Mrs. Patrick Campbell, and, in Japan, for Matsui Sumako whose own life was very similar to that of Magda. The censor soon stopped the play on the grounds that it attacked ideas of filial piety and loyalty and was a danger to the public. The licence was restored eventually, but only on the understanding that an addition be made to the Fourth Act, which then ended with a penitent Magda saying, "It has all happened through my wickedness."

Towards the end of 1907 a letter addressed to the Emperor was delivered at the Japanese Consulate in San Francisco. Written in a disrespectful style it accused the Emperor of responsibility for various crimes (the creation of an aristocracy and of a capitalist class, the subjugation of the Japanese people, the repression of the Socialist party, and others) and ended: "Mr. Mutsuhito [the Emperor's name], poor Mr. Mutsuhito. Night and day we are after you. There are bombs all around you. Very soon they will all go off together. Goodbye, Mr. Mutsuhito." No one could be certain if this were serious or not. Perhaps it was the work of a madman, perhaps a practical joke. Investigations showed that a group of Japanese anarchists were living in San Francisco in a house whose walls were painted red. The significance of the letter lies in its being the first time the Emperor had ever been criticized, and it made the authorities aware that resistance of an extreme, albeit a limited kind certainly existed.

In 1908 the "Red Flags Affair" occurred. Richard Storry's account of it appeared in a chapter entitled "The Golden Years": "In 1908 orthodox opinion in Japan received a further shock when there was a parade in Tokyo of Socialists and Anarcho-syndicalists, carrying red banners and chanting revolutionary songs. Severe police action followed this incident . . ."[14]

Inevitably, given the brevity of treatment, this tends to give the wrong impression of what actually took place. The anarchists had decided to hold a welcome party for one of their members who was being released from prison. Two red banners were prepared, with the words "Anarchy" (*Museifu*) on one and "Anarcho-communism" (*Museifukyōsan*) on the other, the characters sewn in white tape on a red background by the landlady of one of the anarchists (this homely note puts the incident in perspective). As the party came to an end some of the young men picked up the banners and began singing revolutionary songs. The older men tried to restrain them. However, the young men started to leave the meeting place, a smallish restaurant, still with their banners and songs, and as they did so were set upon by the police who had been lying in wait for them. The banner bearers managed in fact to move only about ten paces before being borne to the ground. All the young men, all nine of them, were frog-marched off to the police station, along with four girls who had picked up the banners and refused to hand them over to the police. Here are your Anarcho-syndicalists parading through the streets of Tokyo and chanting their revolutionary songs. A girl who went to see one of them was herself knocked unconscious and thrown into a cell where the arrested, who had been kicked, beaten, and trampled upon, lay nearly unconscious. Sentences of two to two-and-a-half years' hard labor were imposed.[15] This is not being reported seventy years after the event in order to enjoy a sensation of righteous indignation, but to show the ugliness, the pettiness, and the futility of what happened, to indicate the impossibility of protest in a society of that kind.

Two years later there was a roundup of anarchists, a trial behind closed doors, the death sentence passed upon twelve of them, which was then executed with unseemly haste within five days of sentence instead of the customary sixty. People who thought about these things assumed that a serious miscarriage of justice (a frame-up, indeed) had taken place.

The following is the reaction of one man of letters, Nagai Kafū to that event.

Of all the political happenings that I had come across none left such a bad taste in the mouth as this one. What was involved was a matter of intellectual principles, and as a man of letters I should not have remained silent. Had not Zola been forced to flee his country because he insisted on proclaiming the truth during the Dreyfus Affair? And yet I, like all the other literary people, said nothing; and I went through an almost unbearable crisis of conscience over this. I felt an extreme contempt for my role as a man of letters. From then on I decided there was no other way but to let the level of my art return to that of the fiction writers of the Edo period.

Another reaction was this of the poet Ishikawa Takuboku:

With the present social, economic and family systems as they were any attempt to create a rational way of life for oneself had to end in failure. So, almost unbeknown to myself, I became a social revolutionary, and my thought in relation to a whole variety of things took on a socialistic tone. What made me aware of what was happening to me was the High Treason Trial.

Here is another:

The day before yesterday the death sentences were passed on the twenty-four anarchists. This kind of thing is extremely uncommon in Japan. I'm an anarchist myself in a way (although I can't say I think much of present day socialism). Yet really I simply don't want to be bothered with reading about things like this. I don't seem able to manage that kind of curiosity. [16]

This last quotation is taken from the diary of Shiga Naoya for January 20, 1911. The magazine *Shirakaba* had brought out its first number a few months earlier. The next year was the beginning of the Taishō period.

This group of writers came together mostly through a shared background rather than for any ideological reasons. They were all graduates of the Peers School in Tokyo, and the magazine was in effect an amalgamation of three magazines created by three different years at the school. As Satomi Ton recalled later:

If one mentions the word "Shirakaba" people soon start on about its "confrontation" with Naturalism, and, well, one can't say that there wasn't one, but our differences with the Naturalists arose mostly from questions of upbringing. We were aristocrats, whereas "Naturalism," well it meant to us that crowd cooped up in lodgings around Waseda university; and being young, well there didn't seem much chance of our hitting it off mutually. But as far as literature was concerned I don't actually recall any real criticism as such being made. [17]

Although the magazine *Shirakaba* may not have had a distinct set of literary ideas it did have a distinctive tone, stressing self-perfection and self-fulfilment in an overall idealism which had much influence upon the intellectual world of the Taishō period, and which the anarchist Ōsugi Sakae (one of those arrested in the "Red Flags Incident," and who was later to become

a force in the Trade Union movement) referred to as "prison philosophy."[18] Our concern here, however, must be with the one
truly distinguished writer associated with the group, Shiga
Naoya, who wrote a form of fiction which is perhaps the central
one in modern Japanese literature.

The critic Fukuda Tsuneari, who, like many others, wishes
this central tradition were not there, calls Shiga the most "Japanese" of writers since he did not simply lose hold of reality, as
the modern Japanese writer, with few exceptions, tends to do,
but actually and quite deliberately expelled it. He goes on to say:

He pursues his enemy snapping at his heels, but finally becomes
restless, depressed, irritated, and then gives up. He then remains where
he is, squats down, and looks at what is in front of his nose, at those
things which had never been looked at before. In order to look he keeps
his body quite still. He stays motionless, and those things that enter his
field of vision he calls reality. This is Shiga Naoya's realism. What he
desires is not potentiality but certainty, a certainty that he intends to
preserve. He rejects that reality which is constantly changing and escaping one because only this other can bring with it a constant sense of
sureness, of untrembling equilibrium.[19]

This is the terminology in which much of modern Japanese
literary criticism is conducted, and the reader must be asked to
bear with it, as he must also, regrettably, bear with my own style
which has inevitably been stained to some extent by what it
works in. An acquaintance with that modern French literary criticism which has felt the weight of Marxist thought (Sartre,
Barthes) might enable him to feel at home, and temper an impatience which rejects this as the proper function of criticism. The
impatience would be out of place (as it also would in the case of
Sartre and Barthes) since what is being written is perceptive.
This is an acute description of Shiga's writing, if one accepts that
the value judgment may be slipped in so craftily by way of the
amusing dog image. That image with its derogatory implications
will be acceptable to the degree one thinks Shiga's writings good
or bad. If one discounts that, then the description is fair, as almost any of Shiga's writings would bear out.

A story like "Takibi" (The Bonfire)[20] will give some idea of what this kind of writing is like. The style is simple and elegant, the colloquial style ("writing as one talks," although not, of course, exactly like that) written perhaps as well as it ever could be. The situation described is of people, leisured people, doing ordinary things. It rains, so they play cards. When tired of this, they open the shutters and see that it has stopped raining, and enjoy the sweetness of the air here in the mountains. They potter about building a hut, they climb trees, they take a boat out on the lake at night. They notice a furze gatherer who has lit a fire and sleeps beside it, and they make their own fire on an island in the lake. They gossip; the gossip shifts to monsters, to mysterious happenings, but common sense can explain them all, for the monster is one's own shadow cast on the mist, or that of a man's haversack cast enormously on the trees by the light of the match he strikes in its shelter. But there is one story that is different. K (who relates his own story) had been climbing up the snow-deep mountain on his way home. The snow was up to his waist, it was late at night, and he began to feel confused as if he might fall asleep. Later he sees lanterns being carried towards him; it is his brother-in-law and three others come to meet him. His mother had suddenly waked up in the night because she had heard him calling, and sent them out, although K had given no indication that he was coming home that night. The author thinks about K's relationship with his mother. The owls are crying on the island. The bonfire is going out. They throw lit branches across the surface of the lake which flare up and go out. They reenter their boat. The fire of the furze gatherer is also nearly out. The cries of the owls grow more and more distant.

It is possible to recall passages from *L'Éducation sentimentale* or from Proust which have something in common with this (or, in the world of the cinema, from Truffaut's *Jules et Jim*), but in effect they are different since they are always set in a much wider context. Certainly there is more variety to Shiga's work than this implies, and yet the deliberate limitation of material and the narrowness of the kind of sensibility which deals with that material, is what Shiga's work would have meant to a writer like Yokomitsu, although the stylistic achievement would still have been valued most. Hirotsu Kazuo, himself an "I-novelist," pointed out as early as 1919 that Shiga's writing shows a progressive limiting of his sensibility, for he is attempting to escape from an aura of violence which appears in some of his earlier work into a more acceptable world, to exchange discord for harmony, ugliness for beauty, war for peace, motion for quietude. He claimed that Shiga's sentimentality was a result of this.

It will be clear to anyone with even a slight acquaintance with Japanese culture how strongly rooted these attitudes are in the past, in Japanese history and religion; and it is presumably because of this rootedness that this form of writing became what many in the 1920s considered Japanese literature should essentially be. If one is to dismiss this as escapism, then there are wide areas of human experience which will have to be dismissed in the same way, and such a criticism will not do, although the attitudes shown here are not beyond criticism either. This literary attempt of Shiga's also has counterparts in the West, where there is a literature of the exploitation of the self, of life for the sake of art; and yet surely the basic Western reaction is this, by Flaubert, who objects strongly on moral, rather than aesthetic grounds:

J'aime ma petite niece comme si elle était ma fille, et je m'en occupe assez (*activement*) pour prouver que ce ne sont point des phrases. Mais que je suis écorché vif plutot que d'exploiter cela en style!* 21

Flaubert is here referring to the confessional aspects of Romanticism and the achievements of the great Romantic writers are untouched by this criticism, even if it does point to where the cause of some of their weaknesses may lie. Yet Shiga reads nothing like a Romantic writer (not even an unsuccessful one), since he is not simply treating his life as the material out of which art is made. Instead he is treating his life as if it were art already, something out of which nothing needs to be made since it is there, complete, already. His life does not need to be exploited

---

*I love my small niece as if she were my own daughter, and I actively concern myself about her enough to show that these are not mere words. But I would rather be flayed alive than exploit that in fine writing!

since it already is the art form which the Western writer is trying to create.

A tendency to treat details of everyday life as if they were a form of art is perhaps the most distinctive feature of Japanese culture, and the feature by which it most differs from the West where the practice of art is far removed from our everyday acts. That Shiga's writing also conforms to so constant an aspect of Japanese life would account for its power over people. To maintain that such a form of writing can easily degenerate into the gossipy relating of the trivia of everyday life is no real criticism of it, since any way of writing contains its own form of degeneration. What would be more troublesome for a Japanese writer would be that, unless he were a special case as Shiga certainly was, he would feel uncomfortable writing like this, uncomfortable because he would have read Tolstoy and Dostoevsky. For the same reason he would be attracted to it; he would feel this was the real Japanese me, not like those Europeans whom I must stop aping. Then he would feel a revulsion against it. What would be established with the West would be a neurotic relationship; something which has indeed happened and not only in the field of literature. Thus, unless one had Shiga's enormous confidence in one's self, writing like this could mean virtually opting out of the business of being a writer.

This negative implication can be seen clearly in the image of the writer put forward by Kume Masao during the 1920s. For him the writer was a person who wrote popular novels for money, but also wrote *shinkyō shōsetsu* ("State of mind novels," the state of mind being that which the *haiku* poet aimed at in the moment of composition) in order to take into account those feelings one had when waking up in the middle of the night. Thus one is to be a hack writer dabbling in belles lettres on Sundays of the spirit who then cries himself all the way to the bank. These ideas represent a stage in the popularization of literature during the 1920s. Many of the best-known novels of the Meiji period were published in newspapers, but by the time Kume began writing the newspaper novel was becoming a literary form almost in direct opposition to what was now known as serious literature.

For Kume the popular and the serious (or pure) were distinct, and their methods of dealing with reality were opposed. The popular was fictional, the serious or pure was a second look at the self, and must therefore contain nothing of the fabricated. From this point of view *War and Peace* and *Crime and Punishment* had to be relegated to the status of mere popular novels, albeit of a very superior kind.[22]

This is certainly one way of disposing of the masterpieces of the nineteenth century. Unfortunately, by this time the impact of Western literature had simply been too great for any writer to be able to believe in that way except at certain privileged moments. One can see the uneasiness of the position a writer could get himself into, if he were a writer far superior to Kume and more honest and intelligent as a man, by looking at the case of Akutagawa Ryūnosuke in the literary debate he had with Tanizaki Jun'ichirō in 1927, the same year as his suicide.[23]

Tanizaki had maintained that the novel was an achievement of the inventive power of the mind in constructing imaginary events, and that if we removed the interest that resided in the narrative we would be throwing away that which is the distinguishing feature of the novel form. Akutagawa replied:

When I talk about the novel which has no real plot I do not mean just those novels which portray the various disconnected things that happen to the writer. The novel I am talking about is that which of all novels is the closest to poetry. However, it is also something much closer to the novel than what is called the prose poem. Let me say it for the third time: I don't consider the novel without a real plot as the highest form of the novel. Yet if we are thinking from the standpoint of purity, that is in terms of the absence of all aspects of the popular, then this is the novel at its purest.

The work in Japanese which he cites as the best example of such purity is "The Bonfire" by Shiga Naoya, and other short stories of his; he also cites Jules Renard among French writers. The tone, however, is uncertain, which is not surprising, since what he is saying contradicts most of his own creative output. The bulk of his own fiction is certainly fictional (even if a lot of that is borrowed), and one can only assume that he had come to look upon this fiction of his as a form of telling lies. One finds the same uncertainty later in the essay when he writes about the great, disorderly writers, who may well be the greatest writers, and yet:

And yet, if one thinks seriously about this, this confusion can not be considered in the same class as purity. On this point I always feel distrustful of great writers. Of course that sufficed in so far as they were the representatives of their age, yet the extent to which they can move succeeding generations must depend upon to what degree they were pure artists.

One is obliged to see this article as a confession of failure on his part, arising from a feeling that his own literature was not good enough, a feeling in which he was probably justified. On looking at the Japanese literature of his time it must have come to seem to him that the kind of literature which had succeeded was that of Shiga Naoya, and this must have been a conclusion he would not have wanted to make; or rather, as said earlier, one he would have not wanted to make, then to make, then not to make, and so on, and hence the confusions and hesitations in what he writes. Modern Japanese literature had been liberated by the West, and yet where were the Japanese Flauberts, the Japanese Dostoevskys and Tolstoys? The only answer would have been to reject those writers, but this he could not do wholeheartedly. Thus he talks, in that very revealing phrase, of his "distrust" of great writers. Whatever happens the West can not be ignored. Shiga Naoya must then be talked about principally in terms of what he is not (not Flaubert). It is as if one were obliged to think of Shakespeare primarily in terms of his not being Racine. It is this attitude that can justifiably be called neurotic, since an argument (and, more importantly, a state of mind) carried out in negatives can arrive at no conclusion but must always turn in the same self-defeating circle.

For the Naturalist writers European literature had acted as a liberating force, or at least that is how they saw the matter. For later generations it stood as a reproach, an indication of what had not been done, and the lack of confidence which seems to mark modern Japanese literature from this time onwards no doubt accounts for a great deal of the urge to experiment in the 1920s and later.

In addition to this kind of abstract pressure from the West there was that applied by events in the real world. Its most extreme form was the Great Kanto Earthquake of 1923, and in what followed that earthquake. Kikuchi Kan, a leading literary man of the time, reacted thus:

The earthquake showed us human life in its most extreme forms. . . . We thought about nothing but staying alive, about that day's food and that night's sleep. That was enough for us. All that occupied our minds was praying for the safety of our families. Everything beyond that was a luxury. . . .

At the time of the earthquake what I really proposed to do was to lead a more honest kind of life. I wanted to have a way of life that would allow me to look God or man in the face without any feeling of shame, no matter what happened. I wanted to grow my own food for myself. . . . I imagined there would be time, after supplying my personal needs, to occupy myself with the arts.

Akutagawa wrote:

It was the very size of the earthquake that shook us as writers. We experienced violent love, violent hate, pity, anxiety. And yet the image of the human heart we had subscribed to up to then had been, however one looked at it, a very delicate, sensitive one. From now on I imagine the outlines of the emotions will be newly painted with bolder, thicker colors. Also the rebuilt Tokyo is a bleak and tatty affair. We can hardly look outside ourselves for interest as we did before. We will seek whatever happiness there may be within our inner selves. At the least those who are already inclined that way will become even more so. It seems to me that a situation something like that of the Chinese poets who responded to the troubles and confusions of their time by choosing the hermit's life is going to come about here. They withdrew into the task of perfecting their art. [24]

"We will seek whatever happiness there may be within ourselves." Akutagawa found only, as he wrote in the "Epistle to a Friend" left behind at his suicide, "a vague sense of unease towards the future." When he committed suicide in 1927 he admitted that for the past two years he had thought about nothing but death.

In 1929 Hirotsu Kazuo looked back on this period and wrote:

Society was not a matter to be understood. The meaning of life was to know thyself. That was what people said. So each of us, in his different way, set about this task. And so, although the roads might differ, all had set out on the same quest for individuality. My way—well, how shall I explain it—shall I say that it was as if I were to peel off one after another all those various layers that covered the real me. Sometimes I did in fact reflect: "If I keep on like this, peeling off the layers of the self, might it not be that at the end nothing actually living is going to appear; that it will be like peeling an onion and that when one gets to the end one is left holding precisely nothing?"[25]

The earthquake seemed to reveal that kind of nothing. The following year then saw the publication of two new literary magazines: *Bungei Sensen* (Literary Front), the official magazine for proletarian literature; and *Bungei Jidai* (Literary Age), edited by Kawabata Yasunari, Yokomitsu Riichi, and others, the magazine of a group who came to be referred to as the Shinkankakuha. Japanese literature appeared to be taking new directions.

Au dessus de la vie, au dessus du bonheur, il y a quelque chose de bleu et d'incandescent, un grand ciel immuable et subtil dont les rayonnements qui nous arrivent suffisent à animer des mondes. La splendeur du génie n'est que le reflet pâle de ce Verbe caché.

Flaubert*[1]

# Chapter Two: The Sun in Heaven

I was ill for a couple of days and stayed in bed. While I lay there everything looked blue and alive, but when I got up I saw that things were not so. Like a horse at a post station vaguely waiting in boredom for something to come and not knowing what it will be. I see the wind in the sky: the branches of the chestnut, the paulownia, the zelkova, sway in the wind. As if someone were dying in the midday, neglected, castaway.

Yokomitsu[2]

THE ACCEPTED IMAGE of Yokomitsu Riichi is that of a writer who, dissatisfied with the contemporary form of Japanese realism, devoted his early years to various stylistic experiments based upon Western literary models, eventually wearied of this unprofitable task and turned back to a more traditional prose form. This return was not merely stylistic but a question of ideology as well, the West being rejected not only as a basis for literary experiment but its total influence upon all areas of Japanese culture being called in question. This eventually led to his embracing a form of "Japanism," which meant, among other things, Nationalism and support for the war effort. The defeat of all that he had come to believe in destroyed him, and he died a broken man

*Over and above life, above happiness, there is something blue and incandescent, a great, unchanging and subtle sky, and the rays of light from it which reach us are enough to give life to worlds. The splendor of genius is but a pale reflection of this hidden Word.

shortly after. It is also generally accepted that this is a pattern one can see in many modern Japanese writers (and in other
areas of modern Japanese civilization), where an early period of
experimentalism with Western models proves to be unsatisfying,
since it does not touch a writer's real creative depths, and is
eventually replaced in middle age by a period of rejection leading
to a return to the Japanese tradition.[3]

Historicism of this kind has little place in literary studies
since its generalizations are of too sweeping a nature to be of any
real help when one looks at actual texts; it can also be profoundly
dangerous since it provides a continual temptation to edit and
tamper with evidence in order to make it fit ideas which do, after
all, have the attraction of being simple to grasp. The task of literary criticism should be a constant attempt to set such abstractions
against the concrete reality of real works written by real people.
The interest literary criticism shows in biography is obviously
connected with such laudable aims, although it can easily degenerate into the assembling of such facts merely for their own sake,
or even for no good reason at all. In this chapter the question of
foreign influence will be considered by looking at a work which
seems to have been largely created out of such influence, and
thus attempt to see what the concept can mean and what it meant
in this particular case. This necessitates a certain amount of biographical information, although it will be given only insofar as it
can be judged relevant to this actual work.

Yokomitsu was not born at home, but at an inn in one of the
various places his father traveled to because of his work (he was
an enginering contractor involved in railway construction), and
the homelessness which tends to be the theme of much of Yokomitsu's writing (in particular his later long novels) was a constant
experience of his childhood. His relationships with his mother
and father have nothing very remarkable about them, although it
will be maintained later that the death of his father when Yokomitsu was twenty-four years old seems to have been a decisive
event for his literature. His relationship with his one older sister,
on the other hand, probably does need to be noted, for the fact

that they were often separated when they were children and her marriage at the age of seventeen when Yokomitsu himself was only thirteen appears to have made his emotional reliance upon her extremely strong. Apparently she conditioned his image of what a woman should be, but as someone always unavailable. A great deal of the nihilism in his writing which results from an inordinate desire for purity in human relationships can probably be related to that.

Yokomitsu's early writings are, on the whole, in the tradition of Shiga realism,[4] with the result that he soon became dissatisfied with that tradition, coming to believe that the "I-novel" was simply "an enormous lie." Even these early writings, however, are much more "fictional" than that tradition would lead one to expect. This desire to create fictions which would embody what had happened to him and yet also transcend such personal experience is something that marks all his early writing, even though there is considerable variety in the closeness to him of the material to be transformed in this way. Thus Yokomitsu's interest in fiction seems to have been not so much an attempt to create imaginary worlds as to "distance" material which affected him personally in some way. Although this tends to be a motive for a writer in any culture, it still has an intensity of an obsessional kind in its writing which seems to go beyond what might be considered the normal desire to create fictions.

Certainly the desire to fictionalize reality can have two root meanings anywhere and for anyone; namely an attempt to transcend reality in order to arrive at its truth, or merely to escape from it because its truth is unbearable. In any writer these two meanings will probably be mixed, and this is why the charge of escapism can so easily be brought against all art, also why it is so difficult to refute. That this escapist desire was strong in Yokomitsu as a child can be seen in comic form in one of his earliest memories.

Yokomitsu could recall when he was five years old in Kure. The latrines in Kure are pretty deep. One time he fell right in, right up to his neck in fact. His father grabbed hold of him by the collar, dashed him into the sea, and energetically scrubbed him. Yokomitsu used to remark in later years how he could still vividly recall how beautiful the little fish were on the sea floor as they flitted in and out among the sea shells.[5]

This is a parody of the flight from reality to the world of art, and yet it is precisely this movement, in not much less extreme a form, which one can see in the transformation of the world performed in two of the writings of his apprentice period.

During his youth Yokomitsu wrote two longish works as well as a number of short stories, these two being *Kanashimi no Daika* (The Price of Unhappiness) and *Nichirin* (The Sun in Heaven), the latter differing stylistically in a most striking manner from the former, as it also does from those early short stories. No positive dating of either work is possible, but if one assumes, as there are good reasons for assuming, that the former was written before the latter, then it would make the stylistic changes in Yokomitsu's early writing appear as a very logical progression indeed. It could then be argued that the early realistic writing indicates that realism was satisfactorily applied only to material distant (or distanced) from him, and that when the material was close to home and written about as such the resulting literary object and the act of producing that object were unsatisfying, and so he turned to the completely fictional world of *The Sun in Heaven*, which was still not true fiction, but in which everything could be set at the farthest possible distance. The excessive artificiality of this then led to another form of dissatisfaction, for now the material was so transformed that its transformation produced no cathartic effect, and the Shinkankakuha attempt to portray contemporary reality, not in the images of a fictive historical world but in those of the actual world about him (but a world seen as not personally related to him) followed from that sense of failure. Thus *The Sun in Heaven* and the Shinkankakuha writings are two different forms of this flight from reality, as well as two different attempts to go beyond the world of the traditional, realistic novel.

Put baldly, this does indeed sound like the cookery school of literary criticism, where novel writing is reduced to the primitive experimental techniques of a young bride attempting to grasp an art which has never been of any real concern to her. Is it to be Yorkshire pudding or strawberries and cream? Why does the pudding always come out flat? Why are strawberries and cream not enough to fill the stomach? Vary the ingredients, finally despair, then flee to the exotic, deceptive, and basically unsatisfying world of continental cuisine. However, some process of that kind would seem to be going on, and it will be best to state first of all what this reality with which the writer is having so much trouble in fact is.

Yokomitsu left Kyoto to go to Waseda University in April 1916, when he was just eighteen years old, but he suddenly returned home in November of the same year for reasons which are not quite clear, although the principal one seems to have been some form of nervous breakdown. He remained there until April 1918, a period of one year and a half during which he started to write in earnest. On his return to Waseda he made friends with Nakayama Gishū, who was also to become a writer, and who has recorded the following conversation from their student days.

"Nakayama, have you any experience of love?"

"No, not yet. There was a little apprentice geisha in the village back home, and I used to imagine things. . . ."

"Ha, ha, ha, ha. . . . You used to imagine. I suppose you would."

"How about yourself?"

Yokomitsu made no reply to that.

"You know that poet Fujimoto who comes here sometimes?"

"The one with the long hair and the big nose?"

"That's him; that's the man. He stole my girl—cuckolded me in fact."

"And you mean he still keeps on coming here as if nothing had happened?"

"That's got nothing to do with it."

"Nothing to do with it? Why, it's preposterous."

"All right; listen then."

Yokomitsu shook back his long hair.

"I'd been home for the summer holidays and had just got back to Tokyo. So, early in the morning, I get to the house and what do I find? Friend Fujimoto sleeping with my girl. That's it then, I thought, looking at them both sleeping there. It was like gazing at a glass of beer and watching the bubbles disappear one by one."

"That's an interesting image. But what did you do then?"

"It wasn't a question of doing anything. I pushed off, just like that."

"You just pushed off."

I couldn't help admiring him for that.

"So you didn't feel jealousy?"

"Look, lad, jealousy is an appendage of love, an essential bypro-duct. Anyway, since that time I've never trusted anybody, women or friends."

"I suppose one wouldn't. Who was the girl anyway?"

"She was a maid at the boarding house. Sixteen or seventeen. She seemed to like me."

"And you set up house with her?"

"Boarding house life cost too much so three of us decided to rent a house and look after ourselves. That was during the period before this when I first came to Waseda."

"With Fujimoto?"

"And with Fukuda. He's rather dark, and he also has a big nose. He's been here sometimes. You probably know him."

"Yes, I do."

"We rented the house all right but we were a bit stuck about the cooking and laundry since all three of us were too idle to do it. So we took the maid in with us."

"You mean you hired her?"

"No, she wanted to come. She jumped at the chance."

"You were in love with her then?"

"I suppose you could say that, but I don't honestly know."

"Still, just being a servant girl, and you being out of the way, I sup-pose something like that was bound to happen."

"Perhaps."

"Even so, I can't work out the attitude of someone like Fujimoto."

"No, he's all right. It just means that if you want total possession of something, then you're simply going to get yourself into trouble, that's all."

This probably sounds as if I'm trying to expose the "secret" behind Yokomitsu's novels, but the fact is he made use of this "incident" on a number of occasions in his writings. As far as I was concerned it was something restricted to that time and place, but for Yokomitsu it was the one real mistake, the one real failure in the whole forty-nine years of his life.[6]

Since this was written some forty years after the event it is reasonable to question its total validity, but there are no grounds for dismissing the account as a whole, since it keeps appearing in Yokomitsu's writings, the only other account of Yokomitsu's life

records the same incident, and because the overall tone of Nakayama's book is consistently truthful. It is this incident which
forms the basis of *The Price of Unhappiness,* and also of the
rewritten version (in Shinkankakuha style) of that known as "Maketa Otto" (The Defeated Husband).[7] The incident took place in
1916, but the writing of *The Price of Unhappiness* can be dated as
around 1920, at which time he was in love with Kojima Kimiko, a
girl he had met a year earlier (when she was only thirteen) and
who was to become his wife four years later. It is possible to
maintain with conviction that the heroine of this work is not
modelled on the serving maid of 1916 but on the Kimiko of 1920.
The evidence lies in Yokomitsu's letters, since the character of
Kimiko which appears in those letters is identical with the
heroine of this story; and indeed in the revised version, "The
Defeated Husband," words applied to the heroine are almost exactly the same as those written in a letter describing Kimiko.
Thus the novel cannot really be considered as confessional since
it makes use of an incident which has faded enough in the past
to be viewed with a certain detachment, in order to resolve a cur-
rent obsession. The feelings of jealousy evoked by the behavior
of Kimiko are embodied in events that no longer deeply affect
him in an attempt to escape from those present feelings, to escape in the sense of giving them artistic shape and also in the
more obvious meaning of the word; the deep ambiguity of what
Yokomitsu as a writer was up to being apparent here. Certainly
discovering the same pattern in the present as in the past is the
normal human attempt to generalize experience, but this is
hardly what happened in the writing of *The Price of Unhappiness.*
The tone of the writing is extraordinarily obsessive (as quotation
will soon make clear), which shows that the events of the past
have not been coolly detached from the present but are still living
vividly within it; he is opening the sore of an old wound to find
that it still hurts, just like the present one.

The opening one-third of the story is a relating in fictional
terms of the incident told to Nakayama. The hero distrusts his
wife, and this situation is then reflected in his own relationship
with the wife of a book-shop owner, which is pure and disinter-

ested enough in his own eyes, but as he begins to see it through
the eyes of the husband he becomes confused about his own motives. The arrival of his friend Mishima as a lodger tempts him to
see his abstract jealousies in concrete shape. The ambiguity of
the situation is such that he resolves to bring everything into the
open by returning to his mother's house near Kyoto. (There can
be no doubt that the hero is the author, always allowing for a
natural scepticism about the word "is.") When he returns home
his thoughts go to a former sweetheart whom he encounters on
the road to the public bath, and the lukewarm eroticism of this is
described with an intensity which makes it difficult not to assume that the incident is autobiographical. Clearly a number of
events in this work did happen, since they also occur in other
early writings, and the tone of the work certainly encourages the
reader to think so. On his return to Tokyo he finds his wife in
bed with Mishima, although it was a letter from Mishima beg-
ging him to return because he was "in danger" which was the
cause of his witnessing this. He promptly goes back to the
country after coldly rejecting the entreaties of his wife. The final
two-thirds of the work are taken up with his relationship with
his former sweetheart, his offer of marriage to her which she
rejects because she is already betrothed, letters by him, Mishima,
and his wife, and a final reconciliation which leads to his return
to Tokyo, but a return that is without hope. However, the principal events in this section are mental, a long debate in the mind
of the hero about the nature of sexual relations, and of social relations in general.

It was still doubtful to him whether human beings actually possessed a
nature which would allow them to be perfectly happy in any way what-
soever. Still, if one put that doubt to one side for the moment, given that
the happiness of two people was but a private affair of their own, even
so they must surely be the most enviable, the most to be respected of the
whole human race, and at least at this stage it seemed to him that was
undoubtedly the best way for a man, the proper road that he should
take. Rather than grieving over the misfortunes of others or dedicating
themselves to social good, people should rather grieve for their own
misfortunes and strive to attain their own complete happiness. He felt
that ordinary people who did just that, who calculated all in terms of

personal interest, were now more precious to him than ever. In contrast to this he thought of those who had attained to that most self-effacing of all human states, to that perfect love which examined and condemned its own deformities but forgave them in the loved one, and from which love infered their own awakening, and ceaselessly continued that quest for self-perfection which lay in a continual forbearance, a continual concentration of the heart and mind on the beloved object, and achieved psychic complexities beyond this: and it seemed to him certain that a truly human happiness did not lie in that direction for those beings. Even if a form of happiness were there, was it not self-deception, or were they not simply conforming to that power of resignation which had been a part of human psychology throughout the long history of the race, and were thus, unconscious of their own true desires, performing their own suicides.[8]

There has been an attempt to retain the slightly clumsy and convoluted style, since the normal Japanese reader does require more than one attempt to grasp the meaning of this, and the awkward complexity is a part of the meaning of the original. The nagging tone of the style, and the structure of the work with its continual worrying over the same few themes, reflect Yokomitsu's own unceasing concern with this event, and with the other events and ideas related to it. The attempt of *The Price of Unhappiness* is to take a real life event and transfer it to a person who was not involved in that event, his wife-to-be, Kimiko, and to that extent it is a fiction. But it is a fiction to a minor extent only, for the intensity of the letters written in 1920 indicate that this was a continually imagined possibility, so much so as to be an actual part of his life. Since we are surely obliged to assume that the thoughts of the hero are the thoughts of the author himself, we have in effect the classic attempt of Japanese realism, which is to put things down as they happened; in this case the great bulk of the events being mental.

No matter how much one improved the social system even to the extent of creating a perfect communism, one could foresee that the class struggle would be replaced by the more intense one between the beautiful and the ugly rather than between the rich and the poor, and since the ugly people were in a majority they would start a movement to abolish facial discrimination, to adhere to the aesthetic average of those who would never have beauty, and in one stroke destroy the concept of physical perfection which so many centuries had labored to create. And yet even so the fact was that, unless some basic device to eradicate the whole idea of distinction between men could actually be made to work, human suffering would never disappear. As long as this was not so every member of the human race must be aware of the ugliness and wretchedness within him, and the highest morality would become to destroy oneself.[9]

There is not much to distinguish this in tone from what one might find in a letter, or an essay, and the work makes little attempt to organize statements of this kind into an artistic whole. The passage given here is relevant to the story to the extent that the hero reflects upon love and life because of what has happened to him, but then that criterion would permit almost any kind of reflection to be made. In his rewriting of the work ("The Defeated Husband") Yokomitsu would appear to have become aware of the lack of dramatic inevitability in these final two-thirds since he simply removed them, closing the story with the discovery of the two sleeping together and the hero's ambiguous sense of freedom. That the revised version is a superior piece of work to the original in structure and form, and yet much less interesting to read, is a fact of considerable bearing upon the whole of modern Japanese literature, another indication that it is the "I-novel" tradition which lives, those works which are close to autobiography in structure, tone, and generally in content; the attempt to put things down as they were. In the work under discussion its intensity is autobiographical, and its confusion comes from the fact that it is not a wholehearted autobiographical attempt but a confusion of real and imagined happenings which seems to aim at being a fiction. What is fictional, however, is not the fictional achievement of the novel proper, but that mixture of escape from and confrontation with reality which daydreaming is. There is no transcending of the material by creating a fictional world which will mirror the truth of things that had happened. Instead there is a world of daydreams: not things written down as they ever were, but only as they were imagined, brooded over, daydreamed about: not created fiction but lived fantasy.

Among all crimes the most criminal is simply that one is human. I have known this and suffered from it, and yet I still think in terms of having a child of my own. This thought would not leave him, not leave him in peace. When he got home he took his razor and went upstairs to his room. He tried the blade against his member. It was as yet inconceivable that he could go through with this, and it struck him that the need to go through the motions of so doing was absurdly childish in him, and yet he didn't want to put the razor away again. One could never know that one day one might not be able to do it, and it was necessary to be immediately prepared for such a contingency and keep the razor always near one. If one could do it just like that then one would know something harmful in oneself had vanished.

He started having fantasies about himself and Mishima fighting over Tatsuko.[10] Tatsuko suddenly loved him again as she had before their marriage. Mishima left the house in a rage. Tatsuko didn't care: she only loved him more and more. And yet as he became aware that Tatsuko's heart had returned to him he began to lose the power to make love to her. Their married life went on like this for some time, yet Tatsuko was unsatisfied, and when one night she showed she could no longer endure it, he raised himself from his wife's side, stood up, then, in silence, cut off the offending member. As he crouched in his own blood trying to endure the pain his wife asked:

"What's up? What's the matter?"

He looked over his shoulder at her, saw her face half illumined in the glare of the electric light, and saw the desire in it. He picked up his amputated member and cast it at that face. And it struck her cheek, staining it with blood, then bounced back onto the floor and rolled over and over like a dead mouse.

She screamed out, then stayed motionless, her face pale white.

"There's no need for you to love me any more. You can go wherever you want," he said.

When his fantasies reached this point the feeling that he had finally revenged himself upon her surged up within him with a bitter joy. He particularly wanted to see her face in that final moment. Better than that, to see the faces of all the women in the world when all the men in the world did that to them in one fell swoop. If it were only possible, then the scream which would possess the world in that moment. . . .

Yet how could one compare the sufferings of the frenzied women with the cheap momentary satisfaction of the men coldly looking on? What he felt now was not simply that even if he could dismember himself there would be no satisfaction in it for him, but rather the childishness of getting worked up about things in this way, the plain stupidity of it.[11]

One must not assume that the whole work is written at this pitch of intensity, for an extreme passage has been chosen to illustrate in dramatic form the fantasy diary-like nature of the whole. When Kawabata Yasunari praised the work for its honesty [12] it was this kind of intensity he probably had in mind, and a morally evaluative word of that kind seems the right one, since it is a real moral achievement to write down the fantasy world of the self in so precise and truthful a way. Also, his fears that the work might be looked upon as a record of what really happened can be seen as well founded too since, in the sense already given, these events probably did happen, the work being a record of such happenings in the mind.

In a complete contrast is *Nichirin* (The Sun in Heaven), a work which relates events which certainly did not happen, even in the strained sense in which the word has been used here, and which it is reasonable to date as having been written sometime between late 1920 and 1922. It was first published in 1923 in the May number of the leading literary magazine of the time, *Shinshōsetsu* (New Novels), and this, together with the publication of his short story "Hae" ("The Fly") in the magazine *Bungei Shunjū* (Literary Chronicle) at exactly the same time, marks his arrival upon the literary scene at the age of twenty-five. *The Sun in Heaven* can be seen as another attempt to control the material dealt with in *The Price of Unhappiness,* for it reads strangely (given the fact that it is a historical work) like a confessional "I-novel." Even so cautious and level-headed a scholar as Professor Hoshō Masao accepts this last statement, which implies that as an interpretation it is, to say the least, a very likely one. [13] The opposite point of view, that it is a purely fictional attempt to describe the ancient world in imitation of Flaubert's *Salammbô* has never been positively stated, to my knowledge, by anyone writing at length on the subject, although it is still commonly assumed that the style is a direct consequence of reading that novel.

Yokomitsu certainly had read the novel, for in a letter written in the summer of 1919 he mentions having borrowed it from a friend and not yet having given it back. There is also evidence that he was still reading it a year later, which must mean that it made a deep impression upon him. It is also beyond dispute that the style of *The Sun in Heaven* is different from that of *The Price of Unhappiness* and of other of his early writings, as is the fact that it is concerned with ancient Japan in the way that *Salammbô* is about ancient Carthage. Clearly *Salammbô* influenced *The Sun in Heaven:* one could hardly find a clearer case of that nebulous process. The question, however, is what exactly this influence was, and if it was of any real importance. Even if one accords it such importance, is there, can there be, any actual influence upon the style and, if there is, what kind of stylistic influence is it that comes out of a translation?

Ikuta Chōkō's translation of *Salammbô* was first published in 1913 and republished at intervals thereafter.[14] In his translator's preface Ikuta says that he had attempted to make the style actually read like a translation and that, in particular with regard to the conversations, he had tried to use the "unchangeable elements of the Japanese language" and to "deliberately avoid those elements which pertain to the limited Japanese of the past and, if only to a slight extent, to anticipate those elements which will make up the wider scope of the Japanese of the future." What this means is that the method of translation is the common Japanese one of direct translation taken to an almost insane extreme, direct translation being a concentration upon the single word as the primary unit of meaning, a giving progressively less importance to the structure and tone of the phrase, sentence, paragraph, and the work as a whole. In this case there is also a, necessarily limited, attempt to retain certain of the grammatical features of the original, and often to preserve the basic imagery of the single word or phrase. For example, a phrase such as "pétrifié de peur" is put into Japanese, not by choosing the nearest real equivalent, but by directly translating it word for word. In English this produces nothing odd ("petrified with fear") but the resulting Japanese (*"kyōfu ni kaseki shita"*) is very weird and exotic indeed. This does not arise from misunderstanding the original, since a misunderstanding could never be responsible for the appearance of Japanese of such oddity, even if one still maintained that it was a misrepresentation of the original and thus mistaken. However, what it does imply is that a writer who reads this and is influenced by it will concentrate upon that linguistic area which the translator himself has stressed; that is, on the vocabulary. This is not an isolated phenomenon, for if one considers the overall effect of European languages (particularly English) upon modern Japanese, it is the introduction of new vocabulary (not loan words only) which is immediately noticeable; a vocabulary assimilated into the Japanese grammatical structure, which then affects its meaning by this process of assimilation. This is as true of specialized new vocabulary, such as that created to express Kantian concepts, as it is of an everyday loan word like "sense." On the other hand, direct influence upon the grammatical structure is almost non-existent: an extended use of the passive form in partial conformation to English usage is perhaps the one positive example which could be pointed to.

One can certainly see signs of such a stylistic influence upon *The Sun in Heaven*. They are clear; they are also not very important, since what Yokomitsu absorbed from *Salammbô* was something other than a matter of stylistics. Similarities of style, when they do occur, reflect this something other. What that is a study of *The Sun in Heaven* will make clear.

*The Sun in Heaven* is the story of the obsession of a number of men with one woman. She is Himiko, princess of the country of Umi, who is betrothed to a prince of that country. Prince Nagara of the neighboring enemy country of Nakoku, who has seen Himiko and fallen in love with her, invades Umi, kills the betrothed prince as he lies sleeping with Himiko on their marriage night, lays waste the palace, seizes Himiko, and returns with her to Nakoku. Since Nagara's father immediately desires Himiko for himself, Nagara slays him too and, in the resulting confusion, Himiko escapes to the neighboring country of Yamato. The king of that country, Hanya, and his younger brother, Hanye, become similarly enamored of her, and she decides to use them to further her revenge against Nagara. Hanye kills the king, his brother, invades Nakoku at Himiko's command, and finally destroys Nagara, receiving his own death wound at the same time. The tale ends with Himiko's horror at the dreadful toll her vengeance has exacted.

The following extract is from that part of the story where Nagara, Prince of Nakoku, has returned to his native land from a trip to Umi where he had seen Himiko, had his life spared by her intervention, and thus fallen in love with her. An obsessed man, he rejects the wife offered him by his father, claiming that he wishes to sleep. As he retires to rest he is accosted by a young woman, the wife of the High Steward, who offers herself to him.

Nagara mounted the steps of the main hall in silence. The steward's wife seized his arm and pulled at him.

"Prince. Honor me: for this night perchance I die."

The steward seized his wife around the neck and pulled her away.

"Thou hast deceived me. Thou art crazed."

"Unhand me. I am not thy wife."

"Wife. Thou hast deceived me."

As the steward seized her hair and pulled her away the footsteps of some newcomer came stumbling and running towards them. It was Nagara's father, Hitoko no Kami, a wine cup in one hand. He lost his footing, then rose again, one cheek stained with earth.

"Woman. I have sought thee. Thy dance was splendid beyond all others. Come! Tonight I bestow on thee the palace of Nakoku."

Hitoko no Kami seized the woman's arm and was ascending the steps. The steward ran up from behind again and took his wife's hand.

"King. The woman is my wife. Spare my wife."

"Thy wife! So be it."

Hitoko no Kami released the woman and drew his sword. The steward's head fell to the ground. Then his body tumbling from the high veranda into the tall grass grew still there, and gazed upon its own motionless head.

"Come," said Hitoko no Kami to the woman, and took her hand.

"Prince. O prince. Save me."

"Come!"

The woman thrust Hitoko no Kami from her. Hitoko no Kami fell on his back on to the body of the steward, kicked his naked legs into the air, and then stood up again. With the stench of wine still reeking from his mouth he brandished his sword.

"Prince. O prince!" the woman cried and hurled herself upon Nagara's breast. But Nagara's body was unyielding as a tree. The sword fell. The woman's shoulder blades were cleaved in two, and she fell, striking the body of her dead husband.[15]

Perhaps an English reader of this direct translation would be most impressed by the biblical tone of the prose, and its sadistic detachment. Indeed, what is stylistically remarkable in the Bible

(I mean those stylistic features that can be retained in translation) is the briskness of the conversations, and the tendency for the sentence structure, usually a simple one, to repeat itself, thus isolating each sentence more than in normal prose where variety of sentence structure allows the paragraph to establish itself as the stylistic unit. However, the Bible, like the Japanese version of *Salammbô*, is a translation, and Yokomitsu's *Nichirin* is not, even if it has to appear before the English reader as such. The use of such stylistic devices is not brought about as they might be in a translation by the encounter with recalcitrant linguistic material, but by the desire to shape the world in a particular way. The attraction of *Salammbô* would have been that it also appeared to shape the world in that same way.

> "Qui es tu?" dit Mâtho.
> Sans répondre, elle regardait autour d'elle, lentement; puis ses yeux s'arrêtèrent au fond, où, sur un lit en branches de palmier, retombait quelque chose de bleuâtre et de scintillant.
> Elle s'avança vivement. Un cri lui échappa. Mâtho, derrière elle, frappait du pied.
> "Qui t'amène? Pourquoi viens-tu?"
> Elle répondit en montrant le zaïmph:
> "Pour le prendre!" et de l'autre main elle arracha les voiles de sa tête. Il se recula, les coudes en arrière, béant, presque terrifié.*[16]

This certainly does look something like the passage quoted from *The Sun in Heaven:* the short sentences used in conversation, the detachment of each sentence from the next giving a cinematic effect of cutting from one shot to the next. However, one can prove almost anything by the use of short quotations from novels. An overall comparison of the two novels would reveal many more differences than similarities. For example, the extraordinary fifth chapter of *Salammbô*, "Tanit," where Mâtho and Spendius use the aquaduct to gain entry to the palace and so

---

*"Who art thou?" said Matho. Without replying she looked about her, slowly, then her eyes halted at the back of the tent where, on a bed of palm leaves, something bluish and glittering lay. She went forward quickly. She let out a cry. Matho, behind her, stamped his foot. "Who brings thee here? Why hast thou come?" She replied by pointing to the sacred veil. "To get that!" and with her other arm she pulled the veils from her head. He recoiled, his arms thrown back, gaping, almost terrified.

steal the veil of the goddess, is a remarkable sequence of dream imagery which achieves effects of an extensive kind that never appear in the much more short-breathed, sporadic style of Yoko-mitsu. Except for a few pages of fine writing at the beginning of the work he writes only brief descriptive passages: the cumulative effects achieved by Flaubert, and which are perhaps the most noticeable stylistic feature in his work, are not attempted by Yo-komitsu, because the language would hardly permit it. The fact that Ikuta could put such passages by Flaubert into a form of Japanese does not affect this statement since Yokomitsu was writing real language and Ikuta was not. The reason the language would not permit it is that, compared with French, Japanese is, and in its literary tradition has been, a short-breathed language. This is not simply a question of length; *Genji* is a long enough work, and its sentence structures, if one can use that term, are certainly involved ones; but the style is a convoluted one which keeps turning in upon itself and does not achieve the cumulative power which is the mark of most European prose. Also, one has only to glance at the history of Japanese literature to see that the language has chosen the ideogrammatic unmoving image as its focus of meaning, whereas European languages focus on a sequence of images, each image fading into the next, and the structural unit is the paragraph. This is not a question to be argued here: it is a generalization offered to the reader for his assent. Even if he disagrees the fact of the basic differences between the two styles remains, whatever theoretical or historical reasons one may wish to assign to it.

Consequently one is left with similarities in the form the conversations take, and an abnormal use, on Yokomitsu's part, of the past tense. But more important is a most significant attempt in both works to render the whole of the narrative in visual terms, with only the essential minimum of psychological reflection (this last point is more true of Yokomitsu than of Flaubert, although it still holds true for both) which is generally of a very primitive kind. To this extent the literary attempt of both novels is the same; stylistic similarities follow from this basic similarity and in themselves are not that striking. Indeed Yokomitsu could have received identical influences by hearsay, by hearing a friend give a few minutes' description of what *Salammbô* was like, and then working from that. One may argue that this is an absurd hypothesis since it is known that it did not happen, but its aim is to stress what most needs to be stressed, which is that the influence is an abstracted one, a question of aims and possibilities rather than imitated methods, and that this is inevitably the form Western influence takes when it affects Japanese literature.

On a priori grounds the stylistic influence of one language upon another is hardly thinkable, and when it exerts itself through the medium of translation, however direct, it can exist only as a form of abstraction. Even in the field of vocabulary, although it is a fact that modern Japanese is cluttered with a vocabulary formed under the pressure of Western thought, the vocabulary is still a Japanese one and the Western concepts, even when in the form of loan words, are altered by that fact. With a medium as sensitive as literary prose there can be no powerful influences from outside since the Japanese language always asserts itself. For example, the conversations in *The Sun in Heaven* are of a kind that rarely appear in Japanese again, but this can not be explained by stating that Yokomitsu imitated Flaubert, failed, and thus the attempt was discarded, since the conversations in *Salammbô* too are an eccentric kind of French which also does not re-occur elsewhere. The style of these conversations, the form they take, was imposed by the literary attempt; beyond that attempt they have no validity and thus no further use. If one can still see direct imitation here (and it would be unwise to reject the idea outright in this case) it occurs only as a form of failure, the form of one language's failure being taken over into the other, and so exists only on that superficial level. However, it is the literary attempt (not, of course, *en bloc*) which Yokomitsu has taken from Flaubert, a number of semi-conscious suggestions about what literature might be. Some similarities of detail result from this, but they are few and not truly central. Except at the most superficial and momentary of levels, there is no question of imitation.

Flaubert's *Salammbô* is perhaps the most difficult of all his works to read today. The immediate reaction of the Goncourt brothers was that the emphasis upon visual description was boring and most remarkable for producing such minor results, and that the sentiments in it were either banal or general, with no particular relevance to the Carthaginian world.[17] These criticisms were echoed by Sainte-Beuve, who also stressed that although we know nothing of Carthage Flaubert still tells us nothing of any interest, and the exorbitant detail is merely an attempt to veil this nothingness; criticisms which convinced Sainte-Beuve that the historical novel could never be a viable literary form.[18] This critique was then put in a Marxist context by Georg Lukács, who claimed that Flaubert's grasp of history was virtually nil, and so the novel was merely an attempt to give "picturesqueness to a modern sensibility," the heroine being Mme. Bovary in fancy dress.[19]

The obsessive historical factuality of the detail and the modern sensibility accounts for that strange sense of having been here before that one experiences while reading the novel. This is the world of the Hollywood epic where twentieth-century American matrons about to set out on what appears to be a picnic are, in fact, the Israelites dressed with impeccable detail about to cross an authentic Red Sea. That *Salammbô* so often reminds one of cinematic techniques arises from a similarly aggressive concentration on descriptive minutiae, with a similar lack of interest in the human reality of history. The brevity of the conversations also seems to arise from the same fallacy as that embodied on the screen. When historical characters are not deliberately based upon contemporary or near-contemporary parallels (for example, the convention that the Roman Empire was run by people remarkably similar to the Imperial British ruling class), they are given a form of language which represents the primitive dignity of ancient, passionate peoples, a treatment similar to that meted out to Red Indians and Tarzan, as if they did indeed speak one of those imaginary languages consisting of stark one-word commands that Wittgenstein describes in the opening pages of his *Philosophical Investigations*. The fact that *The Sun in Heaven*

should share this Tarzanesque feature does not inevitably have to
be put down to influence (unless one feels it necessary to argue
the influence of Salammbô upon Hollywood, which is unlikely although not absolutely impossible). These are conventions which
arise quite spontaneously out of a use of history for its exoticism,
for its not being the present, and for its ability to transform the
present rather than to provide any understanding of the past.

Flaubert's concern was not with history as it might have
been. Thus he chose to write about Carthage, a civilization about
which nothing is known. His energetic researches into the ar-
chaeological details of the Carthaginian past were attempts to
give this nothing a shape, and a local habitation. "Ce qui me
semble beau, ce que je voudrais faire, c'est un livre sur rien,"[*][20]
was a constant preoccupation of his, as also was the great, subtle,
and unchanging sky which lies above all mere human involvement. His sympathy with the past was with an abstraction as he
assumed it had once existed, with "la tyrranie antique, ce que je
regarde comme la plus belle manifestation de l'homme qui ait
été."[†][21]

The Sun in Heaven is also not concerned with history. It is
true that Himiko was a real historical personnage, the queen
under whose rule various warring states were first formed into
the kingdom of Yamato (or Yamatai), events which took place
towards the end of the second century. Yokomitsu also certainly
read relevant historical works (although with nothing like the
scrupulous passion of Flaubert), and yet, even with the limited
information available to him half a century ago, he could certainly have done better than he did since there is no historical reality in the work, hardly one concrete detail that is right. Salammbô may well have imaginary toads in real gardens, but The
Sun in Heaven has no real garden, the detail being an abstraction
of "the distant past" as much taken from Western sources as from
Japanese ones; so much so that to a Japanese reader it can give a
stronger feeling of ancient Greece than of ancient Japan, and in

---

*What seems to me beautiful, what I want to make, is a book about nothing.
†Ancient tyranny, which I regard as the most beautiful manifestation of man
there has ever been.

the film version the soldiers wear a uniform at least as reminiscent of Imperial Rome as of feudal Japan.

Flaubert's attempt in *Salammbô* is to escape from the degraded and degrading reality of nineteenth-century France which destroys Emma Bovary to a reality which, however authentic in detail it may seem to be, is finally totally imagined. Yokomitsu's attempt is similar, only his is of more direct personal concern, since it is to transform events in his immediate surroundings, in his own actual life. In *Salammbô* the details of carnage, starvation, even an innocent act like eating, are oppressive and disgusting in themselves, but since all is recorded with the same detached tone they form images which leave the reader unmoved, unless he makes the moral effort to concentrate upon their significance, an effort which the style does not invite.

L'Éthiopien tira de sa ceinture un long poignard, et les trois têtes tombèrent. Une d'elles, en rebondissant parmi les épluchures du festin, alla sauter dans la vasque, et elle y flotta quelque temps, la bouche ouverte et les yeux fixes. Les lueurs du matin entraient par les fentes du mur; les trois corps, couchés sur leur poitrine, ruisselaient à gros bouillons comme trois fontaines, et une nappe de sang coulait sur les mosaïques, sablées de poudre bleue. Le Suffète trempa sa main dans cette fange toute chaude, et il s'en frotta les genoux: c'était un remède.*[22]

The similarity between this and the passage already quoted from *The Sun in Heaven* is too palpable to need stressing, as also are the differences: the breath of Yokomitsu's work is shorter and the images clearer in impact, although less detailed. There are also in both works deliberate attempts to set what are conventionally beautiful images (that is, images of things normally accepted as beautiful) against ugly human reality.

On voyait entre les arbres courir les esclaves des cuisines, effarés et à demi nus; les gazelles sur les pelouses s'enfuyaient en bêlant; le soleil se

---

* The Ethiopian drew a long dagger from his belt, and the three heads fell. One of these bounded among the remnants of the feast, then bounced into the basin where it floated for some time, mouth open and eyes staring. Glimmers of morning light came in through the crevices in the wall. The three corpses, laying breast downward, flowed in great bubbles like three wells, and a sheet of blood ran over the mozaic floor sanded with blue powder. The Suffete dipped his hand in this warm sludge and rubbed his knees with it. It was a cure.

couchait et le parfum des citronniers rendait encore plus lourde l'exhalaison de cette foule en sueur.*[23]

This may be seen as ironic contrast, like that used by Eliot in *The Waste Land* to describe the typist ("Her drying combinations touched by the sun's last rays"): but in fact the contrastive intent in Flaubert is not pointed satirically at these details, but simply serves to set them all in a background where they are not evaluated but accepted merely pictorially, a medieval painting of horrors whose pictorial charm is that the horrors have nothing to do with us. In this way human reality is totally distanced, and one notices that the only images which have a real power to hurt the reader are those of the sufferings of beasts, of the sacred fish, of the elephants in battle, since animals are outside of history and have the same reality in that ahistorical world as they have in our own.

This same distancing process can be seen at work in *The Sun in Heaven*.

On the far border the mountain peak sent forth its one jet of smoke. The sun turned to rose color as it sank. Then the field of long grass on the other bank began to whisper. In an instant a flock of water fowl made their disorderly flight high into the sky, and at once thousands of spear points glittered amid the tips of the plumed grasses.[24]

Again, one might interpret this as ironic, dramatic contrast as one might have done with the passage by Flaubert, but here also the principal impact is a pictorial one only, which aims at no contrast, seeing the spear points as the *same kind of thing* as the plumes of grass.

The effort to portray ugly human reality in purely aesthetic terms can be seen in a more positive form in the following example. During her flight from Nakoku to Yamato Himiko is assisted by a man, Kawarō, who has his own reasons for wishing to be revenged on Nagara. The two are captured by Yamato soldiers who are out deer hunting. Kawaro is hung from a tree, then

*The kitchen slaves could be seen running among the trees, frightened and half naked: gazelles fled bleating across the lawns. The sun was setting and the perfume from the citron trees made the exhalations from this sweating mob even more oppressive.

transfixed by an arrow, his death occurring as the mist rises.[25] Himiko demands his body from Prince Hanye, who since he has already fallen in love with her, grants her request, but later decides to dispose of the body, horrified by Himiko's apparent affection for this corpse.

> He crossed the open space, cut through the forest as far as the cliff which suddenly opened out from it, from which height he hurled down the body of Kawarō he had been carrying. Above the hazy far crests of the forest Kawarō's body circled, revolving glittering in the sunlight, until it plunged into the still, green silence.[26]

When Yokomitsu wrote that the great Kanto earthquake destroyed his "faith in beauty" it was this sort of thing he was referring to, the attempt to distance all the disagreeables (to use a Keatsian term) of existence into a far removed pictorial object; to distance them by denuding them of their meaning, their moral significance.

It is in this context that the sadism of Flaubert (and of Yokomitsu) becomes important. It is indisputable that Flaubert was deeply interested in the divine marquis, and although one would not wish to call *Salammbô* a sadistic work, despite the many sadistic elements in it, the dreadful emptiness the reader experiences when he has finished the work is remarkably like that induced by, say, *Justine*. The reason is that the artistic motive is similarly negative, since the style confers no pictorial significance upon the world and denies that anything relates to anything else in any meaningful way. The pictorial significance which exists in a painting is of the same order of significance as that of the moral life (the word "order" is used with circumspection, as I trust it will also be read, since it is not being claimed that the two are the same thing), for it reveals that objects are not arbitrarily there but are connected to one another in some essential relationship which the work of art, the painting, celebrates, being a hymn to this order which relates men to the world of objects in which they live; and the pleasure we take from a painting is the recognition of this order. Didactic paintings, which merely impose order, are offensive because they deny such essential and living connectedness by preferring abstract ones to them. Thus the ideo-

logical order formed out of the demands of social expediency
blots out the order which is the true work of art. Surrealist paintings offend in a similar way since their concern is also ideological, denying any sort of relationship between objects in the world
and so deifying the principle of arbitrariness. *Salammbô* is profoundly anti-didactic, but one can often see in it an attempt to
jumble objects together, removing their significance in a way remarkably close to Surrealism.

On entendait à la fois le claquement des mâchoires, le bruit des paroles,
des chansons, des coupes, le fracas des vases campaniens qui s'écrou-
laient en mille morceaux, ou le son limpide d'un grand plat d'argent.*27

This is a description of soldiers eating given in purely audial
terms, but in a way no human being could ever hear it, or could
hear anything, unless he were in some kind of coma. It is the
profound indifference with which the audial images are presented which is untrue to human experience, and which is also
its attraction. The consciousness apprehending this is distant as
in a drugged state, where words or breaking vases tinkle in the
mind and move it in no way. One might claim this is like the
awakened state of the mystic where all things speak of a transcendental significance in identical ways; and yet, of course, it is
precisely that dimension which is not here. The following is a
description of an army.

Ce tas de piques, de casques, de cuirasses, d'épées et de membres con-
fondus tournait sur soi-même, s'élargissant et se serrant avec des contractions élastiques.†28

In this case the nihilism of what is being attempted is un-
questionable (these are men being described), and both of these
examples stand as clear indication of Flaubert's concern in this
novel to deny any kind of value to human reality. Of interest
here is that this is in almost no way similar to the Yokomitsu of
*The Sun in Heaven*, but is very much like some of the writing of

*One heard at the same time the munching of jaws, the noise of words, of songs,
of blows, the crash of Campanian vases as they crumbled into a thousand fragments, or the limpid sound of a huge silver platter.
†This heap of pikes, helmets, cuirasses, swords and confused limbs turned
round upon itself, stretched and closed up in elastic contractions.

his next, his Shinkankakuha period. This fact is important because the progression from one style to the next is a natural one, and that elements of both can be seen in the same novel by Flaubert supports this point of view. It is also important in making the nature of Flaubert's influence clear. Unless one is to imply that Yokomitsu borrowed some bits of *Salammbô* for imitation now and saved some of the other bits for later, one is obliged to drop the idea of direct influence and accept that of a generalized one which has been stressed throughout this chapter. *The Sun in Heaven* and *Salammbô* resemble each other in their artistic intentions, and Yokomitsu was confirmed in his by the example of Flaubert. Since *Salammbô* is written inevitably in language, and since the Japanese translation is eccentric, various superficial aspects of the style would have echoed in Yokomitsu's head and produced some slight concrete influence. But this occurred at a superficial level only, and the deep meaning of this influence stayed always in the realm of the general and the abstract.

One final quotation from *Salammbô* will suffice here.

Il y avait des Ammoniens aux membres ridés par l'eau chaude des fontaines; des Atarantes, qui maudissent le soleil; des Troglodytes, qui enterrent en riant leurs morts sous des branches d'arbres; et les hideux Auséens, qui mangent des sauterelles; les Adhyrmachides, qui mangent des poux, et les Gysantes, peints de vermillion, qui mangent des singes.*[29]

The resemblance to the style of Paul Morand, dealt with in the next chapter, is striking, in that although the detail is arbitrary (what connection is there between cursing the sun, eating fleas, and burying one's dead, laughing, beneath the branches of trees?), its arbitrariness is functional. Arbitrary detail is chosen because any detail will do, because all detail is meaningless, because everything is meaningless. The artistic endeavor is to create a picture which pays homage to this meaninglessness and

---

*There were Ammonites with limbs wrinkled by the warm water of their hot springs, Atarantes who curse the sun, Troglodytes who cheerfully bury their dead under the branches of trees, and hideous Auseans who eat doves, Adhyrmachides who eat fleas, and Gysantes, painted vermillion, who eat monkeys.

provides us with the momentary shock of pleasure which comes as we recognize the multifarious pointlessness of all that is.

The aim of *The Sun in Heaven* is more limited than this, although, since this was the direction Yokomitsu's writing was to take, a nihilism of the same kind can be seen as latent in this work. Similarly the sadism of Yokomitsu, which may not be of the same obtrusive kind as that in *Salammbô* since its range of objects is more limited, is still unquestionably there, since it is an essential part of the pictorial aesthetic which is the basis of a work of this kind. *The Sun in Heaven* is also a less complex work, since its concern was to grasp at one central fact in Yokomitsu's life (perhaps *the* central fact, but, even so, still not the only one) and fictionalize it. The result is not so much to fictionalize his life as to make nonsense of it, for the novel itself could hardly be called a success. The interest of *The Sun in Heaven* is in what it set out to do, and solely in that: to fictionalize to as extreme a point as possible the world of *The Price of Unhappiness*.

> Hanya, his lips trembling, embraced Himiko's breast. Himiko, indifferent as a stone, entrusted her body to the King of Yamato.
> At that moment the sound of heavy footsteps was heard reverberating outside the room. Then the door was abruptly opened and Hanye was there. Seeing the two of them he stopped upright. And immediately his lower lip trembled with insane jealousy. Wordless, his teeth bared, he hurled himself at Hanya.
> "Go! Go!" Hanya said, raising himself from Himiko's side. Fear written on his face he attempted to flee, but Hanye grasped him and cast him against the log wall. Hanye fell striking the ground head first. Hanye drew the sword from his side. He flourished the naked blade then thrust it into his brother's side. Hanya screamed, then, clutching the blade, attempted to rise. But Hanye again cut him down, this time in the breast. Hanya dragged himself towards Himiko and, clutching at one of her feet, he breathed his last.[30]

This is as much a form of lived fantasy as the daydreaming of *The Price of Unhappiness*, although it has all been put into fancy dress, like Mme Bovary in *Salammbô*. However, if one sets this against the self-castration fantasy of the earlier work, one can notice that this time the author has managed to distance his fantasy, and so avoid his own total involvement in it. The images are coldly set down, and the focus of reader sympathy, of reader involvement, is never fixed or made clear but is constantly blurred and changing. This may have arisen to some extent from the fact that, as already seen in *The Price of Unhappiness,* Yokomitsu does have a grasp of the complexity of moral situations; and yet one must finally maintain that the work deliberately avoids such complexity and instead aims at, and achieves, an aesthetic disinvolvement from moral concerns. It can be noticed, for example, that if one character enlists the reader's sympathy at all it would be Himiko, and yet the amount of sympathy involved is too little to be of any importance. The reader is not involved because the author has been able to disinvolve himself.

Unfortunately, casting out moral reality means casting out human reality. The work is then not only unsatisfactory for the reader, but for the author as well, since it permits him to grasp nothing of what he describes but its pictorial emptiness, the shape that nothing has, and provides no satisfaction for him. The only satisfaction is the empty one of daydreaming, and the whole novel is a long daylit, or moonlit, fantasy. In this respect it is different from *The Price of Unhappiness* in which Yokomitsu had been concerned with grasping his own daydream and gaining the kind of control over it which the act of writing gives. But *The Sun in Heaven* is not the daydream as the material of art but the art object itself, and daydreaming becomes the artistic, creative act. An illusion of this order can leave only a bitter, empty taste, such as Flaubert seems to have experienced in the writing of *Salammbô.*[31] This is not the normal writer's dissatisfaction at the work never coming out as well as it had been imagined, but a fundamental unease about the attempt as a whole. The shadow does not fall between the intention and the act but darkens the intention itself.

If we accept *The Sun in Heaven* as a form of rewriting of *The Price of Unhappiness,* then it is another rewriting, this time a direct one, which shows the direction Yokomitsu's writing was to take. This story, "Maketa Otto" (The Defeated Husband)[32] is a

rewriting of the first third of *The Price of Unhappiness,* ending
with the husband's discovery of his wife in bed with the lodger.
The story uses a slightly more involved time sequence than the
direct, naturalistic one of the early version, and yet the sequence
of events is basically the same. The main differences are that the
rewriting ruthlessly cuts the amount of reflection which goes on
inside the hero's head, uses a shorter sentence, and has much
more conversation. Thus described reality is removed from its
former place inside the hero's mind and put outside into the real
world of spoken language and experienced objects. Since the
final two-thirds of *The Price of Unhappiness* would not have responded to such treatment the attempt was not made, and this
very fact points to a large limitation in the uses of this kind of
writing, a point which will be taken up again in chapter 4, for
here we shall be concerned merely with what the new literature
is like, something which can be seen in contrastive quotation.

The first of the following two quotations is from *The Price of
Unhappiness,* the second from "The Defeated Husband." Both
describe the same event.

One day he came back from a walk and found a letter addressed to
his wife lying face upward on the floor of the hall. Thinking nothing in
particular he was about to pick it up when a feeling of uncertainty
passed through his mind. He withdrew his hand and stared down at the
letter.
"I'll bet it's from a man," he thought. He felt this directly from the
unknown handwriting, but as this suspicion deepened the courage to
pick up the letter and look at the back faded. Indeed, even if he did look
what good would that do? If it was a love letter from a man his name
would hardly be written on the back, and even if it were what could he
do about it. All he could do, in fact, was simply make himself miserable.
Since the only thing to do in this situation was to preserve one's self respect, it was by far the best thing for oneself to just leave the letter as it
was.
He went into his study.

In the marketplace the figs and grapes had disappeared from the
greengrocer's stalls. Persimmons in new boxes were lined up in their
stead. The shadows in the streets fell in new directions, and it became

cold. He wasted almost the whole day in aimless walking. He no longer
went to the bookshop. He drooped, like a summer leaf that feels the
cold. Then one fine day he came home from his walk and found a letter
addressed to his wife fallen face upward in the hallway. Thinking nothing in particular, he reached to pick it up. Suddenly something passed
through his mind. He snatched his hand away and stared down at the
letter.

"I'll bet it's from a man."

Suspicion flickered up at him from the unknown handwriting on
the envelope, and as it deepened he did not feel like turning it over to
see the sender's name.

He went into his study.[33]

The change from an attempt to relate human psychology internally to that of placing it in the outside world is so apparent
that analysis of its details can presumably be left to the reader.
What should be particularly noted is that the inner happenings of
the mind are shown in terms of sensations rather than of ideas; it
is "something," not a feeling of suspicion or uncertainty, which
passes through the hero's mind, for the suspicion has been
placed securely inside an object, the handwriting. The descriptive passage which opens the excerpt has this same function of
relating psychic events through objects in the external world, in
this case being a preliminary indication of the state of mind
which is to come. Thus the first passage accepts what the everyday consciousness relates to itself as the real stuff of experience,
or at least of that experience which can take literary shape,
whereas the second calls this in question, wishing to give back
the realness to the actual world rather than mediate that realness
by way of the mind and so abstract and generalize its reality.
This is similar to much Western writing of the early decades of
the twentieth century, being a concern shared by writers as dis-
similar as Hemingway and Valéry.

Where this differs from *The Sun in Heaven* is that the earlier
work had attempted only to distance reality, to make it cease to
impinge, to objectify it completely, to, indeed, destroy the consciousness which observed it. The attempt of "The Defeated Husband" is not to objectify this outer reality, to reduce it to stone,

but instead to set the inner reality of the mind outside itself into this world of objects which make no particular sense in themselves. What kind of inner reality can be portrayed in this way? This is how "The Defeated Husband" ends:

"I'm free at last. I'm free. Free."
He walked with quick ungainly strides toward the station. He walked energetically, his body leaning forward. He mingled with people whose breath was white in the morning air as they entered briskly through the open gates of a factory. Crowded trams clanged through the confusion of mist and morning sunlight. The horns of passing motorcars splintered delicately about him. Amid the glittering metal and white smoke, people stepped out gaily. He raised his head. Before him a huge building thrust sharply into the sky.[34]

This is no longer the motionless world of *The Sun in Heaven,* nor is it a world from which one is detached. Yet it is still a similar world in the sense that the consciousness, although now certainly involved in the world, does not impose or recognize meanings in it. Thus it is a different consciousness from that of *The Price of Unhappiness* with its continual wrestling with the contingent world in order to establish what it means. When the meaning is intolerable other methods are sought. The end result is this, the consciousness almost rejoicing in the sense of its own nothingness which it sees splintered all around it in the fragments of the phenomenal world.

When he left the house it was already dark outside. He began to walk at once in the direction of the bookshop. A little girl with perfectly normal legs was limping hurriedly along imitating a cripple. After her came a truck racing along jammed tight with policemen. The bunch of policemen stood silently protruding above the cab like black stamens. A car followed after them. There was a girl inside who was tired. The wooden bridge shook as the vehicles passed over. He came to the main road and turned right. Several trams flew by shaking their human bundles to the rear. The crammed flesh ricocheted inside the square trams.[35]

The world can be seen like this, so emptied of meaning that objects take on the aspect of having some new meaning one cannot yet recognize and become isolated, threatening beings as in a nightmare. But this is not realism; it is the world seen through a patently intentional consciousness, a consciousness intent on setting the nothing it feels itself to be into the objective world which presses in upon it. This style is perhaps the basic one of "modernist" literature, and is probably best called "expressionistic" since it can be most readily grasped by a term as imprecise as that. It is the Shinkankakuha style.

Qu'est-ce que c'est beau? Qu'est-ce que c'est laid? Qu'est-ce que c'est grand, fort, faible? Qu'est-ce que c'est Carpentier, Renan, Foch? Connais pas. Qu'est-ce que c'est moi? Connais pas. Connais pas, connais pas, connais pas.

Georges Ribemont-Dessaignes[*1]

# Chapter Three: Shinkankakuha— Background and Theory

IT IS GENERALLY accepted that the years 1918 to 1923 represent a golden age in the world of Japanese letters, and that the period from then on is one of decline, a decline symbolized by the suicide of Akutagawa Ryūnosuke in 1927. It is during this period of decline when it is then maintained that Japanese literature finally catches up with the West, and the two become, for better or worse, true contemporaries. This is a different situation from that of the Naturalist writers for whom Western literature had been a much more generalized presence, with Japanese Naturalism being more a case of performing a Westernization of Japanese literature from a variety of sources, and not a concern with any particular or ideologically consistent aspect of it. It was in this lack of consistency that its strength had resided.

Again, the ideology associated with French Naturalism is obviously of less importance than the works produced by the various Naturalist writers, and it could well be considered as irrelevant, even contradictory, to those works. The novels of Flaubert and Zola are far superior to any role they might be supposed to play as part of a school of

*What is beautiful? What is ugly? What is great, strong, weak? What is Carpentier, Renan, Foch? Don't know. What is me? Don't know. Don't know, don't know, don't know.

writers. However, the various modernist movements in Europe between 1910 and 1925 (Futurism, Cubism, Dadaism, Expressionism, Surrealism) are notable for their ideas about literature rather than for the works they produced. As André Breton wrote: "Le cubisme fut une école de peinture, le futurisme un mouvement politique: DADA est un état d'esprit," and "il serait ridicule d'attendre un chef-d'oeuvre DADA'.*[2] Since these movements were more productive of ideas than of works they were more directly exportable than the literary ideas of the nineteenth century. An idea such as Romanticism might be initially grasped as a few catch phrases by a Japanese writer, but the more he read of the Romantic writers the more he would have to deepen, or abandon, his early ideas until he would end in a richness of confusion in which he would probably discard the word itself. Futurism, however, could be grasped in a few minutes: it would not be well grasped, since the Japanese writer would be cut off from any situation which might give meaning to such ideas, and yet the possibility of developing a deeper awareness of those ideas would not be open to him, since the works did not exist which might have allowed this to happen.

The powerful ideological emphasis in these movements would also ensure that literary ideas would become mixed up with political ones, and the modernist movements in Japan in the early and mid 1920s are closely connected with the most vigorous political ideas of the time, those of anarchism.

What is Poetry? The Poet? We discard all the ideas of the past and boldly proclaim: Poetry is a bomb! The Poet is a black criminal who hurls bombs at the hard walls and door of his cell.[3]

The concern with violence is the same as that of the parent movements in Paris.

Le surréalisme n'ait pas craint de se faire un dogme de la révolte absolue, de l'insoumission totale, du sabotage en règle, et qu'il n'attende encore rien que de la violence. L'acte surréaliste le plus simple consiste, re-

---

*Cubism was a school of painting and Futurism a political movement. Dada is a state of mind. It would be ridiculous to expect a Dada masterpiece.

volvers aux poings, à descendre dans la rue et à tirer au hasard, tout qu'on peut, dans la foule.*[4]

The tendency for this violence to end in the Communist Party or in some form of Fascism is a process one can see as well in Japan as in France, and perhaps the main factor in the early demise of the Shinkankakuha was the conversion of a number of its members to proletarian literature.

The first influential modernist document in Japanese literary history is the *First Manifesto of the Japanese Futurist Movement*, written by Hirato Renkichi and published as a broadsheet in 1921, twelve years after Marinetti's manifesto in *Le Figaro*. Hirato died young, in 1922, at the age of twenty-nine. His principal education in things Western seems to have come about through contact with Christian missionaries, which may account for the slightly religious tone of his manifesto, although it only accentuates a visionary fervor already present in Marinetti.

The mind of the trembling god, the central activity of our humanity, issues forth from the core of our collective life. The city is the motor. Its core is dynamo electric.[5]

The divine attributes have been totally subjugated by the hand of man, and nowadays the engine of god is the motor of the city, and partakes of the activities of humanity's millions.

The instinct of god moves to the city. The dynamo electric of the city stirs the basic instinct of humanity, awakens it, forthrightly demands that we make violent advances.

The realm of god lives in the organic connections of our total lives, and is no more in the darkness of animal behavior, in its frustrations and discord, its condition of servitude, but is now in the impulsive sincerity of the machine, in its light and heat and ceaseless rhythm.

Marinetti—*Après le règne animal, voici le règne mécanique qui commence*.[6]

We dwell in the midst of strong heat and light. We are the children of strong heat and light. We are that strong heat and light itself.

Intellect must give place to intuition. Conceptualization is the artistic enemy of Futurism. We who "since time and space are already dead

---

*Surrealism is not afraid to make a dogma out of absolute revolt, out of a total refusal to submit, out of deliberate sabotage; and all it expects is violence. The simplest surrealist act consists in going out into the streets, a revolver in each hand, and shooting arbitrarily and for as long as one can at the crowd.

dwell in the already and the absolute" must promptly dare to create an appropriate form for ourselves. All that is left to us is that activity of our humanity which gives direct access to the instinct of god, that highest law which transcends the chaos before us.

Most of the graveyards have already lost their usefulness. Libraries, museums, academies, are not worth the roar of a single motor car gliding along the road. Just try smelling the foul stench of piles and piles of books. How many times superior is the freshness of gasoline.

The Futurist poets extol many aspects of our machine culture, those aspects which enter the inner sanctuary of potential future activity, pierce us with their mechanical swift wills, stimulate our ceaseless creation, are the agencies of speed and light and heat and power.

"Chameleon of dancing truth"—variety—complexity—all the chords in the light seen in the confusion of the kaleidoscope.[7]

There are a few more lines in this vein and of an increasing obscurity, and, since the "ideas" being put forward here do not invite discussion, they will not be given any. However, the question which naturally arises is that of the appropriateness of such a state of mind for a young man from the Japanese countryside in 1921. Perhaps all that is truly being expressed here is a longing for that state of mind rather than the thing itself, and perhaps this very craving may have been accentuated by the circumscribed circumstances in which these Japanese modernist writers lived. One can see the unfortunate consequences in the opening lines (there is no need to look further) of a poem by Hirato.

*Motor Car*
whirling, whirling
the voices of battle—
my motor car
dances dances dances
tttttttttt
dddddddddd
ppppppppppp
rrrrrrrrrr
over there over there[8]

This is mere fatuity; whereas the next poem fails in a much more interesting way.

CHORUS (Post Expressionist ANALOGIST poem—*Imagisme +Expressionisme=*
ANALOGISME) Total identification of expressed and expression.

```
DAWN VOICES           BRUUU    ---- UNBB    voices
.       N voices⋛  N⌄⌄⌄⌄⌄   voices
UU      voices⋛  U      dawn + +voices + light light light light
U.      voices N      R      dawn voices
U.      a voice       OBBBB   voice voice voice voice voice voice
R.      voice         V●●●●   voice          aeroplane
B●           ●voice       ...     voice  ...............................
B —     ++++++++++++ voice +++ ploughing man man man man man
BN ..        voice .. voice    tower...........love . man
ND ..        voice + voice + man man ploughing in the heart
UU ..        voice voice + tower of babel .. plough    man
--      voice mountain valley mountain tower of babel dancing man
U            new voice══════════════ TOWER OF BABEL
R.      new voice     S      bell's voice man man
B there is a new voice        ll...........man
      NEW VOICE  ═══════════ towertowertowertowermanmanmanman [9]
```

This is, if read patiently, a description of an actual experience, and the effort to decipher it can indeed give one almost an
affection for it; yet what it truly reads like is a parody written by
a schoolboy who had picked up by hearsay (jocular remarks by
his school teachers, comedy programs on the radio) an image of
what a "modern" poem is like, rather as one could pick up a similar image of "modern" sculpture from cartoons in the popular
press. Naturally it is not implied that Hirato did anything like
that. He certainly was not trying to write parody, but he was in a
similar world of hearsay and ignorance, and his concern seems to
have been less with what modern poetry really should be than
with himself *really* "being a modern poet."

Dadaist Shinkichi (Takahashi Shinkichi) who wrote impressive poems once he escaped from his Dadaist shadow, is a poet
far superior to Hirato. Unlike Hirato Takahashi could read no
French. He admitted in a letter that he had picked up his ideas
about Dada (namely the idea of the arbitrary as the leading principle in literary composition) from an article in a newspaper. He
did not imitate any European Dadaist works since he had read
only one or two (presumably in the same newspaper article); instead he claimed that he caught the essence of the movement and

then worked independently in the same spirit.[10] This supports the basic thesis about Western literary influence put forward in the previous chapter, as also does the contention of Mr. Eto that;

Because the Japanese feel that Western culture is superior to their own, there is a strong sense of obligation to catch up with the West in almost every aspect of daily life. But most Japanese have hardly any direct access to the West per se and hence they abstract what they believe to be the essence of Western culture from occasional rumours or from arbitrary readings in translation, and idealize it or purify it until every substance connected with Western culture has been completely distilled away.[11]

One can see this most clearly in the fact that "Dadaist" Shinkichi's poems are nothing like Dadaist poems. Here is a poem called "Plates" as example:

platesplatesplatesplatesplatesplatesplatesplatesplatesplatesplatesplates
platesplatesplatesplatesplatesplatesplatesplatesplatesplatesplatesplates
Weariness
worm creeping passion on my forehead
Don't wipe the plates
with the apron the color of white rice
woman with the black nest of her nose
Even here jests smoulder
Wash away life in the water
Boredom drifts
in a pot of cold stew
Break the plates
Breaking the plates
lets loose the sound of weariness [12]

This next poem is called "Blind Man."

Snow
Jet black
Radish dark      dirty hands
Burdock bears lewd thoughts
Not a bite of anything nice      Poetry   Death
Sugar beet   people who sleep   the spring of action
Leaning trees rusty nail        woman's thighs
Quarrelling lusts            Hole in my glove
Dropped one of them somewhere
Buried buried buried buried buried
Buried buried      Suburban train suburban train

suburban train   Like ice the fire in the earth
White white white        that is white
That only is white
An eye like the glazed one of a sardine
To be impaled
and grilled
The sky[13]

Neither of these are Dadaist poems, and although that in itself would be no reason for condemning either, it does suggest that the essence of Dada was not so easily to be found in a newspaper article. What we have are "modern" poems, perhaps a little like some of Paul Reverdy, although much closer to what one might find in the school magazine. The following poem, "Dimanche," by Philippe Soupault, is true Dada.

L'avion tisse les fils télégraphiques
et la source chante la même chanson
Au rendez-vous des cochers l'apéritif est orangé
mais les mécaniciens des locomotives ont les yeux blancs
La dame a perdu son sourire dans les bois[14]

[The aeroplane weaves the telegraph wires
and the well-spring sings the same song
At the Coachman's Rest the aperitif is orange-colored
but the locomotive mechanics have white eyes
The lady has lost her smile in the woods]

This is very light and cheerful, far removed from the "Waste Land" gloom of Takahashi, for the essence of Dadaism was that it was funny, a series of happenings rather than works, a series of practical jokes.

As for me, announced as "Dada," I read aloud a newspaper article while an electric bell kept ringing so that no one could hear what I said.

I invented on the occasion of this performance a diabolical machine composed of a klaxon and three successive invisible echoes, for the purpose of impressing on the minds of the audience certain phrases describing the aims of Dada. The ones which created the most sensation were, "Dada is against the high cost of living," and, "Dada is a virgin microbe." We also produced three short plays by Soupault, Breton and Ribemont-Dessaignes and "La Premiere Aventure Céleste de M. Antipyrine" which I had written in 1916. The play is a boxing match with words. The characters, confined in sacks and trunks, recite their parts without moving, and one can easily imagine the effect this produced—performed in a greenish light—on the already excited public. It was impossible to hear a single word of the play.[15]

Such happenings are quite absent from Japanese Dadaism, although five poets did attempt to reproduce Tzara's method of writing poetry, when they wrote their names in roman script, cut them up into single letters, scattered those letters about the room, and then picked them up in the order of those which had fallen farthest from the center. Tzara's own method had been to shuffle about newspaper cuttings in a box, and the intrusion of the logical principle into the Japanese poets' method is perhaps something he would not have been pleased by. Unhappily no example of the works produced by this method is available. Onchi Terutake notes that the poet Don Zakki (an assumed Dadaist name—his real name was Tozaki Tomoo) used to walk along the Ginza in Wellington boots. Since he records nothing more sensational than that one is obliged to conclude that the Japanese Dadaists were not really serious in their attempts to *épater les bourgeois*. Don Zakki's "Wave a Flag at the Earth's Axis" does, however, have something of the authentic Dadaist tone.

It's midnight and
The eyeless pig has ceased to moan
—Buried
The red half moon sobs
The black heart sings
The beggar who walks on his head
    sleeps in the desert wind

Pig-a-back laughs
The third child weeps
    Gentlemen!
Cut off your ears
Material objects have vanished
    To the doldrums—
I wave a flag at the earth's axis[16]

The year after the earthquake, 1924, saw the publication of a number of new poetry magazines, the titles of which are sufficiently illuminating: *Red and Black, Chains, Dumdum, Black*

*Storm Era, MAVO* and *GE; GJMGJGAM; PRRR; GJMGEM* (pronounced in Japanese as Geh; Gimugigamu; Purururu; Gimugemu). One of the poems in this last magazine was called "Crustacean Construction," of which I give the opening section:

Crustaceans are logarithmic
Something like Sin $\frac{\pi}{2}$ Sin $^a$?
Since $\pi$ is a circle
Will it be $3^3$?
No
Isosceles is a battle monad of wire and steel cable
The external combustion engine is heavy on the barometer
Heavy on the winter solstice
Nothing to do with the circle
$A + B = A + 1 + \pi$.[17]

Perhaps the most notable aspect of this poem is that, despite its absurdity, it has a grave air of solemnity about it, the same humorlessness which marks all the manifestoes of the time. "Burn! Burn everything! For the Ideal, for Justice. No! Rather for the final detonation of our festering flesh."[18]

Here we are far from "Dada is a virgin microbe," in a world of total hysteria; and the tone of the next quotation, although recalling statements made by French contemporaries at that time, goes well beyond them in the screaming high pitch of its voice.

Let's chuck out from our minds this bogeyman of "ideas." This hateful specter that has caused us to suffer so long, throw hatred and scorn in his stupid Sophist's face, and laugh when you recall his snivelling. Then in all decency cast him into the rubbish heap marked USELESS.[19]

If one compares this to any of the statements by Breton which are similarly anti-intellectualist in content, one is struck by the reasonableness of his tone even at its most extreme.

This hysteria reaches a high point with the poet Hagiwara Kyōjirō, who had known Hirato, contributed to *Tane maku hito* (The Sower, the first of proletarian literary magazines, but one with a powerful anarchist bias), had created *Red and Black*, and become a kind of Dadaist leader. In 1925 he published a volume of poems called *Shikei Senkoku* (Death Sentence), the preface of which is very much in the tradition established by Hirato Renkichi, and of which I give about one fourth part here.

A poem listens to the music which sounds in our own little box, and also to the sounds of the trains on the overhead railway that mingle with the noises of the city. The sound of the press and the sound of the pen racing beside it are heard as the sound of the one insect. In a momentary spiral, joy, laughter, wrath, pleas, cries, screams and blows explode, revive and run. Thick, billowing yellow smoke compresses the richly discharging heart.

No line of poetry must exhaust itself with the heavy burdens which prose carries.

Discard this role of politely handing things on to the next line! Let each line stand by itself alone. Create a strong, strong sensation!

If this be impossible, if the one line can not yet fully reveal itself, then create a tempo which rushes precipitately into the next line. Thus will the misfired spirit turn and gyrate in the explosion's smoke.

New reality without end, struggle without end, change without end—this is the process which will bring you to that highest interest and intoxication extending even to madness. . . .

Where does our beauty and desire lie? Write from right to left, from left to right, from up down and down up, read from all directions, mix up large and small print, insert illustrations, and spend all your time thus until your enthusiasm exhausts itself; yet still shall you be unable to discover our perfect beauty. . . . It is imperfect and bears an eternally violent form. It journeys through a fearfully resounding tunnel. Amid destruction, revenge, burial, rebirth and momentary acts, our form ascends the raging stream.

Thinking as it thinks, feeling as it feels, it simply moves. It is the latent heat behind movement; it is the dynamic, that aimlessness which has the highest aims. It is an enormous speeding roller crushing the life of the present and the past, crushing hypocrisy and hunger, crushing the husk of the self.

Only the positive!

. . . . . . . .

Freedom! Freedom!

Away with all slaves! [20]

His poems have the same kind of wildness, being either like the one by Hirato already quoted,[21] or like the following, "Walking along the Street with a Man."

You say my face is an octagonal clock!
A ragged leaflet came out of a bat!
Look here, you—
I'll put a hose in your earhole!
Brain coal has a high temperature!
————the noonday gun

Dry the colors!
It's the red flag! The weather forecast's gone crazy!
gnash gnash gnash gnash
The anger and evil of chains meshes together
The train ascends shaking its belly
Look, I'm telling you——you'll get nowhere without the password
It's just a nuisance if your legs aren't artificial!
Have a cigarette!
It's fallen smouldering down into your guts!
Look here you————kokkokkokkokkokkokkok
Language is exterminated
Action is exterminated
So you're the moustache in boots who walks all over our skeletons!
I'm going to do something as certain as using a pistol!
Right and Left   ONE TWO! ONE TWO!
     Doubleuuu    Doubleuuu
     rukrukrukruk
     geckle geckle
   MARUZEN ATHENA INK [22]

The "bat" in line two is probably a reference to a brand of cigarettes ("Golden Bat"), and the "action as certain as using a pistol" is probably refering to that of flushing a (Western-style) toilet, or W.C., since if it does not then one can make no sense of the "double-uuu," although that is perhaps not too powerful an argument in this context. The last two lines would then be the sound of flushing, although the final reference to ink suggests that other interpretations might well be possible.

It is with this kind of literature that charges of imitation start to sound reasonable. The attempts to write "space cubist poems" by using imported typographical arrangements look as preposterous as the attempts of Japanese poets in recent years to write "concrete" poems with typewriters when set against a thousand-year-old tradition of calligraphy which had established the poem as a visual object in a way totally impossible in the West. For these writers their image of writing and the writer is Westernized in the sense that they have a picture of what these things mean in the West, and it is to that picture they wish to conform. "Imitation" is thus not really the appropriate word here, since there is not a sufficient acquaintance with the originals. An abstracted image sways them as they write, and since it must be an up-to-date image, it never has time to establish itself in any depth. The motive force comes from images, ideas, abstractions, rather than from actual works. Since this motive force is thus inevitably superficial, it either produces work of no value or, for a writer who does manage to write comparatively well, it has no real importance for his work as such. Since it could not affect these writers deeply it would leave their creative sources untouched; the danger being that it might cause them to turn away from such true sources.

The writers dealt with so far in this chapter are only, or mainly, of historical importance. They are writers who tell us something about the literary situation in the early 1920s, but in a proper history of modern Japanese poetry they should be little more than a lengthy footnote since the real poems of the time were written by others. One has always to remember that the modernist poets writing in France at the same time were in a tradition at least fifty years old, that their ideological ambitions were never attained (i.e. they did not achieve an aesthetic image of spontaneous thought), and that what is memorable in their work consists mainly of souvenirs and echoes of Romantic and Post-Romantic poetry. A Japanese modernist poet could not be the culmination of a long tradition in that way, and he had no masters of revolt (certainly no masterpieces of revolt) to look to. The poems of Hirato Renkichi and Hagiwara Kyōjirō are connected to nothing and for this reason sound so empty.

These modernist movements in France were anti-novel. There is the famous remark, allegedly by Valéry and quoted with approval by Breton in his first surrealist manifesto, that one could not write "La marquise sortit à cing heures,"* and indeed this manifesto opens with an attack on realism and on that literary form, the novel, in which realism primarily manifests itself. However, the achievements in French writing during the 1920s are surely those of Proust, Gide, du Gard, Radiguet, and

*Her ladyship went out at five o'clock.

Malraux, rather than Valéry, Cocteau, Breton, Éluard, and Aragon. The first concern of the Shinkankakuha was with the novel, with prose, and despite their apparent rejection of the Japanese Naturalists they were still writing in a form which had established itself in the language and produced works of value. To this extent they had a literary instrument, a tradition no matter how brief, which could save them from their own worst ideological excesses.

The magazine *Bungei Shunjū* (Literary Chronicle) appeared in January 1923 and is important in two respects; first, it was a platform for the young writers who were to form the Shinkankakuha in 1924, and second, it was a magazine aimed at a far wider audience than any literary magazine had yet attempted. It still maintains this role of a popular intellectual magazine and it can be seen as the first move in the popularization of literature which is so significant a feature of the Japanese late literary 1920s. The magazine's editor, Kikuchi Kan, is a key figure in this process. Among the contributors to its first number were Yokomitsu and Kawabata. Yokomitsu's contribution was a critical article attacking the class concept of literature; and its appearance indicated that he had started to be an up-and-coming young writer. The same year saw more articles from him, most of which manifest a distaste and irritation with the established literary world, in effect with the Naturalists and "I-Novelists." The attack on them becomes quite open in an article written in that hysterical and confused style,[23] which the reader will by now assume, with some justification but not with complete justice, to be the normal tone of progressive young writers of the time. It includes such phrases as, "What we ask is not to be made to eat your yesterday's shit," and, "To deny the truths you hold we shall create puppets, puppets which have indeed pranced away from your impotences. We will create fictions. To give reality to our fictions we require the cajolement of various puppeteers. For your sake we dare to reject your consciousness." There is not much sense to be made out of these remarks, but one certainly gathers that he is dissatisfied with these people and is not prepared to mince his words about it (at least not in the generally accepted meaning of that phrase).

The first number of *Bungei Jidai* came out in October 1924 as a *"dōjin zasshi,"* a magazine formed by a group of young writers in order to publish their own works, and thus fairly close to the English equivalent of "little magazine," although the coterie nature of the Japanese kind would be stronger. Of the fourteen writers associated with *Bungei Jidai* eight had come from *Bungei Shunjū,* suggesting some form of defection from that magazine.

Editorial duties were performed in turn, with two editors editing three monthly numbers. The first two were Kawabata Yasunari and Kataoka Teppei. It was Kawabata who chose the name of the magazine and wrote its first editorial, in which he pointed out that although "those who love gossip see the creation of *Bungei Jidai* as a challenge presented by the progressive to the established writers," this was not in fact their chief concern since they had no desire,

to hurl stones and meaningless shouts at the spectacle of the literary establishment doing its legless dancer dance. That is something we would rather forget about. However, this sort of commonplace [i.e. progressives versus establishment] doesn't just arise from what is only a literary squabble, is not some kind of exotic ornamentation, but must be, we feel, the result of a deep-rooted demand the age makes upon us. As far as this historical trend is concerned it is more than natural that we, as progressive writers, should feel some sort of responsibility.[24]

This is a fairly definite challenge to the old order, even if it is not made clear exactly what form that challenge is to take.

An article by Kataoka Teppei, which appeared two months later in the December issue, is virtually a manifesto against the old way of writing on behalf of the new, the new having now acquired the name Shinkankakuha, bestowed upon them by a journalist of the time. Kataoka's article begins with one of the opening sentences of a story by Yokomitsu, "Atama narabi ni hara" (Heads and Bellies), which had appeared in the first number. Kataoka quoted the third sentence from the following:

It was noon. The crowded express train raced at full speed. The small wayside station was ignored like a stone. (Or: The small wayside stations were ignored like stones).

Kataoka then comments:

According to one member of the literary establishment this phrase ["ignored like a stone or stones"] is extremely bad. This quest for novelty of expression for its own sake, this self-styled new age that uses such weird methods of depicting the world, this insistence upon the impressionistic is a mistake. There's probably nothing really new in the content either. This impressionistic method is quite unacceptable. As for talking about a new age in this context, what confounded nerve!

Thus spake the member of the literary establishment.[25]

Kataoka coyly refused to say who this was, although it was quite clear from the way he wrote who his informant must be. The informant himself, Hirotsu Kazuo, then replied, stating that the "establishment writer" was Uno Kōji (born in 1891 and one of the best of the "I-Novel" writers), and taking Kataoka to task for encouraging his readers in this guessing game which takes their attention away from the feebleness of his arguments. Hirotsu himself, however, does not deal with these feeble arguments on any theoretical level, but instead criticizes Kataoka for dealing with only one sentence instead of the work as a whole, maintaining that the sensationalist method of the opening is not maintained throughout the whole story. The point is just, and he goes on:

Kataoka, do you really believe that Yokomitsu's *Atama narabi ni hara* represents a victory of the sensationalist method over your so-called "establishment writer"? Do you maintain that this is a work which goes beyond "the various sensations of common sense" to become a method of "projecting upon the external world, glittering and dancing, the poems that are scattered like fireworks within the internal world by collision with objects"?[26]

Hirotsu is on safe ground here, since, like most manifesto statements, Kataoka's look foolishly inflated when set against the work they allegedly refer to. This is a failing basic to so much modernist criticism, for it either precedes the work as a statement of policy which, like similar statements in the political field, must inevitably disappoint in its results, seeming retrospectively to invalidate the earlier statements; or else draws excessively far-reaching conclusions from one work, conclusions which then react upon that work and so belittle it. Polemic has no proper role to play in criticism, although it is the inevitable weapon of literary controversy, and it bedevils all discussion surrounding the creation of the Shinkankakuha. The fact is Kataoka does have something to say about the new literary style he is endorsing (the relevance of these remarks to the literature actually produced will be taken up in the next chapter), and what he says is, on the whole, coherent.

It will be argued that in order to transfer one person's reality to another the best thing to do is use a simple and precise terminology. To transfer the commonplace reality of an express train rushing through a small station this kind of non-commonsense expression is not required. Yet the writer could hardly be satisfied with a plain recital of such "reality." He was aware that, in order to depict in a couple of words or so the relationship among the train, the station, and the impression upon the writer, something strikingly effective, something animated was required.

Something strikingly effective! Something animated! Well then, to portray a material object like a train effectively and animatedly, is something other than a sensationalistic expression likely to succeed? That expressionistic power which mediates between the object and the writer's existence, and which gives this existence its life, is indeed sensation. It is not something else. It is not his feelings nor his mind. If a man's mind or feelings were to mediate between him and the express train, then that would be a secondary existence coming after the sensation. However, our progressive writer sees no need to indulge in this secondary existence. At least there was no intention of thrusting this upon the reader in the very first phrases. All he wished to do was to portray the situation sensationalistically and thus powerfully and strikingly.[27]

The claim made here for the new literature centers on a fairly basic epistemological question of how the world is actually taken in: these new writers deny the common-sense view of the world, which had been the basis of nineteenth-century realism, and reject the mediation of a particular sensibility which organizes the world of brute fact into the "State of mind" or "I novel," claiming instead to give us the actual record of the sensations or sense impressions as received. Now this may be a possible literary program, but, of course, it has meaning, not to the degree to which it makes theoretical sense, but to the extent it can be seen to be carried out in actual works of literature.

Hirotsu, in the article already referred to, maintained that Kataoka was constructing a theory of literature out of the personal necessity of just one writer, Yokomitsu, reflecting his particular view of human life as the human race journeying toward destruction, leaving no project for human beings other than that of enjoying their own sensations. Hirotsu here accuses Yokomitsu of that nihilism and decadence which the proletarian writers were later to point to in his writings; and he ends his article by asking for an art which will revolt against the corruptions of capitalism, not in political but in artistic terms, an argument of such obscurity that it does not permit, probably not even invite, elucidation.[28] Similar sentiments were expressed by Ikuta Chōkō, whom we have already met as the translator of *Salammbô*, but who by this time seems to have forgotten his own alleged interest in the new Japanese language of the future. Now a well-known hatchet man of Japanese letters, famous for his attacks upon the *Shirakabaha*, he led the main onslaught upon *Bungei Jidai* from the pages of the magazine *Shinchō*. The leading point of his polemic is that this movement is no more than an imitation of the French writer Paul Morand, claiming that after that writer's *Ouvert la nuit* had appeared in Japanese translation a "new literary age" had begun, a fact he had learned on authority, although who or what this authority might be he does not specify. In fact most of Ikuta's attack consists of a critique of Morand's novel (a very competent one, it should be added), the implication being (an implication made openly at the end) that these remarks must naturally apply to his Japanese imitators.

Some words may be necessary about Paul Morand, a writer who may not be well-known to English readers. He is in the words of M. Gaëtan Picon, "l'exemple frappant d'une littérature qui se réduit à sa date, 1920."*[29] A Japanese critic has referred to

*a striking example of a literature which can be reduced to its date, that of 1920.

Morand as a "Dadaist novelist," but a Dadaist novelist is a contradiction in terms. Morand himself refers to Dada in amused
tones. He was also a career diplomat, which would have given
him little opportunity to participate in those manifestations
which were the essence of Dada. The term could properly be
applied to him only on the ground that all the true Dadas were
against Dada. However, what *Ouvert la nuit* does offer is a kind
of plain man's modernism, mock Dada without tears (or triple-
echoed klaxons), which uses an expressionistic style in patches
(but never long enough to weary the plain man), but most of the
writing is lucid and ordinary enough. This international best
seller attracted readers by its modish internationalism, its brisk
tour through the countries, customs, and sexual possibilities of
the world. M. Sartre has pointed out that Morand's method of
jumbling together a variety of exotic objects has the same destructive intention as that of Surrealism, its same obsession with
the contradictory, with the bringing together of objects which
negate the meaning of one another.[30] Morand's own comment on
the book (in 1957) was that it was the "De profundis d'une
Europe qui me semblait déjà ne pas pouvoir en réchapper."*[31] It
is, however, a despair that arises out of having experienced all
and understood all, which has its attractions for readers who
have not the good or the bad fortune to be in that position.

Pour les voyageurs, Espagne est un pays comme les autres, avec des
billets de lotterie, des eaux purgatives, des assurances sur la vie, des
parlementaires qui s'embrassent sur la bouche après les discours, et des
ascenseurs dont le plancher s'éclaire dès qu'on y appuie le pied. Un
beau cloaque. Barcelone est un cliché sud-américain. . . .†[32]

The perky *esprit* of this makes it intolerable reading now, but
it would have had its attractions at the time, in particular for people who had not been to Barcelona often enough to think of it as
a South American cliché, or who did not naturally think of places

---

*The *De Profundis* of a Europe which already seemed to me to lack the power to
avoid it.
†For the traveler Spain is a country like any other, with its lottery tickets, its
purgative waters, its life insurances, its senators who kiss each other on the
mouth after speeches, and its elevators whose floors light up when you tread on
them. A lovely cesspool. Barcelona is a South American cliché . . .

in such terms, or who had never been to Barcelona at all. How true this must have been for Japanese intellectuals of that time. Ikuta stresses this when trying to account for its popularity, saying that its interest lies in the information it gives about present-day Europe from a variety of points of view and most of its appeal comes from its being sexually provocative and titillating. He seems to overstress this point, although that in itself may be a significant indication of what Japanese readers got from the book. He quotes from the preface to the novel by its translator Horiguchi Daigaku:

Paul Morand's style astonishes people. Why is this? The answer is perfectly simple. It is that a stylist of great sensitivity and keen powers of observation has created new connections between objects that previous ways of writing would never have attempted to bring together. The connection between objects in the ordinary way of writing is one of "the logic of reason" which links them together. However, in Morand, this "logic of reason" gives place to a "logic of sensation."[33]

Ikuta's answer is that Morand is only using devices already used in poetry, in particular in the Japanese *haiku*, and that although this may be rare in prose it is not new and, more importantly, not good, since these "logic of sensation" *haiku*-like passages make up only a small proportion of the novel and do not fit with its overall realistic tone.

The so-called "logic of sensation" thus works only in parts of the book, and not in the whole. What controls the whole is the "logic of reason" as of old, and when this is set next to the "logic of sensation" it is rather as if the whole thing limped along with one contorted leg.[34]

He then refers to a quotation from *Ouvert la nuit* which Horiguchi had picked out as of special interest:

Un dahlia entra dans ma bouche ouverte jusqu'au gosier. Bataille de fleurs. Un jardin passait dans l'air.*[35]

Ikuta objects that a serious writer would not have put this in the context it has in the book since it sticks out so awkwardly and unintelligibly.[36] He concludes that what is wrong with this "mo-

---

*A dahlia entered my open mouth right down into my throat. Battle of flowers. A garden passed into the air.

mentary" style is precisely that it is momentary and thus cannot be maintained over a few pages, yet alone over a whole book, and consequently destroys the book as a structured whole.[37]

This is an intelligent critique of *Ouvert la nuit*, and since much the same could be said of a great deal of stylistic expressionism in the early years of the twentieth century, clearly certain of these remarks could be considered as applicable to the Shinkankakuha writers. It is a fact, for example, that the flashy opening style of Yokomitsu's "Atama narabi ni hara," the work allegedly under discussion, is not maintained even through a work as short as that, and the implication that, of its very nature, it could not be seems to be a fair one. Exactly the same point was made by a postwar critic, Noma Hiroshi, who saw this as a basic contradiction in the ideology of the movement, which ensured that no new literature could be created that way.[38] However, literature is not made out of ideologies, whether they are basically contradictory or not, and Morand's failure need not imply that of other writers; for even if a similar kind of failure could be seen to exist, one could only maintain that one was suggestive of the other, not that its existence should be thought of as definitive for the other in some causative way. There is nothing to show that Morand's failure is any more than his own, unless one accepts his writings as a prototype on which these other writers formed their own models. Perhaps the most disturbing feature of this literary controversy is that it concerns itself so little with the relevant literature, being about Paul Morand, one sentence by Yokomitsu, and then a mass of abstractions which evade rather than refer to concrete realities. It inevitably ends in condemnatory moralizing, as Ikuta demands a new form of life rather than a new form of art, that pointless rhetoric one learns to dread whenever starting any of the articles involved in this controversy.[39]

In reply, Kataoka Teppei, who repeated his earlier thesis about an assault upon the commonsense view of the world, said, if we are to remain in such a world of common sense, we must arrive at Marxism.[40] Kataoka did, indeed, arrive shortly after this at that very destination, which must imply that he himself remained in the commonsense world despite urging others to remove themselves from it. Of interest, too, is the way the younger writers make great play with imported philosophical terminology in a way that the older writers do not. One reason, of course, is that the supporters of a new literature tend to be happier on a level of abstraction, since such abstractions permit one to do what one likes with them, because they are not yet linked to created works which satisfy, and thus control, those abstractions themselves. Their opponents, however, prefer to stay on a concrete level, since pretensions can always be most easily deflated by pointing to what they have actually given birth to. However, there is more to it than that. The Taishō period was one of a boom in the publication of books of Western philosophy. In academic circles the philosophy of Kant was dominant, although Bergson and Nietzsche were also studied, and it is a truism that there was a connection between the study of German Idealism and the Emperor system, although it would be unwise to claim that this was a government plot to confuse the minds of the young. One can only account for the fact that Ikuta Chōkō, who had translated Nietzsche, uses hardly any specialized philosophical terminology in his writing and that the young men of *Bungei Jidai* use a great deal by assuming that these younger men, unlike their elders, had absorbed this terminology as students and that it had become a real part of the way they thought. How disastrous the consequences of this could be may be seen by looking at what must be considered the central theoretical document of the Shinkankakuha, the "Shinkankakuron," written by Yokomitsu Riichi and published in *Bungei Jidai* in February 1925.[41]

The writing of the article was a rush job, since Yokomitsu had just taken over as editor and the promised lead article had not come, so he had to create something in its place. Still, the article is remarkable for its incompetent usage of the vocabulary of aesthetic theory. That this should be so in a man who, as a writer, was clearly no charlatan and who seems to have thought long and deeply on the problems of his art, is a matter of concern. Professor Hoshō quotes, as an example of the kind of language that disconcerts him, "that which represents the new sensation is a representational capacity as a symbolized complex manifold."[42] Rather than search for other examples, it will be more illuminating to quote at length from the second section of the essay, entitled "Sensation and New Sensation."

Up to now various interpretations have been put forward concerning the role of the sensations in literature. Still, I think one is bound to admit that this interpretative effort has been on a very limited scale. Undoubtedly when criticism is but a limited apprehension of a factor of great potential, the environment conducive to the growth of works of art will be similarly limited in its scope, a fact which one need not illustrate with examples. Thus with regard to the portrayal of the sensations, or sense impressions, in the works of the "New Sensation Group," which has now so suddenly come to the fore, one comes across, at times and in various places, those people of a similarly limited apprehension who, because of their very limitations, direct the most violent hostility towards this factor in the artistic world because of this considerable sensationalistic power it possesses. This was only to be expected, and this is not indicative of any failure of understanding on their part or ours. What has happened is no more than a change in the handling of those sensations which have been described up to now, a change from handling them in an objective manner to a subjective one, describing them at that point where they burst into life. However, it would certainly be onerous to give this new point of view a precise and adequate theoretical form. For example, even if we were first able to make a categorical analysis in objective terms and then to create similar subjective categories, we would still be left with the problem of finding some system of references between the two sets of categories. However, success in such a venture would necessarily lead to the setting of our overall basic aesthetic concepts in order, and to the declaration of the birth of a fundamental revolution in the world of art. I shall limit myself to hints and suggestions only in this matter, prefering the risky business of leaping head first into the adventure of the internal workings of the new sensations.

Indeed my own fundamental idea on sensation, which is the distinctive aspect of the "New Sensation Group" in this respect, is, to put it briefly, that sensation is an intuitive explosion of subjectivity that rips off the external aspects of nature to give direct access to the thing in itself. This is a rather extravagant way of putting it, and as such does not yet enable us to grasp what is actually new in the new sensation. Here there is one essential word, which is the word "subjectivity" in the sense in which it is used here, namely as that which sets in motion those faculties by which we apprehend the various existences of things in themselves. Now, cognition is obviously a synthesis of understanding and sensibility, and yet the question is whether the understanding and the sensibilities which constitute this cognitive faculty which apprehends these various existences, whether these can be said to take on, in conjunction with the development of the subjectivity that directly enters into the thing in itself, a dynamic form which responds in an increased sensationalistic way; a question of considerable import for the elucidation of a new basic concept for the new sensation. Sensation is the representation of that process which controls the representational faculty of external objectivity, and also of pure objectivity which is never an object for subjectivity.

The concept of sensation which operates in literature is generally speaking a simplified form of sensation; that is, not the sensation itself but a sensationalist representation of that sensation. And yet we must make the most definite distinction between the sensation itself and the actual bodily faculties. If we leave this point until later, then what in fact is it that is new in this new sensation we have already talked about? The difference between sensation and new sensation is this: that the objectivity of the object which bursts into life is not purely objective, but is rather the representation of that emotional cognition which has broken away from subjective objectivity, incorporating as it does both a formal appearance and also the idea of a generalized consciousness within it. And it is thus that the new sensationalist method is able to appear in a more dynamic form to the understanding than the sensationalist method by virtue of the fact that it gives a more material representation of an emotional apprehension. Still, one must always point out that, as far as this sensationalist bursting into life is concerned, the distinction between the objective and the subjective form is a real distinction.[43]

It is possible to make sense of this, at least sentence by sentence, but any reader's grasp will loosen as he progresses with it. For example, in the paragraph beginning "Indeed my own fundamental idea . . . ," the gist of the argument is that there is an ordinary cognition (a synthesis of understanding and sensibility), which gives us knowledge of the external world, and also "sensation," which is a direct intuition of that world; the question is whether a combination of these two is possible, and, if it is, would it give us a more dynamic apprehension of reality? Ordinary cognition gives us external objectivity, which is an object for contemplation, whereas direct intuition gives us pure objectivity, the essence of the thing in itself, and that is not available

for contemplation. Having worked things out this far, one
wonders what exactly this has to do with writing, since as aesthetics it is clumsily inconclusive and as literary theory it clarifies
nothing. Yokomitsu has taken the terminology of Western philosophy and aesthetics and then assumed that, since he has this
terminology, the powers of clear logical argument he associates
with it are automatically in his possession as well. This essay
demonstrates only too clearly that that is not necessarily the case,
and it would be of no interest had it not been written by somebody who was an important writer.

Perhaps what is most interesting about the article as a whole
is that it shows how far Yokomitsu is from the position of a "sensationalist" writer. The theoretical confusions may result to a certain extent from an attempt to expand the meaning of the word
"sensation" until it provides a theoretical base wide enough to
contain his own real intuitions about literature. If one thinks of a
"sensationalist" writer, one may think of someone like Hemingway; in this opening passage from *A Farewell to Arms*, for example.

We saw the town with a mist over it that cut off the mountains. We
crossed the river and I saw that it was running high. It had been raining
in the mountains. We came into the town past the factories and then the
houses and villas and I saw that many more houses had been hit. On a
narrow street we passed a British Red Cross ambulance. The driver wore
a cap and his face was thin and very tanned. I did not know him.

This is an attempt, as Kataoka would put it, to transfer the
reality of objects without the secondary existence of the writer's
mind or feelings interposing between the objects and the reader.
Yet this does not, in fact cannot, happen. What instead mediates
is a sensibility that attempts to be as empty as possible, a mind
which refuses as far as possible to give meanings to objects in the
world, or to work out the connections between them; a stunned
and exhausted consciousness which has decided to give up, but
still a consciousness totally imposed upon all it apprehends. Language mediates between men and the objects of their world, and
there is no possible way to prevent this from happening. However, from this essay by Yokomitsu, one gathers he does not have

that kind of ambition, although the fact that his writings themselves seem very close to realizing it is something for the next
chapter. In theory, however, he contrasts the writings of Sei
Shōnagon with those of Matsuo Bashō, saying that the former
give us the world only as it appears to the senses, and are thus
inferior to the complexity of the latter, which allow objects to
take on symbolic meanings; and he calls Bashō's style a truly
"sensationalist" way of writing. One may call this a misuse of
terminology, but it is still clear enough what he requires literature to be, and it is not any literature of sensations. He is seeking
a symbolist literature, a form of writing which will reveal the
truth of things by going beyond surface appearances to arrive at
the thing-in-itself in one sudden and all-inclusive intuition. He
sees the literature of most of the Japanese past as written in a
tradition of elegance (*fūryū*), which always remains on the surface of things, with life shown only in terms of the senses,
whereas Bashō had attempted to break away to a deeper grasp of
the reality of nature beyond mere surface appearance.

   One may doubt the value of talking in such terms, and also
the degree to which Yokomitsu was committed to ideas of this
kind, for they may all have been only a kind of sport to him, totally unrelated to the literature he produced; yet what is certain is
that a standpoint has been reached which is almost directly opposite to a "literature of sensations." Indeed, Yokomitsu himself
admitted in the same essay that "man is a rational being: it
would be quite inconceivable that he should convert this rational
existence into a totally sensational one,"[44] and in the final section
he stated that the word "sensation" was one he had no wish to
keep on using. He concluded with the commonsense and unre-
markable statement that a literature centered upon sensations
will certainly fail, as a literature without them must also.[45]

   Having said all this, what are we left with? We are left with a
dissatisfaction with the realist tradition in literature. Yokomitsu's
statement that he accepted "certain elements of Futurism,
Cubism, Expressionism, Symbolism, Dadaism, Constructivism,
and Ultra-Realism as relevant to New Sensationalism"[46] is something more (although admittedly only a very little more) than a

mere attempt to be modish or to show that he was aware of what
was going on over the water, and should be seen as a desire to
get support from anywhere against the realist tradition. His attempts to fit his *Bungei Jidai* colleagues into various anti-realistic
postures may now look like little else than an attempt to keep the
side together (Kawabata as a Cubist, Kon Tōkō as an Expressionist, Ishihara Kinsaku as a Dadaist, Inukai Takeru as an Ultra-
Realist, Kataoka Teppei and Kaneko Yōbun as Constructivists),
in particular when he speaks of Kon Tōkō and Ishihara Kinsaku
as writers who "not only ignore the consciousness of the empty
spaces of time but hurl point blank at the destruction of all forms
the alternating action of mental images,"[47] we seem to be back in
the lunatic asylum of the Futurists. Yet there is something to be
said for that lunatic asylum. The feeling that the world could no
longer be presented in the commonsense terms of realistic fiction
is the common impulse behind all the modernist movements.
Their failures and absurdities should not blind one to the fact
that they had grasped a genuine problem, even though one they
were unable to solve, or even realize that "problems" of that nature are not there to be solved at all.

Yokomitsu names four writers as precursors of the Shinkankakuha, who may have appeared to him as having solved the
problem. They are Bashō, Shiga Naoya (although only in one or
two of his short stories), Nietzsche in *Also Sprach Zarathustra*,
and the Strindberg of *Inferno*. This may seem an eccentric bringing together of the East and the West, until one realizes that all
four achieved in their writings an attitude towards the external
world which made it appear as though living could be something
beyond what commonsense realism implied, yet in no way denied the ordinary day-to-day reality of that world, achieving
forms of transcendence without the religious significance usually
implied in that. Certainly the world had a spiritual meaning for
Bashō, but his art is a form of momentary rest from quests for
overall meaning, isolated epiphanies which achieved a realistic
revolution in the objects that could be used in poetry. In some of
Shiga Naoya's stories the boring everyday world becomes trans-
figured in certain moments that have no religious overtones and

which always leave that everyday world unaltered. The *Inferno* of
Strindberg is an extraordinary casebook of paranoia in which a
squalid life of boarding houses and strolls about Paris, is, in even
the most trivial of happenings, heavy with meaning because "the
Powers, to realise their plans, have always made use of means
that were very similar. And what are these plans? The perfection
of the human type, the procreation of the *Ubermensch* . . . ."[48]
This is momentary transcendence of the same kind, since the
ideology which makes the transcendence possible cannot be
taken seriously, and the real world comes back. All is done as a
serious piece of play acting: the world is considered as though it
has meaning although it is known that it has not. The basic ideas
of Nietzsche are nightmarish, the acceptance of life as without
meaning, the impossibility of truth, the hell of eternal recur-
rence, and yet the world of Zarathustra is full of light and joy,
something created out of a lived experience of illness, boarding-
houses, conventional breakfast conversations, drugs to stop the
migraine. Here was something to interest a young Japanese
writer in a wretched boardinghouse in Tokyo.

Hirano Ken said that "the constant note of Yokomitsu's writing is his attempt to create an artistic reality different from the
degraded realism which hems in our everyday lives."[49] The main
attempt of Japanese realism, however, is also concerned with
reliving experience in a way which makes it tolerable; that, after
all, is the basic function of the diary as well. For Yokomitsu a
way so naive was not possible, since life had become intolerable,
not something to be reminiscently tolerant about.

The earthquake of 1923 overwhelmed me and this disaster immediately
destroyed the faith in beauty which up to that moment I had held. . . . I
already could not stand the old, sluggish, naturalist style with its concern with outdated emotional entanglements, and I started to fight
against it. At the same time we were immediately involved in the problems of constructing an aesthetic and morality for the new age, but soon
the first manifestations of positivism, that of materialism, appeared in
Japan and assaulted the world of the spirit.[50]

When Nakagawa Yoichi looked back upon the movement in
1950,[51] he said it seemed to have had no real theoretical basis and

to have left no mark upon the present. It had been rather an impassioned art for art's sake movement, which seemed to belong to a literary line beginning with the early writings of Tanizaki and Akutagawa, sharing with those writers a desire to escape from the world of personal confession although remaining uncertain as to what other world they should escape to. This means it stands somewhat outside the mainstream of Japanese letters, although its writers were soon to be reabsorbed into it. The Shinkankakuha appeared at a moment when the "I-novel" seemed to have no more possibilities to offer. Its demise occurred when it became clear (which did not take long) that the Shinkankakuha itself had less.

After a while Tzara asked me, "Has surrealism succeeded in Japan?"

"In Japan the earthquakes provide sufficient surrealism, thus it has not prospered."

Yokomitsu [1]

# Chapter Four:
# Shinkankakuha—Practice

Nul lyrisme, pas de réflexions, personnalité de l'auteur absente.

Flaubert* [2]

THE GREAT KANTO Earthquake of 1923 in which 90,000 people died and more than 680,000 buildings were demolished saw the destruction of the Tokyo of the past, and it might well be considered a decisive event in the history of Japanese literature. Various forms of modernism had been introduced into Japan during the early years of the decade, but their impact had been only superficial. However, in Japan the earthquake reproduced the same social conditions of upheaval out of which the modernist movements in Europe had been created, performing the same function as that of the First World War in Europe by showing concretely in people's surroundings, in the changed forms of their lives, that the old culture had come to an end. The earthquake not only made this destruction and change concrete, but provided the cultural vacuum which encouraged the introduction of such up-to-date Western things as tall buildings, automobiles, cafés, German Expressionist drama, films like *The Cabinet of Dr. Caligari*. This led to actual changes in lived human experience. Stepping out of a taxi into a cafe and chatting with a waitress is very different from drifting around

*No lyricism, no reflections, the author's personality absent.

the pleasure quarter. The whole rhythm of social experience changed, since such relations, no longer rooted in the traditions of the past, took on a new, mechanical nature. The central feeling toward life became a kind of desperate nihilism, as can be seen in the changes in the nature of the heroes of the period cinema, a change that has lasted until the present day. The editors of *Aka to Kuro* (Red and Black) might *talk* about destruction,[3] but with the earthquake here indeed it *was*, not an idea to be toyed with but a reality to live with. Thus the style of the Shinkankakuha arose as a form of necessity created by the new shape of social experience. The "I" is excluded from these writings; even when it does appear it has none of the "dampness" one associates with the confessional "I-Novel," for the surface of the writing is like polished tile.[4] The Shinkankakuha removed the viewpoint from the individual, and made it abstract or attached to things in the world, thus rejecting the idea that the world is revealed through the individual and replacing it by the idea that man is revealed through the world.[5]

This argument is a mixture of the ideas of Sasaki Kiichi in the article referred to (which can also be found in numerous other places) and my own given on N.H.K. television in the autumn of 1971. It is tempting to think in this way, and the ideas cannot be summarily dismissed. They are exciting ideas. They seem to dignify the act of literary criticism by giving it an importance and a confidence which do not truly belong to it. They are easily communicable to people who have little or no acquaintance with the literature under discussion. They also have a clear, simple logic which one is loath to destroy and, even better, they are not completely untrue. Unfortunately they can be retained only in the inflated form into which they inevitably develop by keeping one's eyes away from the literary works they claim to be elucidating. The temptation to hold on to them comes from the fact that they do arise out of the actual experience of reading, are real insights which are then linked with social questions (a valid enough concern of literary criticism, although not its primary one), which then inflate and vulgarize those insights to the point where they cease to be true. The reason is not so much the incompetence of the critic (although one should never discount that), but comes rather from the poverty of the literature he is criticizing. One of the marks of a second-rate literature is that on second reading (not only on second reading but often, indeed, on the next page) it contradicts the insights one thought one had had about it, whereas a really achieved literature tends to confirm, deepen, and add new insights when reread. In the latter case the literature dominates the critic because it always holds his attention: in the former case the literature lacks this power, and the focus of interest becomes what the critic can make out of that literature, a creation which he dignifies by reinforcing it from extra-literary sources. This is a considerable labor, and the critic becomes obstinate about giving up something so painstakingly arrived at, and also so patently his own. Certainly one changes one's mind in the reading of Shakespeare, since his is a richness which perpetually provides, but there is little sense of being forced to give up what one had previously thought. Since the literature itself dominates, it does not (or should not) tempt the reader/critic into daring intellectual flights as a form of compensation for what the reading experience does not provide. Perhaps the unsatisfactory nature of so much criticism of contemporary Japanese literature arises because it is concerned with works which do not respond in this way. One can see something of the same in the kind of thing that tends to be written about Shelley.

This way of thinking is not to be totally rejected however; only the rigorous, false logical connectedness needs to be weakened since it is not true to the act of reading which these works inspire. One need not deny that the landscape was altered during the 1920s, nor that this caused actual changes in experience. Yet the statement made in that form sounds more absolute than it should. The roots of social experience are not changed in any radical way, and this was as true of the earthquake as it has been of more disastrous happenings since then. One may stress the transforming power of such experience, of the unique sense of *angst* which destruction on such a scale gave with its months of uncertainty about the surface of the earth, its fear and violence. But having said that one has said too much, because ordinary life asserts itself. A different tone is added, abstractions take on lived, concrete form perhaps; but the basic act of living is not stood on its head. The world does not become surrealist because if it did it would end.

One may notice, for example, different styles of living, but it would be false to give them much weight. It is a fact that the earthquake did produce a vacuum in the arts, particularly in the performing ones, since performances were inevitably discontinued. Given this vacuum it became easier for different performing modes to be introduced. Thus the Tsukiji Little Theater in its production of Reinhard Goering's *Seeschlact*,[6] with the action taking place in the gun turret of a battleship, with completely new lighting and a remarkable set, with the lines hurled at the audience in staccato, almost unintelligible fashion, provided an intimate contact with modernist European literature which up to that time had been unavailable, as did films like *The Cabinet of Dr. Caligari*. This was an experience of the new in the arts in Europe of a kind quite different from that gained by reading a newspaper article about Dadaism and working on one's own from there. It is also true that the Shinkankakuha writers, Yokomitsu in particular, were deeply interested in the theatre and the cinema. Yokomitsu wrote a number of plays, and the group even formed a cinematic association to make their own films. One, *Kurutta Ippeiji* (A Page of Madness), directed by Kinugasa Teinosuke, with a script by Kawabata Yasunari, is a really accomplished piece of work, now well-known in film society circles in a number of countries. Certainly the brisk, mechanical tone of the conversations and other aspects of the style of Yokomitsu and others in the group during this period are reminiscent of German Expressionist drama, and the publisher of *Bungei Jidai* brought out a number of translations of these writers. None of this should be denied importance, nor should the nature of this importance be forgotten. One has entered the world of cause and effect, always a near fantasy world in questions of literature, which can never provide any of the certitudes it seems to have. All that is certain is what gets written down. When what is written occupies the critic's attention this unreal world of causes and effects can cast some form of light upon the real world he is dealing with. When his concern slips away from that real world, the fantasy world can take on an absurd realness, almost as if one came to believe in the conversations one might have with a ghost, and forgot that a ghost says what one expects to hear.

Probably all Japanese critics agree that the modernist movement which began with the Shinkankakuha was a failure, something rootless and unproductive, a literary movement alienated from society, with no impact upon it.[7] The very form of such a statement implies a belief in literary historical processes one may not be willing to share, and it is given here purely as a value judgement, an indication of the general consensus of opinion on the worth of the literature produced by that movement. Any serious treatment of the Shinkankakuha normally restricts itself to literary theorizing, concerning itself with the theories on writing which the group allegedly had,[8] staying as far as possible on that abstract level, where the fact of the literature, the question of whether it has anything to do with these theories or not, does not intrude. Even this kind of rarified treatment has to end by admitting the literature is in fact there, and the word "failure" is bestowed upon it.

However, when the first number of *Bungei Jidai* came out in October 1924, it was certainly read with eagerness by many people: "This was the new literature that we of the younger generation had been longing and thirsting for. Surely all young people interested in literature like myself responded in the same way."[9] This is a clear enough reaction and causes some concern to Sasaki Kiichi since, if the movement had been of no importance, how does one account for this shock of recognition?[10] Of course, how seriously one can take literary reminiscences written decades after the event is a legitimate source of doubt, and this may well be no more than a case of a writer persuading himself into remembering the kind of experience a young writer is expected to have. This scepticism deepens if one looks at the contents of this first number, for there is virtually nothing new about them,[11] except the critical article by Kawabata already referred to and an eccentric short story "Atama narabi ni hara" (Heads and Bellies) by Yokomitsu, which must be considered incompetent and bad by anybody's standards. In fact, these "new" writers themselves, although young, were certainly established figures in the literary world. Similar writings from the same hands had appeared the previous year, not to mention the "modernist" literature already dealt with in chapter 3. Perhaps the one thing which might really have impressed with its newness was the expressionistic front cover,[12] a picture difficult to make out, but which has a cloud-like squiggle at the top, something like a drawn curtain to the left, an unmistakable Western-style toilet at bottom center, with what appears to be a bunch of grapes spilling out of it, and some dark, ragged but geometrical shapes occupying center, bottom right center, and right. The overall impression is one of embarrassing fatuity, although some of the covers for later numbers are quite pleasing.

Takami, like the rest of his "younger generation," was apparently looking for something new and was willing to assume that he had found it, as the excellent sales in both Tokyo and the provinces indicate. The stage, the audience, for a new literature were there, and its appearance was expected. One's scepticism is then properly directed at the idea that this expectation was satisfied and, if it was, whether it was legitimately satisifed or not. That scepticism then leads to a more important one about the reality of this group as an actual literary movement, suggesting that one's focus of attention should move away from the group as such and instead be placed upon the one writer among them who can be said to have written modernist prose seriously, Yokomitsu Riichi. If this fact is obscured by accumulations of useless historical detail about movements, trends, theories, influences, then the one fact of true historical importance, the fact that Yokomitsu Ricchi is modernism in Japanese literary prose, becomes lost. In order to justify this procedure a look at some of the writings by other members of the group is called for first.

If one looks at the contents of the first number of *Bungei Jidai*, for example, it is the lack of "newness" which is probably most remarkable, if one excludes the eccentric piece by Yokomitsu. Two stories in this first number were praised at the time, "Dora" (The Gong) by Suga Tadao, and "Kōjitsu" (Idle Days) by Sasaki Mosaku, and there is nothing remarkable, certainly not stylistically, about either of them. The milieu of Suga's story is aggressively up-to-date and Westernized, even the names of meals, but in terms of method it risks nothing, and the story by Sasaki, which is well done, is an old-fashioned piece of realism about whether somebody is to get married to somebody else, having the tone of an "I-Novel" even if not strictly belonging to that genre.

One can hardly imagine anyone hungering and thirsting after that, although the second number has works which may have satisfied that thirst better. "Gunkan" (The Warship) by Kon Tōkō is the most recognizably modernist of them, and the same label could be fixed on "Yūreisen" (The Ghost Ship) by Kataoka Teppei. "Shishū serareta yasai" (Embroidered Vegetables) by Nakagawa Yoichi certainly sounds the part, but on reading it one discovers an "I-Novel" which makes only a light pretence of modernism in the beginning. Since the degree of modernism seems to determine the degree of badness in these works, we shall start with the most modernist, "The Warship."

Certainly this work is modernist, the kind of thing the literary polemics of the time would lead one to expect. The opening pages describe the drawing office of a huge shipyard in terms of the tools used in it rather than of the people who use those tools, since "man is revealed through objects in the world." However, this revelation does not take place, since the tools are simply tools which tell us nothing about man in any intelligible sense, for when people are described they are cut off from all this by way of a sentimental ideology about them. Kon's descriptions, after his opening *tour de force*, concentrate upon the dehumanization of the process of work; human relationships are shown as brutal; horrible accidents are regarded with inhuman interest by others; there are continual uses of bird's eye views in which the workers appear as ants. This is no concrete world since it is not the world at all, but the world of capitalism where everything is underlined and distorted by an ideology. It is not a world of things, but of abstract and sentimental concepts. It comes as no surprise that Kon became a proletarian writer, since here he is already one. Certainly only the nihilistic, apocalyptic aspects of Marxism are present, there being no sense that things ever might be, or even ought to be, different; as if this parlous state of affairs was described, rejoiced in, for its own sake. The human portraiture is so crude, however, that it is difficult to believe the author is serious, anymore than his alienated ideology can be considered as seriously held. He is playing at literature. Since he is young he is playing at being an "experimental" writer, and this experimentalism arises from no attempt to grasp a world which will no longer respond to those realist methods used in the past, but is purely modish. Here is the final paragraph:

> There were times when just a hand, or maybe a bloody leg, maybe something else, would plonk down. Something heavy had fallen on it or maybe it had been ripped off by a cogwheel.
> Rose colored viscera.
> The Chief Engineer's dreams—
> The guns caved right into the belly of the warship.
> Flowers of splintered silver.
> Armored plate, floor boards, girders, square props, steps.
> Spars, round props, chimneys, red flags.
> The conning tower.
> Steel doors of the embrasure, protective covering.
> 12 inch guns, 5.6 inch guns, 4.7 inch guns.
> Torpedoes.
> Black smoke.
> Rudder, windlass, antenna masts.
> Admirals, captains.
> Searchlights.
> Screams.
> Howls.
> Weeping.
> Laughter . . .
> The slush of bloody guts.
> Beetle.
> Warship.
> War.
> Fool! Fool!
> Damn!! [13]

One could hardly have a more patent example of "being a modern writer." It is true that the whole story is not like this, it hardly could be; and yet the very fact that someone wished to write in this way indicates how very thin his literary motives must have been. He is presenting himself in as modish a guise as possible, and obtaining a cheap satisfaction from so doing; although it must be added that he soon stopped, and other works show him as a writer of genuine talent.

The same tendency to give up experimentation appears in Nakagawa Yoichi, where the contrast between what a writer might persuade himself he was up to, and what he could actually do, can be seen in two stories of his, "Kōru Butōjo" (The Frozen Ballroom) and "Embroidered Vegetables."[14] The former is another example of the kind of failure which the literary expectations of the time encouraged writers to make and the latter of that being resisted.

"The Frozen Ballroom" has a Westernized, though unspecified, setting, somewhere in a cold northern country. It is the deep continental winter. There is one place of warmth and light in these wastes of snow, the ballroom. The dance is described in mechanical terms, as are the short conversations which make up the bulk of the story and are concerned with sexual intrigue. Various intrigues go on, and finally a young officer breaks a window to let in some fresh air. The cold air enters like a scalpel. It fells the officer. The humid warm air turns into a cold mist, ascending to the domed ceiling whence it falls as snow. The snow falls steadily. Outside the cold moon shines. A confusion of people rush in and out under the snow. The globes of the lamps freeze and crack open. The lights go out one by one. The snow falls. The moonlight shines. The hall is transformed. The powder of the women stains the snow lightly as their faces are transformed into perpetual beauty.

One may be reminded here of the surrealist image of the woman with an umbrella, the rain falling under the umbrella. An image of that kind can have a disturbing effect in paint, but can hardly stand the weight of language which has too much of the real in it. What the story gives is a fashionable nihilism and the empty triumph of art. It is reminiscent of Yokomitsu's *The Sun in Heaven* in this respect and, like that story, it has to use an unreal locale and "foreign" people. The refusal to describe people's consciousnesses, the setting of everything in external description and conversation are the characteristics described in chapter 2. Again, in this limited sense, one can see aspects held in common by Nakagawa and Yokomitsu and other members of the group, and might thus be considered as making the use of the word "movement" valid. It would, however, be another mistake to stress this, since these shared characteristics are only sources of failure, a failure which arises from, in this case, the fact that Nakagawa does not truly see the world in this way. All his Shinkankakuha writings except these two were excluded from his *Collected Works* because, as his remarks about the movement show clearly enough, he understood that all this was a technique of self-deception.

In contrast, "Embroidered Vegetables" gives a good picture of how life really looked to him, and, although it is certainly only a slight work, it is still a real achievement.

The title and the opening of the story may give one the impression that it is going to be almost offensively "modernist." The work is to be the record, so it says, of happenings in a poor kitchen, a hymn to the beauty of the woman of that kitchen, this to be done by way of the various vegetables, fruit, and fish with which she comes into contact. Man is again being revealed through objects in the world, and yet the elegiac, muted tones of the style give much more the impression of mainstream Japanese realism than these ideological preoccupations might lead one to expect. What we are given is, indeed, an "I-Novel," since Nakagawa is describing himself and his wife.

The first sight of the wife comes as she returns from shopping. She is dressed Japanese style, and the movement of the dress is described with the sexy aestheticism Japanese writers seem to enjoy. What should be noted here is that this is the tradition of "elegance" (*fūryū*) which Yokomitsu had condemned in his "Shinkankakuron." Then the vegetables she carries are described as if weighing down her beauty. She takes the fruit out of the basket and deftly peels an apple. The way the glow of the apple is replaced by its own whiteness as the skin comes off is written with great sensitivity, although it needs considerable empathy on the reader's part to see this as anything like the act of embroidery. The husband then bites into the apple, and as he does so the wife describes the great beauty of the white radish in the market. Then the figure of the black overseer, always inspecting the vegetables and the women handling them, comes into her mind. He is like someone watching over his slaves. She feels a repugnance against men. She notices a black mark on her husband's cheek and points it out to him. He laughs and she falls silent.

This is an outline of the first two sections of the story (four generously printed pages in a twenty-two-page work). One can see that the setting of mental events into the world of objects has to a certain extent been achieved; the sexual implications of the apple, the repulsion of the wife shown by way of the black spot on her husband's face. However, the world of objects by no means reveals all, and as the story proceeds one realizes they are concerned only with showing a very commonplace fact indeed, the pathos of a young bride obliged to sweat over a hot stove all day. The function of the kitchen and the objects in it is not so much to reveal man through them as to stress the incongruity which, for a young married couple, the kitchen can represent on a level of experience where it has only a very minor, even negative role. The great momentary beauty this incongruity can give, the new domestic role of a romantically seen person, is a commonplace fact of life, although saying so does not deny its depth or its importance. But the story shows this commonplace as commonplace, and nothing else is stressed. The tight structure which would be needed to fulfil the symbolist aims the story apparently had in its opening pages is not there. A loose, rambling, diarylike structure takes over; events occur for their own sake and carry little meaning except that of themselves. For example, the irritating noise of a neighbour's piano which appears on the first page and seems, in that context, to have some meaningful weight attached to it, is in fact only there as an absence to be regretted later in the story. Similarly the vegetables gradually lose their former symbolist functions, drop out of the story in fact, and are replaced by the neighborhood children who dance about the house and dirty it, then by the next door dog who had become attached to the wife, whose owner moves, and who returns one wet night and muddies up the whole kitchen.

The incidents do have a very light symbolic role, as has the gradual roughening of the wife's hands, an image on which the story ends. They are Life wearing Beauty down, and they reflect the husband who is also a representative of that destructive abstraction. But the connections are only lightly made, and the sense that this is simply how things are (or, in the diary sense, how they were, how they happened) is the central tone of the work. As a description of life it is pleasant, and as a work of literature it comes off; but the achievement is not much and one that needed no Shinkankakuha to create. What is achieved is purely traditional, and this is particularly true of the sensibility which dominates, indeed is the work. It is this sensibility, a rather cheerful sentimentality, a sense of the pain of life which cheers one up rather than otherwise, which Nakagawa was later to exploit in his best-selling novels.

Possibly the finest work published in the early numbers of *Bungei Jidai* is "Aokusa" (Green Grass) by Jūichiya Gisaburō,[15] a work completely within the realist tradition, as are also other fine short stories by him. That the realist tradition is the only one which really means anything to these writers can be seen in a short story by Suga Tadao (author of "The Gong") called "Utsukushii Ane no Koto" (About his Beautiful Sister), in which the emotional relations are the staple ones of earlier fiction, and the style, although it is not the heavy one of Naturalism, is virtually the same as that established by Shiga Naoya.

The next morning he had his usual breakfast and left the house. Although it was now winter the wind even in the shadows was not cold. As he came out onto the main road he raised his hand to shield his eyes and looked up at the blue sky. It was because of the sound of an aeroplane in the far blue sky. A warm day of a kind to make one regret a Sunday wasted like this.[16]

This is brisk enough and it tries to keep things on the surface, but it has nothing whatever to do with modernism. The fact
is that Suga, like the others, had never truly attempted anything
but this. The early attempt to handle up-to-date sensibilities is
soon abandoned for a concern with the things he really knows
about, and those things have no genuine connection with the
polemical statements being hurled about in the magazines of the
time. Suga's "modernism" is that, and only that.

Considered in this way the Shinkankakuha does indeed
seem to have no meaning, except as a wrong road a few writers
took, but only for a short time; and this is the status which literary history has given it. *Bungei Jidai* was created by a group of
young writers who wanted the freedom of their own magazine.
To launch it various polemical statements were felt to be in order.
A friendly critic gave them a title which Yokomitsu and Kawabata eagerly adopted. This invoked a fairly serious squabble in
the literary world, which dismayed some of the writers in the
group who had no serious desire to be iconoclastic, and who had
begun to understand that it was the literature of one of them,
Yokomitsu Riichi, which was getting them all a bad name.[17]
Quite early there were sounds of dissent from some of the lesser
members, and this led to a gradual defection and a turning toward proletarian literature. The magazine began to lose any function it might have had as the organ of a group and eventually
ceased. Thus the group never existed in any true sense of the
word. Even at the time this fact was acknowledged, since all the
polemic was directed at one writer and at one story by him,
"Heads and Bellies," which must be seen as a failure and as inferior to the selection of his earlier stories which came out in May
that same year. Is one then merely in the presence of a literary
blunder, for there is no question that Yokomitsu damaged his
reputation with what he wrote during the sparse period of 1925
and half of 1926, sparse because he was occupied with his dying
wife?

One might well accept the implied answer to this question if
one concentrated attention only upon the place where it has

always tended to be, upon the story "Heads and Bellies" over which the controversy of the time expended itself. However, that would be a needless concession to the accidents of history and fashion. The story is one with only polemical intentions of representing the "new literature," The suggestion that it might have had an even more limited and exhortatory function and was aimed at Kikuchi Kan [18] does not seem an unreasonable one. It was Kikuchi Kan from whose magazine Yokomitsu and the others had just defected, the man to whom Yokomitsu was deeply indebted as the one who had launched him as a writer, in order to show him that a new magazine really was required for such a patently new literature. Of course it is impossible to know whether such an assumption could be true or not, and the motive behind it is sly and satirical, its chief interest being that the story is feeble enough to encourage assumptions of that kind. A serious consideration of Yokomitsu's works is therefore well advised to ignore it. [19]

The next work published appeared in the following (October 1924) number of *Bungei Jidai,* "Ai No Maki" (The Scroll of Love), later retitled "Maketa Otto" (The Defeated Husband). (This rewriting of *The Price of Unhappiness* was discussed in chapter 2, the implication being that it was probably the first Shinkankaku work.) The next to appear was in *Shinchō* for January 1925, "Hyōgenha no Yakusha" (The Expressionist Actor). In the same month Yokomitsu's mother suddenly died. His "Shinkankakuron," the article on the theory of the new literature, appeared in the February number of *Bungei Jidai,* and these months before and after the New Year of 1925 are the period during which the controversy surrounding the movement was at its height.

The extreme nature of some of the writing in "The Expressionist Actor" can perhaps be put down to the fact that controversy was going on, although the real eccentricity of "Heads and Bellies" is not there, or, if it is, not to a particularly upsetting extent. Like that work it is a fiction, but the hero approaches quite close to what Yokomitsu himself was, which can not be said of the idiot hero of the other story. The opening is in the style already analyzed at the end of chapter 2, with its short sentences, slightly surreal images, brisk conversations, and an overall sense of connections not being made.

The paving stones became uneven. It's cold. He stepped into the shadow of the building. Carriages pass. The sole of his shoe flapped like a piece of bind-weed. A girl was smiling behind glass. The fallen leaves are a cursed nuisance. The stone lines of the building thrust into the sky.

"You're just like a horse,' Midori said.

"The damn sole has come off."

"Exactly like a horse."

"What is?"

"Walking along clip clop clip clop clip clop."

"The sole's come off."

"You shouldn't scuff along like that."

"Get me a flower for my buttonhole."

"We've already passed the flower shop."

The automobiles are like crabs. The glass windows shine. He must buy one pistol and one pair of shoes. And one Pompaean Massage Cream for Midori. She's starting to get eczema. The two turned the corner. The wind struck their faces. On the bright street Midori's white stockings[20] collected dust. He stretched his neck above the collar of his overcoat. Wait a minute, that's a very good idea I've just had.

"Look, darling, when you hit me today would you mind doing it a bit more gently. It hurts the next day."[21]

"All right then; and the same when you kiss me."

"Oh, come off it."

"It's better that way in rehearsal."

"For heaven's sake."

"You're going to be in trouble if you don't clear up that eczema."

"I know. It's always like this in winter. My skin chaps easily, that's why."

"In winter?"

"Does it bother you?"

The leaves were falling from these trees too. The street rattled: the North wind struck the windows.

"Yes, it does."

"I walked by the sea last night. It was so cold."

"All by yourself."

"Yes, I've just started going to piano lessons."

That's why she hadn't come last night. A lie of course. She'd been infecting someone with her eczema. That old bourgeois pig again. How much did she get? And I'm in love with her! Money. I need money, I tell you, and the cushions all gone flat with the stuffing out of them.[22]

The reader is reminded that he is reading a translation, and thus reading something which is a form of description of the work rather than the work itself. The first paragraph, for example, besides creating the eternal problems of tense and number (the tense problems solved by literal translation, which solves nothing, and the number problems by ear, "building" but "carriages" when there is nothing to prevent "buildings" and "a carriage"), has a particularly striking final image which disappears in translation. This is the verb *kirimusubu* ("cut" "bind together"), a term used in sword fighting, the swords being linked together in tension before the fight starts again, and it contains not only a precise visual image of the hard line of a stone building (particularly hard when seen against a background of wooden ones) but also a sense of barely contained violence which is right for the image of the town here presented. One might argue that the image seems too sought after to be really "right," but one could not argue that the writer was not actually *writing*. The use of the language is sensitive, but it comes out in English as cliché; "The buildings thrust their way into the sky" might be considered fine writing by a third-rate journalist. If one had slipped in the word "together," more of the original might come through, but then only if one knew the original. One could use the word "clash" to bring out more clearly the idea of struggle, but that would only produce a similarly over-stressed form of journalese. If one expanded the phrase to "the buildings thrust together like swords into the sky," one would have an over-stress again, since one would be writing out in English what is only implied in the Japanese.

This is not meant to be yet another stanza in that old favorite, "The Translator's Lament," but a reminder that the literature being dealt with is indeed written, and that the form it takes here can only primarily be a description of it. No attempt has been made to recreate this literature in a shape that might better reproduce the experience of reading it, since presentation in extracts makes such an attempt meaningless, and also because the real concern is to bring out the stylistic feel of the original, to show that it does have this kind of image, this kind of verbal structure. Obviously the original is much more than these limited concerns, but then literature always is more than what can be said about it, and translation is perhaps closer to "saying about" than to actual "being." When dealing with a literature in translation one gets that literature not as it really is, but by way of the concerns of the person who presents it, and thus through the limitations of his vision.

Readers may now suspect that they are being subjected to a concealed piece of special pleading. Here what looks like a fairly ordinary piece of writing is presented as of the same order of complexity as a Shakespearean sonnet which will give up its secrets only to detailed analysis. Even if this were true, they may ask, why is it being said here, and why was this cautious, courteous treatment not also meted out to the hapless Kon? Surely its being placed here is an attempt to sway the evidence, or at least the way in which the reader will respond to that evidence, in Yokomitsu's favor? Well, there is some truth in that, since an attempt is being made to enlist sympathy, an attempt not made when other writers were dealt with earlier in this chapter, and the extract given from "The Warship" is no more the work itself than this extract is. For example, the rebarbative clusters of ideograms which technical terms in Japanese require is not shown in an English term like "windlass" with its pleasant, pastoral, eighteenth-century ring. Also, it could be maintained that Kon actually looks better in English than he does in Japanese (at least that might be said of the extract in question), but even if it could or could not it would not matter. What precedes the description of any work is a judgment about it, and the work is then presented in such a way as to support that judgment. It would be absurd to claim complete objectivity for this, except that kind one expects from any critic since one assumes he aims at the truth.

The tendency to sway the evidence is unavoidably there in any critical venture, but how much more so in dealing with a foreign literature, since the writer would actually like to be, may even imagine he is, objective. The fact that the material dealt with is an unknown for his readers confronts the writer with the importance, the duty indeed, of showing things as they are; and this very importance may persuade him, and his readers, that an objective account is being achieved. Also, the writer will be aware that criticism is dialogue, and that the truth of critical opinions is established by debate, not by individual pontification (debate on the printed page, or in seminar, or in the minds of readers), and that debate depends upon the parties concerned having equal possession of the relevant information, which is the experience of having read the work or works in question. This being so the critic must be aware of the vanity of presenting critical propositions for which this can not be true, and so his role appears to be solely descriptive, since what else can he do? Yet this is precisely what he cannot do, for there is nothing to be described which would permit this objective description, other than the so-called facts of literary history, since the facts of literature are works as they are read, and these cannot be objectively handed over. Everything is filtered through the writer's judgment, a judgment which is *a priori* suspect since it is aimed at a literature in which he can never feel truly at home; and the act of judgment underlies every descriptive gesture he makes. It also looms much larger in this kind of undertaking than it would in the normal critical attempt aimed at one's own literature, since in the latter case the evaluative faculty is always held in check by the possibility of the evaluations of others, the possibility of dialogue. It is true that the writer can create a form of mock dialogue (as can be seen in this work, at this moment indeed, when occasional men of straw are variously knocked down), but it need have no more validity than a small child triumphantly winning game after game of chess with a teddy bear. The writer, will he nill he, has the reader in his hand.

These remarks should not be taken as implying that a high valuation has been placed upon the work under discussion. Despite the power the writer may have he can never totally dictate to his readers. He may sway the evidence, but evidence of a kind is there, and even if readers assent to the statement that they are not reading the real thing, they will hardly imagine they are reading the completely unreal thing. "The Expressionist Actor" is not a great, not even a particularly good work; but it is real, even if only a real failure, in a sense in which the other "modernist" works dealt with so far have never been real. The author is engaged in what he is doing, even if he is not doing it that well. The very sensitive nature of the language shows this, being not basically modish or chic; not "being a modern writer," but a true attempt to create a work of art and not simply an image of oneself as an up-to-date creator.

The opening sentence of the story sets its central theme, the relationship between this man and that woman. This man may well be modelled on one of Yokomitsu's friends, although since friends at that age (Yokomutsu was twenty-four at the time he knew the man in question) tend to interest to the extent they reflect one's self, there is a clear tendency for this hero to become Yokomitsu, even if there is as strong a tendency for the story to remain on a satirical level. The concern of this actor with his face, for example, echoes a similar worry in Yokomitsu's early short stories which can be assumed as autobiographical, and can thus be thought of as something like his private problem even if not exactly the same thing, Yokomitsu's face being the masculine equivalent of the *jolie laide,* a face which certainly attracted women but would not have repayed study in a mirror. Now, it is true that this concern is not being put down just for its own sake, is not confessional, since it stands for something and has a meaning beyond itself. It is something which the hero often sees quite literally reflected in the outside world, and it is the form which his alienation takes, for he is the useless misfit, the *type foutu* of M. Sartre's writings and those of many modern novelists. The following passage occurs six pages (i.e. half-way through) after that already quoted, just after he has said goodbye to the girl Midori.

The lights had come on in the streets. A man with St. Vitus' dance can walk twelve steps in an hour and a half. The moon was reflected in the canal. It's beggars who look at the moon. A good-looking bit strutted by giving off whiffs of perfume. One of those curt, snappish faces, looking as if she was well aware of the natural law that there's always a bigger fish in the sea. O God, please, make me the handsomest man in the world. In gratitude for that I would become the greatest of your prophets. There's my face again. Glass windows in the street have given the human race a sense of objectivity. And what if my shape exists in a corner of the vast city? Men, despise me not! I appear at the end of a long tradition. I am the culminating point of history. Gentlemen, pray observe these postures as yet unseen by human eyes. Yet it's not me who's turning the wheels that make me go. Who is it then? Who? The English Labor Party has been defeated. The front line in China has collapsed. A death ray has been invented.[23] My feet run only over my own footsteps.[24]

The virtue of having an actor as one's hero is that it makes histrionics of this kind plausible, the hysteria, the near-falsities, the posturing, all serve as comment upon what he is. The objection to this, however, is that it is much too easy to do, as fledgling novelists portray stupid, boring people in a stupid, boring way and feel they must be above criticism. It also becomes self-defeating, since it makes it difficult for the writer to move away from that level, for move away he must. As long as the actor broods over himself in his room, as long as he stays on the level of the actor, then he is acceptable. Thus on the stage he shouts, "Dog, Cat, Pig, your wanton blood has defiled the color of righteousness," a splendidly ludicrous line which makes a good, ironic contrast with the way he can actually speak to Midori, whose wanton blood he feels has done the same thing. And yet all such a contrast can really achieve is to set the relationship on the comic or histrionic "I-don't-believe-it-all-it's-all-only-acting" level, and stop it from going further.

When he gets back to his room, that little room full of torn-up scraps of paper which appears in most of his writing of this period and which is unarguably autobiographical, he finds a fan letter from a woman who signs herself "Machiko." The tone of the letter is slightly too serious, and the reader is prepared for the later disclosure that Midori herself had written it (this also seems to be an autobiographical detail, Kimiko having played the same joke on Yokomitsu). The letter proposes a rendezvous for that evening by the lake in the park. Before he meets her he acts out the meeting, practising puffing at his pipe, twirling his stick, all of which is fairly funny. When Midori turns up they quarrel, but are then reconciled, although he knows this is only acting on his part. She agrees to marry him, but once she agrees he no longer wants to marry, and so he insults her and she goes off in a huff. He wanders about the town and meets her again, but this only results in his saying "Hi" and her saying "You still around?", and they pass. The story then ends:

> When I come home all that cries for me is that dark stairway. My dad drunk himself to death. Mum sits and stares at the old fur scarf he used to wear. Yet her son is an Expressionist actor. He smokes his pipe and is made a fool of by the side of the lake. Yet tomorrow when the sun rises he will no doubt shout out "I'm great!" [25]

What has gone wrong with this is a question of tone. It is not simply that one is not sure whether to laugh or not, but the way in which one is not sure. In Kafka, for example, the real power of the work comes from that uncertainty, for is a large beetle staring out of the window as twilight falls a melancholy, poetic object, or is it something horrifyingly funny? The answer is that it is both. Yokomitsu was too innocent a writer to be able to manage high comedy of that kind, and thus his actor looks neither tragic nor comic nor both but, finally, simply rather silly. In comparison with the literature already dealt with this story may look appreciably better, but one can hardly maintain that it succeeds in any real sense. It is the cause of failure that is of interest, since it fails in its satirical intentions rather than because of any misplaced ideas about style. Satire is the comic as a reasoned comment upon human actions and requires a strong moral sense of what human existence should be, against which norm human aberrations are set. This is what Yokomitsu does not have, for although he has a rich comic sense and a feeling for the absurd, he has nothing that would permit the writing of such satire, and it is questionable whether any Japanese writer has ever had it. Japanese norms are mainly social ones, and they allow broad comedy of a tolerant nature; but the objective moral norms out of which satires are produced are not clearly there, and thus the satirical attempt usually turns into a form of personal griping, of self-indulgence, as it seems to be in Akutagawa's *Kappa*.

One feels this in "The Expressionist Actor," since the author appears to be enjoying the sense of alienation he experiences through his hero, and thus it all turns into no more than a kind of posturing. Certainly actors posture as they also act, but, if that is what the story is primarily about, one can not seen why it should have been written. Such doubts about the purposes of the story extend to the style. Why is the world dislocated in this way? Why should the hero's "good idea" at the beginning not be expressed but merely broken into by the remark of the girl, which then acts as an absurd comment upon that unexpressed idea? Why should the hero's reply to her question "Does it bother you?" be held up by a paragraph of impressions, whose purpose is to dislocate, and thus to empty of meaning, what is going on? Even if an actor is to have an actor's consciousness why must it be this dislocated one? The style, in fact, does not present sensations, but an image of the world, a point made at the end of chapter 2 with reference to "The Defeated Husband." What one should notice is that, although things have now actually been set within someone's consciousness, that consciousness has to be a playacting one (drugged, hysterical, or mad), since the presentation of the world must be dislocated and is, consequently, hardly suited to this sentimental type of tale. It also becomes quite clear what the style cannot do, that is, to handle a human being in relationship to anyone else, for it can only describe an isolated consciousness which relates to nothing. The relationship between the man and the woman, despite the adept way in which the conversations are written, never properly comes alive, and the references to Mum and Dad in the final paragraph seem extraordinarily out of place, as if one were seriously to entitle a surrealist painting as *When Did You Last See Your Father*.

This scepticism about the limited possibilities of the style becomes deeper if one looks at another story, "Sono" (The Garden), which was published three months later in *Bungei Jidai* for April 1925. One of the interests of this story is that it deals in fictionalized form with a problem close to Yokomitsu, the illness and possible death of his wife. It is fairly, although not absolutely, certain that symptoms of consumption had appeared quite plainly by this time, and, even if they had not, the fact that Kimiko's sister had already died of the disease makes it likely that consumption and an early death as real possibilities for her should have been present somewhere in his mind.

In "The Garden" the consumptive who is to die soon is the hero's younger sister, the elder brother having already died. The hero himself has the same disease and the question for him, soon to be answered, is who will die first. The hero has a last meeting with his girl in which the whole stress is upon not daring to touch her for fear of infecting her. It was in this year that Yokomitsu wrote two stories of a direct, "I-Novel" kind about Kimiko (something he had never done before), and thus it seems reasonable to assume that this story too is written out of a sense of personal necessity at least. Whether one could go so far as to maintain that Yokomitsu directly transferred his fears about his wife to himself and a non-existent younger sister, and thus also expressed his own fear of being infected by his wife, is an open question. Perhaps one could go so far, although the question at stake here is whether or not this is another fictional attempt to distance the events of his own life, and it would surely be excessively rigorous to say that this was not proven. The pattern shown here is of a style formed out of deep personal concerns in a rewriting of *The Price of Unhappiness,* a process which is repeated in attempts to write of his father's death in 1922 (these works will be dealt with shortly), and these are interspersed with attempts to write actual fiction ("Heads and Bellies," "The Expressionist Actor"—only to some extent—"Silent Ranks"),[26] although these never quite work. The events of real life intrude so much (his mother's death in the same month as the publication of "The Expressionist Actor," for example, although he never wrote about it) that he keeps returning to these events in the desire to distance them as fiction of a kind. "The Garden" can be seen as one step in this pattern or process which finally works itself out in the works dealt with in the next chapter.

"The Garden" is the same mixture of success and failure as "The Expressionist Actor," and it is so because it is, although to a different degree, a similar kind of mixed fictional mode. It reflects concerns of Yokomitsu about his own life, but it is also sufficiently distanced for it to appear to be a "real fiction." I use the term "real fiction" in a naive sense that would be arguable outside this context, in the sense of a made-up story, whereas "fictionalizing" is here used as meaning the attempt of the author to take the events of his own life and make them into a "fiction" rather than into an "I-Novel." Thus both "The Expressionist Actor" and "The Garden" are mixed modes, with the former closer to "real fiction" and the latter closer to "fictionalization." Again, the Shinkankaku style is used as sensitively in this work as in the former, but with the same kind of limitations appearing, as if the style could not handle such material, and a heavy handed sentimentalism takes over to exploit what is cheap and easy in the material, just as a pat, ambivalent nihilism had done in the former. "The Garden" opens thus:

The doctor came out of his sister's room, looking as if he had been doing something wrong. He didn't enjoy scrutinizing the doctor's face. The doctor's nose tended to twitch. When his nostrils dilated it was clear that he was going to tell a lie.

"How is she?"

"No change apparently."

A lie. The doctor took his pulse in a cursory way. Pointless. This patient has already been killed by eugenics.

"Coughed any blood?"

"Not today."

The snow of the orchard was reflected in the doctor's spectacles. The spectrum that flowed from the lenses weakened and dissolved in the pattern on the wall.

"Temperature's gone down, hasn't it?"

"Which of us is first?"

"What?"

"All right."

His face became red. Yet he had the desire to make the healthy man ridiculous.

"I'm talking about dying, that's what."

The doctor stared at him, compressed his mouth, and was silent.

"My sister goes first, no doubt."

The doctor smiled openly. In fact the walls of the lungs of both brother and sister were rotting away. That was so. They had been infected by their dead brother.

The doctor dilated his nostrils, stared at the rifle on the wall, and left. Hurrying out as if advising them to call in a priest. Outside black birds disturbed the snow. The lighthouse started to flash out above the rocks on the shore.[27]

Readers may be reminded of Virginia Woolf, perhaps largely for an accidental reason (the image of the lighthouse), although there seems to be more to it than that. If one looks, however, at a page of, say, *To the Lighthouse,* it is soon apparent that Virginia Woolf is nothing like this.[28] What has happened is that the act of reading the above is similar, not to the act of reading Virginia Woolf but to the after effects of such a reading, to the writing of Virginia Woolf as reminiscence rather than as the writing itself and the experience of reading it. Various images have been left in the mind in the isolated state that similar images also share in the actual style of the passage from Yokomitsu. However, the remembered images of Virginia Woolf have achieved that presence since they have been stressed in a style which emphasizes continuity, and have thus achieved symbolic weight. The aftereffect of reading the Yokomitsu of this period is not one of a number of images but a tone of voice, a generalized atmosphere like a painting which has been recalled in terms of its color. Virginia Woolf's style is a consciousness which connects things, and "stream of consciousness" is not a misnomer, at least not insofar as the "stream" aspect of the style is concerned, although the implication that the consciousness is indeed like that is certainly a dubious one with which we are luckily not concerned here. The consciousness as a stream, as an activity linking objects together, imposing meanings upon them (even if that meaning is that finally the world has no meaning) is what her style is about, what, in fact, it is. Yokomitsu's style, or at least the one we are concerned with here, does not connect things.

Outside black birds disturbed the snow. The lighthouse started to flash out above the rocks on the shore.

It takes little ingenuity to turn that into this:

Late evening snow
Disturbed by black birds over which
The lighthouse starts to flash.

The *haiku*-like nature of the passage with its fixed images, images staying still and not flowing but cutting (in the cinematic sense) into each other, is apparent and hardly requires three lines of *pastiche* to make clear.

Yokomitsu may well have been related to the greatest *haiku* poet, Matsuo Bashō, on his mother's side; and he was aware of this connection although he never attempted to confirm its truth. Nakayama Gishū maintains that there are real similarities between Yokomitsu and Bashō and that his writing after the Pacific War indicates a "return to Bashō," to which his sudden death unfortunately put an end.[29] Yokomitsu wrote that he had read Bashō occasionally although he was not really well acquainted with him, but the state of mind required for writing *haiku* was quite alien to that needed for the writing of novels.[30] In his "Shinkankakuron," it will be remembered, Bashō had been mentioned as one of the four precursors of the Shinkankakuha, and his symbolist use of the image had been contrasted with the merely descriptive images in the writings of Sei Shōnagon.

The image of the *haiku* is one exclusively concentrated upon; the state of mind it relies upon can be created, at least in a superficial form, by concentrating one's mind for a minute or so upon any single, unmoving object, particularly one that is often in movement but is now stationary. Its pathos is achieved by this concentration upon objects which are normally in motion, either in space or in time, at that point where motion has temporarily come to an end, and thus at that moment when they reveal their true natures as in a Joycean epiphany. That a novel cannot work like this is what Yokomitsu meant when he said the state of mind was alien to novel writing, and he was right. This does not mean that such images cannot occur in a novel, since indeed they may well be what some novels most wish to attain, as seems to be the case with *A Portrait of the Artist as a Young Man;* but as a method, as a style, such discontinuity and perpetual stopping would not allow the form of the novel to get into motion, and if it does not get into motion the still point of the epiphany has no context in which to become remarkable.

It is here that one can see what is fundamentally wrong with the Shinkankaku style. In the *haiku* there is a stress upon the epiphany as containing the truth of life, a truth appearing in isolated and privileged moments; but there is no implication that this is what lived life, lived temporal life, is like. The *haiku* often looks best in a context (the travels of Bashō, for example), and even without this it fairly invites the reader to give it one since the act of reading it is not a movement forward but a fixed brooding upon the image, the *haiku* being so brief. Certainly Japanese writers have no monopoly of this state of mind and Keats probably meant something very similar with his remarks about "dreaming" over poetry, and Mallarmé, too, with his constant use of the word *"rêve,"* not an idle reverie, but deep, unmoving attention upon the object. However, in the world of created literary objects, there is nothing comparable in the West. In particular this cannot exist in the world of prose since the *haiku* style apprehension will then *become* the context and cease to be what the context unfolds; the unmoving images become the very structure of the world and *not* the meaning it reveals, the meaning then revealed is that the world is meaningless—nothing connects in it. The succession of isolated images imposes an ideological nihilism, whereas the *haiku* is obliged to do nothing of the sort. The "emptiness" of the *haiku* form is a mode of apprehension; emptiness is a form of getting at the truth, not a statement that emptiness is the real stuff of the world. It is similar to the Zen *kōan* where the nonsense form is not saying that the world *is* nonsense, but is a discipline to open the mind, not to nonsense but to what is real. But a novel uses time; it gives life a structure, since it is a temporal form, and a *haiku*-like stress on emptiness will thus cease to be a method of apprehending the stuff of the world but become that stuff itself. It will only describe the world as not making sense.

Since the world cannot be described at length as not making sense (if it truly does not make sense then it cannot be described), the style must be self-defeating. Either it is modified or dropped, or it ceases to function seriously and becomes a form of nervous tic. It looks well enough in short extracts, but the pointless, habit-like nature becomes oppressive in extended form.

A bell tinkled from the road that rose up to the marsh. It was Machiko's sleigh. He stood up and moved away from the fireplace. The blue lantern of the sleigh came swaying through the snow. He turned down his page and went outside. The snow fell and settled upon his eyebrows. As he descended the path his terrier dog dashed upon him like a wave. He stopped, looking gloomily at the blue lantern of the sleigh as it descended from the marsh.

The sleigh stopped. He saw the figure of Machiko getting out from beneath the hood. Behind her the bay lay darkly silent. He turned his eyes away. He regretted he had to see her.

The terrier leaped up at him and rubbed his snow-covered head against his lap.

Machiko came up to him and stopped, saying nothing. At the distant wharf a patrol boat lay frozen aslant.

"It's nice there's no wind."

Machiko threw her dangling scarf back over her shoulder. The empty sleigh moved off back toward the harbor.

"Why are you standing here like this?"

"Are you going somewhere?"

"Shouldn't I have come?"

He didn't reply but moved towards the door. The snow sounded beneath his feet. He knew that if he saw her now he would want to see her again. Machiko was standing on the step brushing the snow off herself.

"Why were you standing out there?"

"I thought things would be worse if you came."

"Are you so afraid of me?"

"Come on in then."

He entered the house and put more coal on the fire. Machiko sat in a chair and, as he crouched down, she rested her hand upon his rounded back.

"I wrote a letter to you yesterday. Then I decided I didn't want to send it."

"I wrote a letter to you too, yesterday.

"What sort of letter? Tell me. You didn't send it, I suppose."[31]

This passage is certainly not a series of fixed images only, but then no literature has the purity which critical generalizations require, a fact which does not make such generalizations untrue but simply underlines what they are, things that need continual modification in concrete situations, continual exposure to such situations. It is the disconnectedness of the images and the very slight amount of inner consciousness (not none at all since that would be impossible) which the generalization has attempted to point to. This disconnectedness appears even in the conversations, where sentences are dropped into silence and do not make that music which real talk has but remain closed in upon themselves. A sleigh, a hood, a girl, a bay, darkness, silence, turning the eyes away, regret, a terrier's snow-covered head, a patrol boat aslant in the frozen sea; this is the world shown to us, and the background is the cold waste of winter whiteness, where nothing is happening and where what does happen takes on the same immobility.

The style can describe only what is stationary, being still life. If not stationary, it is concerned with repetitive movements which are also a form of stillness, such as waves, snow, the over and over again movements of machines, automobiles passing in the streets. But the movement of real life is beyond it. The talk is of the same quality, and it is here one can see, with these people all isolated within their own language, real similarities (even if only at an abstracted level) or rather links with Western modernist writing, the conversations in the novels of Virginia Woolf, for example, or those in *The Waste Land*. It is true that this can be a real vision of life which, even if it can not be maintained for very long, at least has the power to create actual works of art. However, like any ideological stance towards existence, it always tends to become frozen and immobile, and eventually as meaningless as the life it purports to describe. It turns in upon itself; it ceases to be open to alteration from outside and thus does not develop; this gives it the perfection and completeness of any closed system of thought, and also deprives it of life. The attraction of *The Waste Land* for an adolescent is that it reads like a complete description of the truth of life; if one accepts that world it gives the comfort of not having to ask any more questions. The world is like that, and one has acquired an attitude of mind which sets one at ease before what then becomes an unreal form of despair. *To the Lighthouse* has similar completeness which, as in the case of *The Waste Land* too, does not come from any perfection as a work of art, but from its complete picture of the world, its shaped ideology. This is not to say that its picture of the world is clear, but only that it is total. It is possible to walk around in a Virginia Woolf world for days, weeks, perhaps even months or years, and this is even more true of *The Waste Land*, although it is surely not true of a work like *King Lear*.

In chapter 3 the ideological nature of Modernist writing was stressed, and the point being made here is that in actual modernist works one can see this as a question of the style itself. A picture of the world creates a style and that style then maintains a picture of the world. It is a circular motion (one would not wish to say a vicious circle) out of which it may be possible to break, but within which there is little chance of progression. There is little real development in Virginia Woolf's writing, despite the constant obsession shown with always trying to do something else. The same could be said of T. S. Eliot. The sections which work in the *Four Quartets* are those based on the lilac-garden motif, always present in his writing.

This is not an attempt to condemn either of these writers, nor is it to claim that the literature of Yokomitsu is like theirs; since indeed it is no more like than it is like Flaubert's, and in that case it was difference which was primarily stressed. However, there are things in common, and what is most in common is a total picture of the world, a picture that does not alter and that determines the style and is in turn determined by it. This does not necessarily imply success or failure in the literature, but it does indicate the form such success or failure will take. It is a limited art form, but limitations do not prevent art from being great, for it would be difficult to imagine a more limited form of poetry than that of Mallarmé (and here I am not speaking of what is the material of that poetry but what the poetry itself is, for most of human experience is there in Mallarmé if one looks for it), but it is at least arguable that his is the greatest poetry in the

French language. The problem with a limited art is just that it is, indeed, limited, demanding purity and not inclusiveness. In contrast, the art of Dickens or Hardy is not seriously harmed by elements which may be awkward failures in themselves, for they are generous art forms encouraging a generous receptivity on the part of the reader. Exclusive art forms, such as those being dealt with, have an opposite effect. For example, although one can feel an affection for the sentimentality in Dickens while also seeing it as a blot upon his work (so much so that one begins to wonder if it really is a blot), the passages which fail in *The Waste Land* (the preposterous pub scene, for example) are offensive and seriously disturb the work, as does the obtrusively confessional tone of certain passages and relationships in *To the Lighthouse*. This is an art form which always has a sense of strain about it, making such works susceptible to being knocked off balance. Symbolist/modernist literature implies a closed-in picture of the world, and closed-in pictures of the world need to keep things out.

To what degree Yokomitsu's writing of this period should be thought of as a similar kind of literature can be seen by looking at those works of his which deal with personal, almost confessional subject matter, an enquiry which will continue through this chapter and the next.

Three works of his deal directly with his journey to Korea to bring back the remains of his father: a short travelogue, a longish "I-Novel" kind of story, and a Shinkankaku-style story.[32] There are also stories which deal with his way of life, or state of mind, after his return from Korea in the autumn of 1922, and one of these will be dealt with here as a specimen of Shinkankaku literature.[33] The two Shinkankaku stories are rewritings of an experience previously set down "as it happened," and thus the relationship is similar to that between "The Defeated Husband" and *The Price of Unhappiness,* although it is by no means exactly the same, since the original, "After Picking up a Blue Stone," shares certain stylistic features with its re-written versions. Admittedly whole passages of *The Price of Unhappiness* were transferred to

"The Defeated Husband" virtually unaltered, but this only underlined the inconsistency of the style of the later work, and the
"essence" of the style of "The Defeated Husband" is quite opposed to the earlier work, as the final pages of chapter 2 should
have shown.

The short travelogue will be dealt with first. Here Yokomitsu
alters his experience by the simple method of being dishonest
about it, and it serves as a reminder of how bad this kind of literature can be. The translation is in full.

*Ginseng* [34] *and Sky and People*

I have come to Korea. We get down to the wharf by a gangplank
eighteen inches wide. Along that eighteen-inch gangplank bombs,
ideas, *ginseng*, germs, suicide squads of Asian nationalists, war, contempt and oppression ascend and descend. Ceremonious Customs Of-
ficers, Quarantine Inspectors and policemen wait at the bottom of the
gangplank. How many inches can their insight infiltrate through the
clothes and mask faces of the people ascending and descending? For a
start I had better assume a ceremonious expression and a lying tongue.
From an island country to the continent. If one walks the streets, pears,
pears, pears, pears. Beneath the lights the continual pear trees are like a
river bed. The white clothes flutter beneath the full yellow faces. The
footwear is superbly clogs.

'Ooooh, Ooooh.' Everybody talks like cows.

I once had the following dream. A dream about hell. And yet in this
hell people were selling pears. Were these people living or dead? Then
one noticed that nobody smiled. One felt they had been oppressed for
too long by the wide air, by the over extensiveness of the great sky. And
yet the "savage wind" can hardly be this. The race has become worn out
at the very peak of its history. And the cause of this is the sky. A sky
that puts an end to laughter. A frigid sky, a sky that is wholly contemp-
tuous of man. Beneath that sky which never tells one which way the
wind is blowing, a people have no chance of progress. A never intimate
sky. A clear, negative, unsupporting sky. If the sky clouded over one
would be afraid to look up.

One can notice some fathers who are like this. In some households
all hope of change must be put away until the father dies; the household
must accept that. That form of acceptance is in this sky. The sky makes
one accept everything. Nothing will ever change. All that really
flourishes beneath that sky is the *ginseng*, and the fact is that the most
fertile *ginseng* is mysteriously that whose shape is most like a man, and

that the secret of its growth is that it escapes into the soil fleeing from the sky it fears. It makes one feel that even these Korean carrots are aware of the fate of this people on this peninsula.
'Where is *The Tiger*?'
'Behind that hill.'
The rocks on the hill are like fangs.[35]

This is not so much about Korea as about Yokomitsu himself, and in this sense it has things in common with the journal he was to write much later on his journey to Europe, which is concerned with "Europe" in much the same way that this is concerned with "Asia," both being abstractions whose sole function is that of defining a sense of alienation. This is what the impressionistic writing at the beginning of this piece is up to; nothing makes sense, all is foreign, and confronted with this unintelligibility the writer assumes a pose. All the talk about bombs, Asian nationalists, ominous officials, and his own lying tongue, is, however, a deliberately willed sense of alienation. Yokomitsu had a perfectly valid reason for going to Korea, which was to collect his father's remains. No smuggler or revolutionary he, but a student at a distinguished Japanese university on a mission of filial piety. What did he have to lie to the police about? How could he have been more respectable in their eyes?

The Korea he sees is pear trees, yellow faces, white clothes, carrots, clogs; the exotic other than himself, as far removed as it would be for a Western tourist. But mainly it is the sky, put in nightmare form since what is real is nightmare. The statements about the sky are not in themselves that fanciful, since almost any Japanese who has lived on the continent says the same sort of thing. Yokomitsu, however, is not really writing about that sky but about the sky he carries within him, which is not now the pure, blue dome (the art of Flaubert, the achievement of perfected beauty) which he had wished to seek in earlier days, but a desolate blankness reflecting the emptiness of all that human life is. Japanese life is domestic, closed in; the towns are collections of houses and streets, never a complete city; and in this closed-in life one hardly notices the sky in its fulness. The streets open no prospects, the attention of the eye is always to what is near at hand, its focus shortsighted. What is striking about photographs of bombed Hiroshima or of Tokyo after the fire raids or the earth-quake is that the sky has been revealed. Yokomitsu's nagging talk about the sky may well get on one's nerves, but its impor-tance for him is easy to understand, in the same way that the ref-erence to households and dead fathers may seem almost ridicu-lously obscure, although his reasons for talking about that are obvious enough.

Once a real image of alienation, the sky, has been written out, a comic image, that of the carrot, is brought in to put every-thing on an ironical level, and the sketch ends with a scrap of conversation pregnant with undivulged meaning and a forced image about rocks like tigers' fangs. Everything has been made comfortable; the alienation is distanced, made commonplace, fashionable, cozy.

This is a trifling, affected piece of writing, although it is about things which were serious to him, and again here, as with the style of *The Sun in Heaven*, life has not been transformed into some meaningful shape but merely into evasive falsehood. Writ-ing thus only vulgarizes his insights into a schoolboyish piece of posing.

"After Picking up a Blue Stone" has nothing of the poseur about it and is very close to autobiography. It is true that it does not have the slack, rambling tone of the classic "I-Novel," since he was always enough of an artist to wish to give structure to his experience; but it is close enough to that experience, sufficiently unstructured in fact, for the term "I-Novel" to be descriptive. Nakayama Gishū refers to it as something directly created from Yokomitsu's life and uses the term "elegy" to describe it.[36] An English translation of this and the other works dealt with here is available,[37] but since the overall feel of the work can be gained by a descriptive summary one will be given here, and detailed consideration of certain passages will be kept for comparison with the other two stories.

The hero, "I," stumbles over a blue stone on his way to the

Public Bath in broad daylight, and cuts his foot. He picks up the stone and has his bath. The incident gives him a generalized feeling of anger towards everything.

He visits his girl, then suddenly feels the desire to go home, "home" being his sister's house in Kobe. As soon as he gets there a telegram arrives from Korea telling of his father's death. He goes to Seoul where he is met by his mother. His father has left no money, so he writes to his girl, "K," saying they can not get married. Now they need money just to get home, so he starts dunning his father's debtors. One of these lives in the house next door, but the man is dying and the wife (not the true mother of the children but a former servant) is playing around with another man. There are two lonely children. He begins to wonder at himself and at what he is doing.

His mother's comment on his father's death, as she thinks about the man next door, is that it was lucky he didn't have a long illness since they couldn't have afforded it. He wonders if this is what forty years of married life means.

There is a long comic scene as he attempts to get money out of a man who is never in. After this he inspects his father's remains. This ash and clinking sound is what father is, but he is also not this. Father's death has not been experienced by him and so it is not real. The reality of that death for him is that he has become a creditor dunning those who owe him money. Living is a question of material connections only, the sequence of cause and effect which means he cannot marry "K." Death itself is a dead beggar lying in a puddle in the street; after the body has been removed passersby step in the puddle where it had been.

He manages to collect two-thirds of the money, and he and his mother return to Japan. The structure becomes even looser at this point, and there is even an attempt to add a morally positive note by the remark that the house next door (which had still not paid up) meant most to him.

A letter arrives from Kobe saying the little girl Mah is ill with dysentery. He visits the hospital where children are dying like flies and feels his body is like a substance which scatters death about it wherever it goes. The little girl gets better, but the dying captain, the next-door debtor in Korea, dies. All the money he had collected in Korea must be given to his brother-in-law, who is his creditor, having supported him at the university, and who needs the money now. All these debtor/creditor connections are imposed, contingent, and inescapable ones.

He finally returns to Tokyo exactly one month after he had picked up the blue stone. His friends visit him. One is just back from Shanghai, another perpetually plays *La Paloma* on the violin, a third is an Expressionist actor, a fourth is a cinema enthusiast, and the fifth is a socialist who always goes on about the Third International. Thus his days are spent going from concerts to Expressionist plays to films to socialist meetings. Eventually the oldest friend returns to Shanghai and the others stop coming.

He has no money, so nothing to eat. He envies the laborers the rice they eat. He also has nothing to do. He can no longer think about anything since thought hurts his head. He returns to his room and contemplates suicide. Outside a blind masseur passes, and children walk behind him mimicking his walk.

He enjoys the smells of the vegetable market, which is his sole pleasure in life; that, and going up on the hill to lie down in the long grass. His father's life was cursed by his mother, as his own life has been cursed by "K." While in this state of mind the money due him from the house in Korea arrives. This saves him. The story ends on this positive note.

"The Pale Captain" is a rewriting of the Korean section of this. The differences are not as extreme as those between *The Price of Unhappiness* and "The Defeated Husband," but the pattern of change, with shorter sentences, less going on in the hero's head, abstractions changed into visual images, more conversation, and a shortening and tightening up of the structure, is the same. The opening of "The Pale Captain" is very brisk indeed.

Father suddenly died. I crossed the straits, eating bananas for four days, and arrived at an unknown town. Mother was in a weird, triangular house that was all glass windows, on a street corner, sitting like a table doing nothing.[38]

This covers material which takes twenty times as much space in "After Picking up a Blue Stone," and all sentimental associations have been ruthlessly cut away. For example, the mentioning of the bananas with its slightly desperate association (not eating proper meals) is a transformation of what had been the occasion of a sentimental (the word not here being used in a condemnatory sense) scene in the earlier work. The girl Mah had received a banana from her uncle before he went to Korea, and it is the thing she recalls about him when he goes to visit her at the hospital. The scene is not presented sentimentally but given coldly and quite straight without any response from the author/hero, but its effect in that context is, and clearly was meant to be, moving, and it is that kind of thing that occurs nowhere in the rewriting, which goes on from the above quotation as follows:

"Well?"
"He's dead."
That he certainly was.

This is so brisk and unemotional that one might well call it the Shinkankaku style in its extreme purity, which does not imply any value judgment, but only that it is a step, or steps, farther on than the style of "After Picking up a Blue Stone." Certainly the style of that earlier work has its Shinkankaku elements, but it is still not that far removed from the world of Shiga Naoya, as its opening lines will show. (This remark is even truer of later passages in the work).

I was walking along in Tokyo in broad daylight flourishing my towel. Then I fell over. I had tripped over a stone. Blood was coming out from my shin. I picked up the small, pale blue stone that had cut my shin and went into the bath. As I poured the water over my naked body I had a continuous feeling of anger toward the world.

I left the bath and went straight over to K's house. The shadow of her house seemed to have something oppressively blue about it. K was sitting in a corner of her silent room powdering her face.[39]

In this story, unlike in "The Pale Captain," his mother meets him at the station, takes him to the house whose oddness is not stressed, and the following scene occurs.

Mother got out a fan.

"The place is rotten with flies," she said. There was a persistent smell of carbolic.

"That's carbolic, isn't it, that stink?"

"It stinks all right. They've got dysentery next door, and someone, I don't know who, splashed the stuff all round here."

"Gets on your nerves."

"Stinks the place out," mother said.

After a while she produced a gold watch and chain.

"Your father thought very highly of this. You can have it."

"It's gold, isn't it?" I put it down gingerly.

"You hungry?"

"Yes."

"There's nothing much here." She went to the cupboard and brought out some fishpaste.

We sat at the table and started to eat. Then the grief welled up within me. I wanted to spit the food out of my mouth so I threw down my chopsticks and went to the lavatory. I started to sob, long, drawn out. I supported myself with my right hand, stared at the wall, and held my breath. Smaller sobs escaped through my nostrils. When the feeling in my stomach had quieted down, I went back to mother and picked up my chopsticks. The same thing happened again. This time I ran outside into the road. I ran noiselessly sobbing in the middle of the twilit road. The pale road trembled through my tears. I turned off the main road into a filthy back alley. A Chinese and a Korean were hitting each other in the narrow lane. The Korean was struck in the face by a stone and knocked down into a rubbish heap by the side of the lane. His legs stuck up and his face was red. A lot of Koreans were silently looking on, towels tied round their heads. And then, "Dad's dead, Dad's dead," someone started singing, over and over, in the middle of my head.[40]

"The Pale Captain" differs from this in that the logic behind the style has been fully carried out, the structure and described content being changed rather than the basic linguistic expression. Nothing is to be seen as trembling through tears, and the images are not to be given in the form that real life gave but in a form which comments on and alters that real life. For example, although nearly the whole of that scene has been cut out of "The Pale Captain," since the realistic, confessional tone is to be avoided, the fight between the Korean and the Chinese is still there. The hero has been examining the remains of his father (a scene which is in the earlier work too, but comes later, for in

"The Pale Captain" the structure of the real life events has been altered in order to give them an imposed significance).

> I picked father's bones up one by one and tossed them back into the box. Father made a cheerful, jingling sound. I remembered wrestling with him and throwing him down.
> Outside, a Chinese and a Korean were hitting each other. The Korean was pushed and fell in some rubbish. One leg stuck up and he howled pathetically.[41]

One could well maintain that those few brisk sentences represent the whole of the passage given from the earlier work, since in both cases it is the realization of his father's death which is being recorded. And yet how different is the way in which this is done, particularly the way in which the fight is linked with his father's death and the implications it makes about it. In the earlier work all is given as a deep, tearful realization, where the Korean's falling over is no comment upon death but only an accidental happening in the outside world which makes that death seem real for the first time. It is the comic irrelevance of the incident which deepens the sense of the tragic relevance of the father's death, and the prevailing tone of the scene is heavily emotional.

In "The Pale Captain," however, the father's death is shown as not grasped. The warm remembrance (but how coldly written) of wrestling with him is then given immediate ironic comment in the scene outside whose blundering absurdity is now stressed, for the Korean is simply pushed down (not struck by a stone, since that would be something more painful which might imply sympathy), and one leg sticks up and he howls pathetically. The world is presented in frigid images, and the images have been so arranged as to form a structure of meaning. Of course, the fact that the images are cold does not have to imply that they cannot be moving, for one might well feel that the "dry" attempt of the later work is in effect more powerful as it avoids the deliberate creation of the emotional tone of the earlier work.

If we return to the beginning of "The Pale Captain" it continues thus (i.e., following the two earlier quotations with no intermission).

That he certainly was. From that day on my life as a creditor, my dunning life began.

"Pay up. Dad's dead."

"Hand it over. Dad's dead."

That was how the dun chorus went.

First, I parleyed with a local law official, a mechanic at the steel works, a secretary at the County Council, and the owner of a watchmaker's. Yet money never dances to a clumsy dun chorus. Then I ignored the demands of decency and started having a go at the house next door, my weakest opponent. He was a retired captain. Now I learned he was ill with dysentery, and dying. His two children, a boy and an older girl, were in the dark kitchen baking buns for the shop in silence. I was sick of dancing for money.[42]

In "The Pale Captain" this girl plays a more important role than she had in the earlier work, and it is through her attitude towards her dying father that the hero tries to define his own attitude to his dead one. The relationship between the girl and the hero is shown through conversation. She hates her stepmother and is indifferent to her father, an attitude he tries to argue her out of, but she will not budge. Her indifference is, in fact, the true tone of the story, of the style which presents that story and which, like her indifference, never alters. All the images are in fixed postures, like the opening image of his mother in the house of glass. The hero's attitudes are fixed in the same way; the money collecting, for example, is dealt with only at the level of farce. Human relations are mechanical, human postures have the repetitive meaninglessness of a machine. The beggar who appeared only briefly in the earlier work as a corpse to be dragged away here has a main function. He appears a number of times, but always in the same fixed image, a heap of rags sitting in filth, continually injecting himself with cocaine. It is his death which then becomes the focus of meaning in the work. When he dies he leaves the imprint of his face in the mud, a death mask. The hero wants to show the girl what death is, and since it is dark he is obliged to strike match after match in this quest for the real face of death. When he eventually finds it, however, it is his own face which stares up at him from the death mask of the other. When he returns home his mother's ashen face seems like a gravestone, and there the work ends.

How well this works it is hard to say. It may be that prose cannot handle the symbolic weight laid upon it here, and that as one ends the work it is with an irritated sense of having had one's nose rubbed in a death mask of "meaningfulness," of having been imposed upon by the author in the same way that he has imposed meanings upon his material, which dominates, a sense that there is a rigidity in all this more appropriate to a corpse than to a living body of literature. One can certainly say the style has achieved a purity of presentation, a logic in the structure of the material it presents, at which it seemed to have been aiming, and thus that the inner logic of the style has indeed been worked out. However, the question is whether such purity was worth achieving, whether the rambling realism of "After Picking up a Blue Stone" with its occasional bits of Shinkankaku style is not really a superior achievement. Has everything then ended, as in *The Sun in Heaven*, with life being given, not so much the shaped truth of fiction as the empty postures of untruth? When questioning reaches this point it is answerable only by putting an end to reasons and trying to let the literature speak for itself, inasmuch as a translation can be said to do that. "The Depths of the Town" ("Machi no Soko") is a rehandling of the material dealt with in the final pages of "After Picking up a Blue Stone," and is given in full.[43]

There was a shoemaker's on the corner. The place was packed with shoes from floor to ceiling. Between the black, closed walls of shoes the head of the shopgirl perpetually drooped down. Next door a watchmaker's with its watches spread out in a dense pattern. Next door to that an egg shop, an old man squatting in a foam of innumerable eggs, a towel tied round his bald head. Next a crockery shop, in the midst of whose frigid hospital whiteness the lady of the place, still young and gay, seemed as if she were about to kick over the columns of plates.

Next a flower shop. The girl was grubbier than the flowers, among which appeared from time to time the rapt, idiot face of some small boy. Next a dressmaker's with headless bodies dangling; and the owner poked a bloodless finger into his ear and sniffed the odour from the cafe. Next a bookshop, like a suit of armor, opened its mouth.[44] There was a draper's next to the bookshop. Like the dark bottom of the sea, its mountains of muslins, beside which a thin, pregnant woman was sinking, a flatfish with glittering eyes.

Next to that the gate of a girls' school. At three o'clock a multicolored wave of girls poured out. Next to that was a public bath. Beyond the glass, mermaids were broiled, their fresh naked bodies cast down on wooden slabs. Next a fruit shop. The son kicked the fruit with a foot made powerful by prolonged pedalling. There was a doctor's next door. The heads which hung by its windows seemed always to have a ripeness in their indolence.

Every day he passed those shops in silence, then climbed up to the top of the green hill beyond. The hill was a cone of thick, green grass jostled and contained by the straight line of the main road. Its grass bent softly to the air. He lay in the grass beaten by the light, unmoving, attempting to drink in hopefulness from the hopeful tones of the streets.

He couldn't move. If he moved, the accompanying effort of thought hurt his brain. Because of this he couldn't eat. He had to learn to live in useless glory on this hill. From here one had two choices of vision, and the various objects of the town competed for his attention.

On the high ground to the north stood the spacious residences of the well-to-do. There the breeze and sunlight entered at will. A dignitary with his lady rushed his car between the stone gates of his mansion, pondering the gravitational facts of his own body. Then, like a bouquet of flowers, gaudy dancing girls were crammed in and sent away. Then a polished silk hat, then a frock coat like a bird. But he was thinking of nothing.

He looked southward to the bottom of the narrow valley. Here fumes of carbon dioxide built up pressure; what freely entered was only dust blown by the east wind, typhus, factory smoke. Nothing grew here. A collection of tiles and germs and empty bottles, market leftovers, workers, whores, and rats.

What should I think about? he thought.

He needed ten sen. If he had that, he could get through the day without thinking. If he didn't think, he could get well. If he moved, his stomach would feel empty. If his stomach felt empty, ten sen would not be enough. Thus he lay all day, his face grey, like an insect that hopes to acquire protective coloring in the green grass on the hill.

As evening approached he went down from the hill and entered the streets. Sometimes he would be caught up in a crowd of workers, grey black, an avalanche of weariness, and borne along with them. They had been making boots all day standing in a row, and yet they flowed in procession, heads bowed at times as in a funeral, toward the center of the lower streets.

At times he was drawn along by them in their group hunger to enter silently an eating shop. Meat and rice. The heads of pigs and cows, the skin flayed off, rolled over on the kitchen table like sleeping human heads. The workers lined up in silence between the cramped tables.

When the food was slow in coming they beat their rice bowls with their chopsticks. When the place was full of steam their faces reddened, widened, and grew small.

He filled his stomach with cow's head, threw down his ten sen, and went back alone to his backstreet home. He rented a three mat room. The pillar that propped the roof was splintered and askew. The wall was blackened like the inside of an oven; the rain had drawn a pattern on it like a map, in which the muck of flies was etched in little spots. He leaned his head back against the pillar, kicked aside the torn-up sheets of paper with his foot, and brooded on the glories of suicide. Outside, children were swaying the fence, playing zoo. A blind masseur passed along the narrow lane calling for custom. The children started to creep along one by one behind him mimicking his walk.

He lay down and lay still. From where he lay he could see the broken back wall of the house across the way. Through one chink he could see a pendent female breast. It belonged to a pale, sick woman who lay eternally in the same posture. The one thing he could be certain of seeing when he came home was that immodest breast. The breast had virtually become an intimate of his. He longed just once to see the owner's face. Yet whenever he looked, the breast lay squarely beyond the chink in the wall, fallen, spread out, unmoving. Always seeing it, it was as if the world had become one gigantic breast alone, and twilight was falling. The electric light came on over the mountain breast, drawing extravagant patterns over what had fallen under its own heavy gravity, casting the shadow of a smashed gun turret, face down and out.

When it became dark he went out. The sunken street, a heap of rubbish by day, glittered like a festival. Stalls were set out beneath the low roofs, and heaps of cheap toys and metal objects flickered and shone. He strolled along, looking, breathing in the fresh air, past the stalls lined up by the muddy ditch, toward the vegetable market. Here was the unexpected, a vegetable garden which drank in the acetylene light set greenly on the road at the bottom of the town. The rows of freshly watered vegetables were like a field, a continual source of fresh, green, gentle air that drifted among the passersby with the scent of coolness.

He rejoiced in his own rare lightness of heart and glanced affectionately at the mountains of copper coins that had collected on the straw mats. The jammed heaps of copper possessed a form of elegance, like mysterious towers. He felt the dynamism of their presence, here slumbering at the bottom of the town, as a kind of pin or nail that held together the various conical inclines that were the town itself.

"That's it. And suppose one drew out that pin?"

He imagined the whole town spread out in fragments, and that pleased him, so once again he went and jostled shoulders with people. And yet amid the smell of human bodies he was overwhelmed by an unexpected and unexplained sadness. The misery of momentary life flashed out at him, the sudden cross-section sight of a blunt heavy boat opened to the view. Still one grinned and went on walking. He passed between warehouses full of empty bottles and went home, got into bed as he was, and curled up.

He knew he could make ten sen a day if he sold three magazines. As long as he kept hold of this principle, life would not be terrifying. One day he picked up the coin obtained from selling three magazines and prepared to go out. There in front of the door was a blind old woman he had never seen before, standing dirty, solitary, and barefoot. She held a brush in one hand, bowed severely, and began her spiel. She kept on bowing.

"I'm seventy years old, sir, and my husband's died at the age of seventy, and I had an only son, sir, but he's dead too, sir. The police won't let me beg, sir, so please won't you be so good as to buy one of these brushes? I've got money for myself but the old man's funeral will cost eighteen yen and I don't have a copper toward it, sir. I have to pay thirty eight sen a night for my lodging, sir, and if I can't pay that I don't know what I shall do. Please be so good as to buy one of these brushes, sir."

He folded the ten sen into her dry palm and went out. He was going to sit in the grass on the green hill.

Whatever he thought about, his head hurt. He stood on the sunlit road. The town spread out with himself as its center. There was the shoemaker's on the corner. The shopgirl was silent among the shoes. Next to that was the geometrical watchmaker's. Among the innumerable angles of the clocks and watches the moving hands were at three. He stopped in front of the girls' school. A wave of brilliant girls poured from the school gates, glancing at him. A stake washed by the overwhelming sea, he stood and watched. The wave of girls broke into two at his breast. Like a waving field of flowers they flowed serenely on.

If this style can produce successful literature, then this sort of thing will be it. Yet if it is successful, what a small, closed-in success it is. Yokomitsu, when writing about these two stories,[45] compared them with an earlier story, "The Child Who Was Laughed At,"[46] a story which he sometimes felt was the best thing he had yet done, although it was the sort of thing he had no wish to write again. He rejected it because it had no surface brilliance or light (*hikari*), although internally it has such brilliance. Yokomitsu is writing here with his usual inability (perhaps refusal) to organize what he is saying, but his meaning can be understood. He then says that of his latest works it is these two, "The Depths of the Town" and "The Pale Captain" he likes most because they have this surface brilliance.

The symbol is the surface brilliance which allows the inner life to shine forth. This is why I want above all symbols that shine. That which attempts the most brilliance in its symbols I have come to call the Shinkankakuha. There is absolutely none of the Shinkankakuha enterprise in "The Child Who Was Laughed At." For this reason I maintain that is is an art of the past.[47]

This is, despite its brevity, a good description of *Shinkankaku* writing, at least as Yokomitsu wrote it, and, since it has been maintained that only he wrote it, one can not hope for a more relevant description. As a form of symbolist writing it is to that extent within the same tradition as European modernism; although it is not *in* that tradition in any profound sense for the simple fact that it is Japanese, and calling it "symbolist" says nothing about its value. Does this "surface brilliance" in face point to anything other than itself? Does the "inner life shine forth"? I had meant to translate the word *hikari* as "life," but that idea had to be dropped since it is precisely life which this kind of literature seems not to have.

plus de vie pour
moi
et je me sens
couché en la tombe
à côté de toi
Mallarmé*[1]

# Chapter Five:
# The Death of a Wife

KIMICHAN WAS RATHER dark like her brother, and slim; a gentle, kind girl. Since mother was not happy about the marriage Kimi was always having to be careful about her. I can remember going up to Tokyo once and going out shopping with her and mother to Hoteiya in Shinjuku (the present day Isetan). Riichi didn't come because of mother. Kimi said there was an umbrella and scarf she'd been wanting for ages, and she was terribly happy when I bought them for her, trying on the scarf and laughing and playing about. She was writing children's stories for a magazine ("I've got my own work, you know"), and she showed me copies with her own things published in them. At that time she didn't look all that well, and mother told me that Kimi sometimes complained of pains in her stomach, and that if she caught cold she would spit up blood with the phlegm. From then on I began to be secretly worried.[2]

Yokomitsu's first wife Kimiko remains, like most people after they have died, an indistinct figure. Except for her appearances in Yokomitsu's literature there are few descriptions of her. There are not even photographs available (as there are of his second wife) and the imagination has nothing to grasp at. The above description by Yokomitsu's elder sister is the clearest that we have, a clear picture of normality, of a small, dark, lively girl interested in shopping and the innocent world of children. In Yo-

*no more life for/me/and I feel myself/lying in the tomb/beside you

komitsu's stories she appears as an image of naive life, a force of
great energy which attracts whatever is about it and becomes the
amoral source of moral complexities, "amoral" in the sense that
the pure existence she is is neither good nor bad (even Himiko in
*The Sun in Heaven* does not appear in any moral light, although
the actions of the people around her do, a characteristic she
shares with the heroine of *The Price of Unhappiness*). The final
image in "The Depths of the Town," of the young girls like the
sea, is the role she plays in his literature, and this is presumably
what her existence in its deepest sense meant to him.

Muramatsu Shofū's account of Yokomitsu's life does not describe her, and the fuller account by Nakayama Gishū mentions
her only slightly, mainly because he was not living in Tokyo during the period when she was Yokomitsu's wife and so had no occasion to meet her. He describes his one visit (in 1924, probably
late September) to the two rooms in which Yokomitsu had set up
house with mother and wife shortly after the earthquake,[3] the
house he would soon leave. Nakayama's impression of this slum-
like area was a cheerful one, although he attributed it to the early
autumn weather. His impression of Kimiko was equally cheerful;
with a red scarf around her head she was the very image of the
happy new bride bustling about doing the housework. He was
moved by a sense of happiness and life about her, a deep contrast to his own wife who was ill in bed at home. He had seen
her occasionally before, at the Kojima home during his and Yokomitsu's student days, and thus he knew her (and she him), but
they had rarely spoken to each other. When he heard that Yokomitsu was out, he paid his respects and left. It did not seem possible that this could be the girl whom Yokomitsu had married,
since he remembered her as a mere child. As he left he reflected
not only on the fact that a successful young writer could be considerably poorer than a schoolteacher like himself, but also on
the brilliant happiness in Kimiko's face. He went on to visit
Kojima Tsutomu (Kimiko's brother and a student friend of his)
and realized that he and Yokomitsu were now completely estranged from each other, not only because of his opposition to
the marriage but also for literary reasons. The group of students

all three had belonged to while at Waseda had now split into two factions, one devoted to "socially-concerned" literature, and the other to literature as "art." The age was moving in that direction.

He visited Yokomitsu again early in 1925 in the house he had moved into a few months before, in Nakano in the suburbs.[4] His visit was just after the death of Yokomitsu's mother. It is the happiness of the house he stresses, although most of what he says is literary shop talk or is about his envy of Yokomitsu who, in his eyes at least, was now the "top" new writer. Nakayama must have been there at a lucky moment, and one can assume that Yokomitsu's literary success (in contrast to his own discarded literary ambitions) had cast a glory over all the objects in the house, since in Yokomitsu's memory his wife became ill immediately after his mother's death, this house was for him one of illness, and illness only. However this may be a case of seeing misfortunes retrospectively as coming thick upon each other. The truth probably is that Kimiko, as the recollections of his sister imply, already had symptoms of consumption when they married in the spring of 1924, that they got worse, that the clear, dry air of the autumn and winter of 1924–25 gave them some respite, and that with the coming of the humid air of spring and then of the rainy season in June they reached the point where she was obliged to take permanently to her bed. The first story to mention her in a direct, "I-Novel" way, "Tsuma" (Wife), October 1925,[5] has her in bed during the rainy season, and the first indication in the letters that she had taken to her bed is also in June of that year. These letters continue until April of the next year (1926), but then there is a virtual hiatus for nearly two years. Thus the only account we have of these crucial months in his life is in his literature, which admittedly becomes more confessional during this period. Consequently one is as nearly in the dark about the "reality" being transformed in the works dealt with in this chapter as one was with those considered in chapter 2.

An outline of the biography over the five years from 1922 to 1927 would be as follows. In May 1922 (twenty-four years old) Yokomitsu, Nakayama, Kojima, and others brought out a little magazine called *Tō* (The Tower, the front cover having a drawing

of the Tower of Babel). On August 29 of the same year Yokomitsu's father died in Seoul, and in September he went there to
bring back the remains. As a result he was penniless and thus
unable to marry Kimiko (born in 1906 and so sixteen at the time).
This is the period covered by the works dealt with at the end of
chapter 4. From January of the next year (1923) the monthly magazine *Bungei Shunjū* was brought out under the editorship of
Kikuchi Kan (1888–1948, i.e., ten years older than Yokomitsu),
and Yokomitsu, Kawabata, and other younger writers who were
to form *Bungei Jidai* in the next year were "members" of it. Yokomitsu, now under Kikuchi's wing, was becoming a known young
writer, a position confirmed by the publication of *The Sun in
Heaven* in May of that year. Thus he was able to tell his mother
during a visit home (to Kyoto) in June of this year that he wished
to marry Kimiko, a suggestion she violently opposed, since she
was involved in arrangements of her own with a distant relative,
and photographs had even been exchanged. Yokomitsu's sister
landed the task of talking her around, and eventually the mother
grudgingly consented to go to Tokyo in order to have somewhere
to live with her son. The exact date is not at all clear, but late 1923
(the earthquake was in September of that year) or early 1924 seem
likely dates, the latter more likely than the earlier. The date of the
marriage is not clear either, the only positive piece of evidence
being a letter dated May 1924 which says Kimiko is living with
him and the Kojimas still won't accept it.[6] The two women did
not get on well, as Yokomitsu's literature makes only too clear.
The year 1924 also saw the publication of Yokomitsu's first volume of short stories and of *The Sun in Heaven* in book form. It
was in August of this year that Yokomitsu's sister saw Kimiko for
the last time. Yokomitsu had been to Kyushu (his father's birth-
place) for military registration, and on his return he took Kimiko
(who had been in his sister's house in Kobe) to Ōtsu on the
shores of Lake Biwa. This was where Yokomitsu had lived as a
child and where his sister had been living when she first married, and of all the places associated with his past this was the
one with the happiest memories. They rented rooms for a month
in the house next door to the one he had lived in as a child. His

sister visited them there and has recorded how happy they were, the happiest they ever had been and the last time they were to be so. Indeed he must have been happy, for he was now successful as a writer (not yet in terms of money, yet by no means poor) and his ambitions and hopes must have seemed capable of realization. How short and unreal this happiness must have come to seem to him can be realized by the fact that it never once occurs in his writing.

After their return to Tokyo in September they moved to Nakano, in the suburbs, but at that time still real country. *Bungei Jidai* was to come out in October. They had been deeply attracted by the external appearance of the house, by its garden full of flowers; but when they started to live there they found themselves oppressed by the atmosphere, a strange darkness inside in contrast to the cheerfulness outside. There were no windows on the north side, only a long expanse of wall.[7] Immediately after they moved Yokomitsu was ill for two months. In January (1925) his mother suddenly died, and the final illness of his wife began. In an essay published in September of that year he recalled how his mother had told him as a child that when the "wind of transience" blew somebody would die.[8] He reflected that such a wind had been blowing through his life since 1922. One of the interests of this essay is the depth of superstitious belief it reveals in him, ideas which seem to be at odds with his modernist literary ambitions. He, of course, would not have seen these ideas as superstitions since that would have been a way of getting rid of them. In his youth, he wrote, he had discarded this belief in "the wind of transience," but had now taken it up again out of a realization that places and landscapes do indeed affect the life that is lived in them. What the essay reveals is his acceptance of the fact that such truths exist on a level beyond the grasp of reason, and a contentment that they should remain on that ungraspable level.

Both he and his wife grew to hate the house, and in October (1925) moved to the country, to Hayama on the sea coast south of Tokyo, not just for the sake of moving, but to allow Kimiko to get better in clean, healthy air, for the doctor had diagnosed her illness as bronchial catarrh. By this time he was finding it impossible to work, and plans for forming a theatre group had been abandoned. From this time on his letters express anxieties about what was happening to *Bungei Jidai*, for both he and Kawabata were now living outside Tokyo, and there are many apologies for not sending manuscripts on time or not sending them at all. In February of 1926 he mentions that the maid had run away, presumably because she had found the nursing too much. Yokomitsu and his wife had originally lived together in a part of a house, but eventually she was obliged to move to a hospital (probably merely a doctor's house with one or two rooms available for patients). Even so Yokomitsu had to visit her every day to do most of the nursing, something he seems to have continued to do virtually single-handed until she died. The last letter, to Kawabata in April 1926, is full of the most tragic hope.[9] He admits that all the doctors up to now have been no good, but the present one is a "good man" who has assured him that the lungs can mend. The letter, like the others written before it, is courteous, considerate, and humorous; he had been nursing a carbuncle on his face which had finally broken, leaving his face as swollen and exaggerated as his own writing. It also contains some advice about sleeping with the window open but with the head away from it, since if one did not do so one would be caught in the wind, the wind of transience. If one slept in the right position one would not get ill. It is interesting how a piece of ordinary and sensible medical advice is seized upon and then transformed into a magical device to ward off the evil. Life had reached a point where only magical alternatives remained, since what was happening was beyond thought. Kimiko finally died on June 24, 1926. She was twenty.

After her death he returned to Tokyo, to the house of his wife's family, but quarrelled with his mother-in-law, who had suggested, not a strange suggestion in Japan, that he marry the remaining younger daughter. He left the house with no possessions except a single towel and stayed in a room in the *Bungei Shunjū* offices. There he wrote "Haru wa Basha ni Notte" (Spring Riding in a Carriage), an account of his wife's death, which

seems to be relating things as they really did happen. It was published in August. In February of the next year he remarried, this
time a girl of twenty-six (Yokomitsu himself became twenty-nine
in March of that year) called Chiyoko, who had come to know
him through her admiration for his writing. Yokomitsu was now
becoming famous. *Bungei Jidai* brought out its final number in
May of the same year. Chiyoko was the very model of a Japanese
wife; judging by photographs she was very beautiful, with that
deep calm arising from a self-denial which appears to be natural
and easy. The marriage was a success; the enthusiasm of the two
sons for their parents is the best indication,[10] and when he was
in Europe he wrote very tender letters to her. She gave birth to a
son in November of that same year, 1927.

Yet even this happy marriage seems to have been a form of
resignation for Yokomitsu, as if life were not really to be lived
any more.[11] Kimiko's death (as his constant observation of the
anniversary of it shows) opened passages into a darkness within
him that nothing—wife, children, success—was to close. "Hana-
zono no Shisō" (Ideas of a Flower Garden), an attempt to look at
that darkness and the experience which had produced it, was
published in February 1927, the same month as his second marriage, and presumably completed just before it. Like "Spring
Riding in a Carriage" it describes his wife's illness, although
unlike that story it continues to the moment of death. However,
its real difference from the earlier work is of the same kind as
that between "The Pale Captain" and "After Picking up a Blue
Stone." The elegiac reminiscence is transformed into the different world of fictionalized reality.

Nakayama Gishū classifies "Spring Riding in a Carriage"
with "After Picking up a Blue Stone" as an elegy about Yokomitsu's own life, in contrast with "Ideas of a Flower Garden,"
which he considers as something not created directly from life
but as a world of abstractions and generalities.[12] This is a true
distinction, but it does not mean that the former work is a
straightforward piece of autobiography any more than "After
Picking up a Blue Stone" had been. The desire to create fictions
is always there, but, as already seen, with material taken from

his own life his normal process is, first, to write it out in a form
close to that experience, then rewrite it and distance it. But Yokomitsu did not write mainstream "I-Novels," even when he chose
a theme so much a staple of the genre as the Sick-Wife-Novel,
which might almost be considered a literary genre in itself. This
theme suits the "I-Novel" well, a clear case of one's flattering
image of oneself as loving and kind, severely knocked down by
the ugly reality of illness, bad temper, desire to be alone, loath-
ing for a loved one (or one who should be loved) which the situation imposes. It is the complete confessional situation, and it will
put Yokomitsu's literature into perspective if one considers a
classic of this genre.

Kambayashi Akatsuki wrote his "Sei Yohane Byōin nite"
(At the St. John's Hospital) in 1946.[13] Kambayashi is quite confidently and unashamedly an "I-Novel" writer of the confessional
type, literature for him being a second look at, or even reliving
of, one's own life, in particular the shabbier aspects of it. One's
evaluation of him will depend on one's evaluation of the mainstream of which he is a part. Even if one regrets the existence of
this tradition (as so many Japanese critics do), it is still within it
that the modern Japanese writer has been most at ease, producing works that do not have that sense of strain, of attempting
what is finally not achieved, which marks a more ambitious literature such as that of Yokomitsu. Evaluation is difficult, because
Yokomitsu is clearly a greater writer than Kambayashi and his
stories about the death of his wife are more important than Kambayashi's about his. And yet Kambayashi's writing on this subject could be considered superior as writing. One is continually
being brought up against this contradiction, and it does not seem
to be one that can be resolved. It is not just a question of the attempt of criticism to make sense out of such writing, but of the
actual experience of reading it. Yokomitsu's writing engages and
disappoints the reader; Kambayashi's satisfies, but then leaves
one feeling indifferent, wishing for something else, aware that
literature should surely be something other than this.

"At the St. John's Hospital" has the misery and confusion of
the immediate postwar period for its background, but it hardly

stresses this, because its writer/hero is so completely closed up within himself. He appears in the story as a writer since he is merely being himself. He is forty-three years old and obliged to go into the hospital to nurse a wife with whom he has not slept for seven years. This wife has provided the material for several other works of his, as he is at some pains to remind his reader. He goes into the hospital resolved, since this may well be the end of their married life together, to make the period as "beautiful" as possible. She is blind and in the mental ward of the hospital because she cannot look after herself; and because the nurses cannot look after her all the time the husband must do so. No details are spared: she fouls herself at the toilet, she knocks things over and breaks them. But the writer does not rub the reader's face in these details. They are merely presented to him. Life is like that if one is blind and helpless, and the tone is always detached and cool. This tone is the great achievement of the "I-Novel," and there is no attempt to assault the reader in any way.

This very modesty of treatment is reminiscent of the chaste camera work in the cinema of Ozu Yasujirō, a modesty which arises from a real wisdom about life and which, in Ozu's case, constitutes a truly considerable artistic achievement. This modesty in the "I-Novel," however, gives rise to doubts about it as such an achievement. One feels that the enormous resources of language, of language in the full and precise form of literature, are not being employed, and this then appears in that literature as a lack, as something missing. In the cinema the camera brings in the whole world just by the act of pointing at it; techniques of restraint are essential to control this. But language has continually to remake the world; and to assume that the bare and intermittent charting of one man's course through a world he has not yet remade is adequate as an artistic construct indicates a misunderstanding of the nature of language. Picking up a pen does not switch on the experienced world as a camera does, but only permits it to be redrawn, like a painting. The "I-Novel" implies that there is nothing to draw, since lived life is not simply the material of art but the work of art itself. It does not believe in writing as a process of transfiguring, but as one of letting things be. That writing simply *cannot* let things be, that it must alter and create, is the contradiction which makes it finally mistaken as a literary genre.

Despite Kambayashi's desire to care for his wife, he is soon confronted by the fact that he really does not want to. When the doctor tells him his wife cannot recover, he accepts the blow quite cheerfully and thinks more about the troubles that will arise out of her death than of the death itself. Certainly he is ashamed of this feeling, but not that much. He realizes he knows nothing about her childhood and decides he had better get it written down now or it will be lost to posterity. He asks her to recall what she can, but she refuses, since she has, understandably, had enough of being turned into stories for publication. This makes him ashamed of himself, of his despicable novelistic tendencies.

The story then centers on food. He quarrels with his wife because she eats his breakfast. After quarrelling he walks outside and feels bad about things. He recalls his resolution to make life beautiful and finally resolves to keep his own rice in a box in his pocket. While this reflects the nature of real life decisions, it is only a gesture of resignation made acceptable by the fact that everything is kept on a comic, ruefully tolerant level. This continual lowering of the atmosphere is another apparently inevitable aspect of the "I-Novel," for the "I" of another is intolerable (at least within Japanese and Anglo-Saxon cultures) unless it is tempered by devices of understatement, irony, modesty. Admittedly the "I" of the Romantic poet is not restrained in that way, but then that "I" is a literary construct, as a comparison of the "I" of Keats's poems and that of his letters will show. It is true the two "I"'s are not always kept apart, which accounts for the repellent tone of some of Shelley, and for Keats's remarks on the egotistical sublime in Wordsworth, but essentially Romanticism does imply a distinction between the two. The "I-Novel" does not imply this distinction, although it may at times occur, and the low-key atmosphere is a direct consequence of this.

In the next scene of Kambayashi's work (and the thinness of the structure will now be apparent) the hero is mistaken by a girl for a lunatic because he is playing with some acorns. The mistake is cleared up; the girl had seen him coming out of the mental ward where his wife is and had thus come to that conclusion. However, he now comes to have doubts about his own sanity, particularly after meeting a real mental patient who is, in fact, only a little odd. This section is well done, but its tenuous connections with what has gone before and what comes after limit its impact. This does not mean that there is no connection: the scene stresses the pleasure of having one's own thoughts, of brooding happily over what madness is. This cozy pleasure of having one's own life on one's own, of thinking about oneself and sitting lazily in the sunshine, is rudely disturbed by a nurse who scolds him because his wife has fouled the toilet again. He is back to reality after his brief escape into the world of pleasant artistic thoughts. It is this contrast between his own private mental world and the inescapable outer reality of the mental ward which holds the work together; that, and the personality of the author, mainly the personality. So arbitrary a principle, however, gives no true shape to what is supposed to be, after all, a literary artifact. One can take or leave that personality, find it charmingly sympathetic or nauseously intimate. True literature would never allow such arbitrariness to have so essential a role in holding a work together. The success of *Hamlet* or *King Lear* does not depend upon one's liking the hero (indeed the concept is absurdly out of place in such a context), but Kambayashi's work does require that the reader like him or the work ceases to please or even to exist.

A number of scenes of disconnected connectedness follow. In one he escapes from his wife with his food, then watches her blind gropings as she searches for him. He goes outside and later returns to see a nurse leading her back to her own room. That evening at home there is a power cut and he experiences the sightless world of his wife. When power is restored he feels the desire to stay at home even more strongly.

The story winds up with his reading the afterword to his latest volume of stories which he is proofreading. He reads it aloud to his wife, but he doesn't actually read what is there (since it is all about her and her probable death) but a much simpler, made-up version which has nothing about her in it at all. This is a fine, if unconscious, comment on the whole "truth-telling" function of this form of literature. The work finally ends with his wife's being well enough to move to another hospital, and she is trundled there in a kind of pushcart. This comic scene is described almost lyrically, with a strong sense of the freedom that is in the outside world, and the story ends on that note.

A description of this kind can hardly show the virtues of this sort of literature, although what, in an abstract sense, this literature is, what kind of literary attempt it represents, can perhaps be understood from this; and while Yokomitsu's "Spring Riding in a Carriage" may have things in common with it, it is not the same. The whole of "At the St John's Hospital" maintains a constant, unruffled tone and is a form of reverie in which everything is shown through the medium of that reverie. The world fits the consciousness which dreams it, and the harmony and lack of tension show the total pervasiveness of that harmonizing consciousness. Certainly the theme of the story may look something like a conflict—the control over the hero's own consciousness being disturbed or contradicted by the tough reality of the world. But these apparent conflicts take on no disturbing shape; everything is accepted, the disturbances are shown as in the past and as after the event (all is over and done with since this is a second look at, a reliving of, one's life), and by that time the consciousness has absorbed them. The tone is one of acceptance, resignation, ordinariness, everydayness. Nothing tragic appears as tragic, even if one's wife is blind and going to die. Since no one is close to the hero no loss can be felt as real loss. This egoism, this locking of oneself up within one's own experience in order to become at one with that experience, this attempt to turn all discords into harmonies has already been noted in dealing with the writings of Shiga Naoya in chapter 1. It is the central attempt of the "I-Novel," a form of literature which does not wish tragedy to exist as tragedy. Its wisdom is everyday; no matter what happens you eventually get over it, it is all water under the bridge, and nothing really happens anyway. The structure and style of the "I-Novel," which refuses to stress anything, refuses to seek out certain events as meaning more than others, refuses to impose emphases which might give a structure of meaning to those events, refuses to give anything a status slightly approaching the symbolic, is the reflection of this commonplace wisdom. This is why Yokomitsu considered it an "enormous lie." His own experience of life was that tragedy was real and the water did not flow away under the bridge. His everyday life had little to do with this everyday wisdom whose literary form is the coziness of the "I-Novel," a wisdom meaning resignation which has, consciously or unconsciously, social harmony as its aim.

Tragedy seen as tragedy emphasizes the opposite of harmony and acceptance; it shows what has happened as something not to be explained or allowed to drift away. Tragedy shows the real lack of harmony between the individual, lived misfortune, and the undisturbed society enclosing it; between the individual death and the permanence of nature. It is not denied that the form tragedy takes can create a sense of harmony, of tensions resolved in the perfected structure of the work of art; but this is not the harmony the "I-Novel" aims at. The "I-Novel" resolves no tensions, but dissolves them by playing them down; it shows no consciousness coming to terms with such tensions but one which merely absorbs them into itself. It does not understand the world but merely fills it with itself. This is why the master of this form, Shiga Naoya, gives one so oppressive a sense of overpowering egotism. This is also why, as a literary form, it looks so much like a form of action, a transforming of the past; something achieved not by changing it into a work of art but by seeing it as a work of art already. Nothing need be done about such a world since, on reliving it, one sees it as all right as it was, and is.

In "Spring Riding in a Carriage" Yokomitsu shows the illness of his wife in terms quite similar to those of Kambayashi. He describes quarrels of an ugly kind; the hero is repelled by his wife; there is even the same emphasis upon food. But all this is presented tragically, as the way the world should not be. The wife is shown as loved by the hero even when hated; the physical distaste he feels for her is put on a tragic level by his real closeness to her. In Kambayashi's work the hero is close to no one, and the wife has not been slept with for seven years. Her situation may be shown as pathetic, as sympathized with; but it does not attack the hero at the center of his being, for that is always shown as unshaken. This is not to accuse Kambayashi of being untruthful, for the everyday world is not untrue even if it is not the whole truth either. Everydayness is a surrounding harmony capable of being broken, and a deeply true art should show that as well.

Kambayashi is close to his world, he enjoys nature, he is pleased by the everyday manifestations of social life. Yokomitsu's world is not like that, for he is alienated from it, and the images of the natural world in his story are all coldly detached from him. The opening, for example, goes thus:

The cold late-autumn wind began to sound among the pine trees on the shore. In a corner of the garden a clump of small dahlias shrank in upon themselves.[14]

This is how Kambayashi describes nature:

The tree shrubs had already put forth buds, but they were still hard. Ahead there was a forest of towering red pines. The birds were singing. I walked along the path, all anger forgotten, and simply holding to me my accumulated grief.[15]

This is nature in its everyday (which does not, of course, mean superficial) aspect as a comforter. Yokomitsu's nature is apart from him, almost as if it were behind glass: it is the world he is cut off from by his wife's illness. It is also representative of the objective, detached consciousness he would like to achieve and yet can not. It has, indeed, a complex role, and one could say more about it. Kambayashi's nature invites no comment since it is just nature. None of these remarks need imply value judgments.

Out at sea the afternoon waves broke on the rocks and scattered. A boat leaned and rounded the sharp point of the headland. Down on the beach two children sat like scraps of paper, steaming potatoes in their hands, against a background of deep, surging blue.

The waves after waves of suffering that came in upon him had never been something to be evaded. The origin of those waves of suffering, each different in each onslaught, existed in his very flesh, had been there from the beginning. He had decided to taste this suffering as the tongue tastes sugar, to scrutinize it with the total light of his senses. Which would taste best in the end? My body is a scientific flask; the most important thing is absolute clarity.[16]

Here the clarity of the images at the beginning, their almost surreal detachment from one another, is the same attempt as the sensibility in the second paragraph to stay detached, transparent, objective, and unmoved. The distance from the outside world is the same as he wants to achieve from his own experience. The images of nature are being made to work in this style in a way quite different from that in Kambayashi's realism where no such demands are made of them.

The style is the Shinkankaku one already described, although what this story shows is that that style, and thus the detachment it implies, does not work. He is not like a scientific flask; he quarrels with his wife, and as a result has to sit up all night nursing her. This pattern dominates the story, and has led critics to claim the work should not be considered *Shinkankaku* at all since most of the time the characteristics of that style are not present.[17] This criticism is partly true, but it is not much to the point, because it is not any absence of that style which we have here, but a demonstration of its inability to function, and that is not the same thing. The story is about the attempt of the mind to transform a reality it can not accept, but it fails in this since the reality proves too great for it. The style reflects this, but it does not imply that the style as such has been disposed of.

Attempts at transformation are inevitably shown as doomed to failure. The husband describes the food his wife eats (directly to his wife rather than to the reader) in fanciful, affected terms which hide (and since they fail they do not hide) that she, a dying animal, is eating dead animals.[18] This is followed by the reading of a passage from the Bible, another (particularly for Japanese ears) stylistic transformation and distancing of experience.

But immediately the cough gets worse, with the pain and the ugly quarreling,[19] and it is this ugly reality which occupies most of the story.

The conflict is resolved when the doctor tells him plainly his wife will die, causing a resignation in the hero which puts an end to discord.[20] The story then ends on a note of fantasy. Spring has come and he takes her some flowers. He says that the flowers have climbed into a carriage and driven here from the borders of the sea. The wife puts her face into the flowers in ecstasy.

This ending reads with a sentimentality which may grate on Western ears, but it would be a misreading, for the pathos comes from the fact that this creation of a fantasy world cannot work in the face of what is real. The efforts of both husband and wife to respond to this fantasy world are a form of resignation, an admittance that it has no real existence but will do since nothing now will do. The story ends with a tragic realization, not a sentimental evasion, and it is not surprising that many Japanese critics should cite it as the finest single work he ever wrote. It is the existence of stories of this kind which allows one to speak of a major talent, for here, as elsewhere, it can be seen as truly realized.

"Ideas of a Flower Garden" takes this situation and transforms it.[21] The very locale is different, being an up-to-date Western-style sanatorium where the patients are clearly well-to-do. This is a quite different world from that of real life in rented rooms, where the maid runs away and the husband, a carbuncle on his face, tries to write to make money. It is also different from that of "Spring Riding in a Carriage," which had been close to that real world, with its quarrels, publisher's deadlines, visits to the butcher's to buy giblets. There is no quarrelling in this work, and the tone of the conversations is always under control. We are not given a record of real life but an attempt to make sense of what actually happened in that life; not, however, to make sense of it by drawing conclusions from it, but by giving it the meaningful shape of art. The success or failure of such an attempt can be seen only by considering it as a whole structure. Thus a fairly lengthy account will be required here, although the reader who is able to do so is asked to read the whole work at this point. The story is in thirteen sections, and one can show what the style is like simply by quoting the opening section, for in this work the style is maintained throughout, as it had not been in earlier, more experimental writings of his.

> The clear windows of the sun room glittered among the flowers on the top of the hill. The steps leading up to the balcony stuck out like a white backbone.
> He was returning from the seashore up the road that led to the sanatorium. Sometimes he would leave his wife's bedside and go out walking, then to return and see her face anew. Each time the face had advanced closer to death's border, a maintained and definite pace, each time a stage nearer. Suddenly from the brick building farther up a group of nurses swarmed out.
> "Goodbye."
> "Goodbye."
> A patient was leaving, and they followed him, running and glittering in the sun like a white mantle on the road. They circled the bed of roses in the front courtyard, forming a ring, a single flower.
> "Goodbye."
> "Goodbye."
> New, white patients lay sunbathing on the sloping lawn like heaps of fruit. He threaded gently through their fantasies toward the corridor. From the windows of the rooms along the corridor a column of eyes shining with despair pursued him.
> He opened the door of his wife's room. Her face was still, a heartbreaking serenity in it, like the air filled and confused with flower petals.
> She was probably going to die.
> He watched her from the side of the bed. He recalled the virgin beauty given to him on their marriage night, and the face of that time floated before him, a pale blue outline fitting perfectly on this present profile.[22]

The second, third, and fourth sections deal with his sense of exhaustion, the resignation of his wife, and with his attempts to fill up the blankness in both their lives with flowers. In the fifth section the ambiguity of the flower as an image of life is deepened by connecting it with the healthy nurses who are symbols of that love which is only destructive of health in this flower garden. In section six the people of the fishing village below declare war on the sanatorium (its unhealthy presence is bad for their market reputation) by assaulting it with the stench from the dead fish, and then with flies and smoke. In section seven he is told that his wife is to die, and he decides that the only way to accept this truth is by pretending that it is its opposite, for there is nothing which says we must experience misfortune as misfortune, and so we can experience a funeral as if it were a wedding.

In section eight his wife's face starts to change into a soft, peach-like bloom, as she lies there surrounded by flowers, although she objects to the oppressive scent of some of them. In section nine, after an unsuccessful attempt to stop a young man raising smoke from a bonfire, he goes down to the fishing village and the following description is given, one obviously meant to have strong symbolic implications.

He didn't wait for an answer but went down from the hill toward the fishing ground. On that level space was a forest of bare, bronze, powerful thighs. They were drawing the fish from the nets, and then they would dash back with the nets into the sea, scattering foam above their heads. The children on the shore picked up trembling jellyfish and hurled them at one another. Barrels and thighs, then tunny, sea bream, and bonito, glittering with the color of the sea, poured out of the boats. Suddenly the fishery was brilliant as in the light of an unnatural dawn. The hairy thighs twisted and turned here and there among the waves of fish. Bestridden by those powerful thighs, the bream resigned themselves like rose-colored girls; the tunny were quietly lined up, like shells stored up in readiness. Sometimes the erect forest of thighs would waver and the evening sun pierce through, scattering phosphorescence on the billowing crests of the fish like the slash of a knife.

From among the fish he looked up at the hill. The flower beds on the hill rose up magically among the waves of fish. Roses, tunny, peonies, bream, marguerites; and above those succesive layers the always many-angled face of the sun room glittering in the evening, flashing off rays of light like eyes.

"The sanatorium is a castle besieged by these waves after waves of fish. And the first to die in that siege will be my wife."

The fish were really an innumerable and intrepid host who hastened her death amid their smoke. They were also healing physicians who shortened the period of her suffering. Then the dull ranks of the tunny lined up like shells took on a different, disturbing meaning; became a black, black silence, and only that.[23]

In section ten he starts to question the wisdom of trying to keep his wife alive as the symptoms of her death become clearer. He reminisces to her about the past, and then the fact of her dying becomes real to him.

He was in danger of weeping again, so he stepped down among the flowers, his eyes brimming with tears. He buried his face in the crowds of night flowers. Then the tears poured over. As he wept he passed his face from one cold flower to another, drinking in their perfume like an insect. As he smelled the perfume he began to start praying violently.
"Please, God, save her. Please, God, save her."
He picked up a handful of primroses and wiped his face with them. The sea was pale and secret before the rise of the moon. A night crow drew an uncanny curve in the air, then flew over the flower beds like a sharp shadow. Like grief itself he walked countless times around the quiet fountain, until his own heart quieted too.[24]

In section eleven the wife's mother arrives, bursting with possessive love. Two healthy nurses walking among the flowers contrast with the sick patients. In section twelve he again attempts to think about her dying in time and of his living in it, in this surrealist passage:

The number of injections made in his wife's arm increased every day. All she now had for nourishment was water.
One day at dusk he climbed up to the balcony to look down on the deepening twilit sea below. He was thinking.
"All I am doing is waiting on her death. What do I expect to get out of moments like these?"
He knew nothing. All he felt was that the unmoving balcony on which he was riding was perpetually voyaging above time.
He watched the pace of the sun's half-circle as it sank beneath the sea's horizon.
"This is the pace at which her life is worn away."
One could see the process. The sun swayed and trembled, then was swallowed by the horizon. The surface of the sea was a chopping board over which the blood ran. The sun stifled a cry, and sank. On the sea's surface boats lay unmoving like fallen birds.[25]

This section then gives what seems to be a very real account of another scene of reconciliation between husband and wife (all in conversation); and the death described in the next section reads much the same way. The closing lines of the work again show how the story has been concerned with making something out of this death, although one hesitates to use a phrase like "give it a meaning," since this kind of literature seems not to be trying to do that.

> She nodded and gazed all round the room with wide eyes. A crow took up the sounds of the husband and mother and cried above the flower garden. His wife gave a smile of loving recognition and murmured: "Clever crow, to be so quick. He has cried already."
>
> He bowed his head before the greatness of her prepared spirit. He wept no longer.
>
> After a while she said, "Goodbye".
>
> "Yes. Goodbye," he replied.
>
> Her mother called her name.
>
> But there was no reply. Her breathing had changed into great, violent spurts of breath. As her head gradually declined the grasp upon his hands stiffened like wood, then grew slack. Then death came suddenly over her face like a vivid dawn.
>
> That is it.
>
> He remained awhile absorbed in the beauty of this death before him, then stood up entranced, and drifted, a scrap of blown paper, down into the garden.[26]

Yura Kimiyoshi, an authority on the "new criticism," has written a long analysis of this story, in which he stresses structure, symbolic meanings, repetitive patterns, the work as a body, as a structure, of meaning. Clearly it invites this sort of treatment, since the work itself seems to be attempting to stress those very things. The slightly unreal nature of the setting allows the symbolic potentiality of objects to be stressed, stresses the symbolic content of words like "flower," "hill," "sea," "fish," "bird," and so on in a way the "I-Novel" does not for it simply presents things as themselves. The relationship of the sanatorium to the village is given the same form of stress by seeing it in mechanistic war-like terms or as the similarly automatic connections of the organs of the body. The objections one could make to Professor Yura's analysis are those one could always make to such explicative analyses, in that they tend to produce painstaking accounts of the obvious, or discover meanings which are not in fact there since they have no proper place in the act of reading; and it is this last failing which is the most dangerous. Yura, for example, discovers a meaning in the use of thirteen sections, seeing it as a symbol of the irrational and anti-scientific.[28] One could argue that the most likely interpretation seems to be the ordinary idea of thirteen as unlucky. The fact that Yokomitsu quotes the Bible twice at length in the companion work, "Spring Riding in a Carriage," could be proof that he may well have been thinking in such terms. This rejoinder, however, would also be beside the point, since the structure of thirteen sections does nothing in the story. It may well have been part of the author's "intention" that it carry some kind of meaning, but considerations of that kind mean little when one is concerned with the completed work. What role does the structure of thirteen sections have, and, indeed, what role could it have? The answer is none, except, perhaps, that of giving the busy critic a bone to nibble at and then cast away. If it has any sort of role then it is simply that the narrative is broken up in this way, and the numbering thus stresses the dislocated nature of the structure. The thread of the story is broken, and we are given a series of sketches which invite symbolic interpretation because of the isolation imposed upon them. One can say no more than that.

This minor point has been stressed because a major principle is involved here. The story may well be aiming at symbolic meanings, but it is most unwise of criticism to assume that they must have been achieved. Either analysis is evalutive about this, or it can say nothing. With the use of flower symbols, for example, are we in the presence of some over-stress here? Even if we are not, do they express anything more than a platitude? If symbols are to be stressed in this way they need to carry a deep and deepening meaning, and they will do this only if their use creates a development and is not simple repetition only. Do the symbols work like that here?

It is clear from a number of his stories that Yokomitsu associated flowers with his wife, and that he should have done so is natural enough. Because of the extreme nature of their climate the death associations of flowers are very apparent to the Japanese. The flowers bloom and fade quickly and may be destroyed by strong winds and heavy rains. The three-day cherry blossom scattered by a spring gale or with a late snowfall upon it is a classic example. In this story the flowers carry that kind of meaning, and carry it as a paradox, since flowers are associated with death, with rotting lungs. The flower is thus concealed death, the attempt to create a world of beauty (Yokomitsu's world of art) which will reject the deadly outside world, and which yet also is that death. The real livingness of the outside world is shown in the fish and in the living beings who subjugate those fish; images of rape are strong here, in contrast to the hero who cannot embrace his wife but can only lift her up like a bunch of flowers. The decorating of her sick room with flowers not only serves to give life to the lifeless face of his wife, but is also an attempt to convey timelessness to that face, as in a still-life work of art,[29] since it is time in its dead, mechanical sense which the hero is trying to combat. The story opens with flowers and a group of young girls like flowers: it ends with the flowers withered.

One could go on almost indefinitely with an analysis of this kind, discovering subtlety after subtlety; but a return to the actual experience of the work (rather than an inquisitive excavation of it) would cause some doubts about the relevance of what one was doing. The actual use of the symbol in the story does not in fact permit that weight of meaning; the weight of meaning is given to it by the critic, whereas his function ought not to be that of imposing meanings upon things but rather of discovering what is really there. For example, to note that the word "goodbye" occurs at the beginning and the end of the work ought not to convince one that the structure is circular, or even that it has any successful and firm structure at all. The word "goodbye" said at the beginning has a simple function, for someone is getting out of the place, which emphasizes the fact that "she" and "he" are not. One could perhaps maintain that "goodbye" has the same meaning in the final death scene, but then "goodbye" is said only to people who are leaving (that is what the word means: this form of criticism always pushes one towards these obvious statements), and it would be perverse to ignore the fact that the word functions differently in each context and that only ingeniousness would suggest that either use suggests or recalls the other. One might maintain one gets a hint (even an ironic hint) in the first "goodbye" of the last "goodbye," but what purpose could such a remark serve? For example, one can notice in *King Lear* that an impressive phrase toward the end of the play, "Or image of that horror" (v.iii.264), has occured much earlier as "the image and horror of it" (i.ii.178), but I believe no one has been rash enough to accord any significance to this. The echo is interesting, but no more than that. It is no more because the time gap between the two occurences and the structure of the whole, which gives no emphasis to this echo, do not permit any significance to be drawn.

This point needs to be given particular stress here. The structure of Yokomitsu's work is a dislocated one, and it reads as a set of fragments. The symbolic weight the objects should take on does not materialize, since the work does not become a unified body of meaning. To analyze it as if it had done so is to be untrue to it. What holds the work together is the autobiographical fact, but the thoughts and reflections stay isolated from one another. They are all on the same theme, that of death, but they achieve no sort of cumulative effect. The ideas stay as isolated as the isolated images of the style; nothing leads into anything else. When one has finished the work no ideas or images of death remain; one has simply the blankness (so deeply shown at the end of section nine). That death is a blankness is acceptable enough, and I would not wish to deny the great power this story achieves in showing just that; but the question at issue is whether the symbolism of the story is working in the way it seems to be trying to work and, if it is not, what justification does it have for being there?

A look at an example of true symbolist writing can show one what Yokomitsu does not have. It is by the greatest of all symbolist poets.

*Tombeau* [30]
Le noir roc courroucé que la bise le roule
Ne s'arrêtera ni sous de pieuses mains
Tâtant sa ressemblance avec les maux humains
Comme pour en bénir quelque funeste moule.

Ici presque toujours si le ramier roucoule
Cet immatériel deuil opprime de maints
Nubiles plis l'astre mûri des lendemains
Dont un scintillement argentera la foule.

Qui cherche, parcourant le solitaire bond
Tantôt extérieur de notre vagabond—
Verlaine? Il est caché parmi l'herbe, Verlaine

À ne surprendre que naïvement d'accord
La lèvre sans y boire ou tarir son haleine
Un peu profond ruisseau calomnié la mort.

*Tomb*
Angered by the cold north wind the black rock rolls
And will not cease, nor under pious hands
Searching its resemblances to human ills
As if to bless some fateful form of them.

Here almost always if the dove should call
This immaterial mourning will oppress
With countless nubile folds tomorrows'
Ripening star, whose shining silvers all.

Who seeks, following the solitary leap
Erstwhile exterior of our vagabond—
Verlaine? He is hidden in the grass, Verlaine

Only to surprise naively in agreement
The lip not drinking there nor drying up its breath
A stream ill spoken of nor really deep, of death.

Mallarmé is not relying upon the traditional meanings of his objects here, and the obscurity and grammatical complexity serve to focus the reader's attention upon things which thus have a deep, so deep as almost to be hidden, meaning. This is what symbolism implies, a long look at objects until their meanings are achieved, even if not totally revealed. The poem then becomes a celebration of the fact that something has been understood, that all those painfully half grasped and always escaping ideas about death, ideas which turn in upon and negate themselves and then become transformed, are here caught in a shape where they can be apprehended. They are caught not so much as ideas but as the objects which alone can fully represent those ideas. The obscurity of the poem, its tendency to slip away from the reader, to elude him, is not its confusion but its truth.

"Ideas of a Flower Garden" does not do this: Yokomitsu's objects show no complex grasp of artistic truth but rather a poignant awareness that it is, after all, not to be grasped. If one looks closely at any one passage this will be seen to be true, and it also explains why the structure as a whole cannot hang together. For example, in section twelve, the hero reflects upon time and that he is living real time (unlike the living time of emotionally lived life), and there is a dramatic description of the sun setting, with images of the sea as a chopping board, the sun stifling a cry, ships (or a ship) like fallen birds (or a bird). The images, although precise, relate nothing; they have, it is true, connections with other images (the bird image with a death meaning is used before and after this scene), but no statement is being made. They are an insight into that nothing seen as the heart of existence; the images occur as not being able to grasp what is there. The attempt of art is shown as failure, as the attempt to cure his wife is also failure. The hero's aim is to pretend things are other than they are, to apprehend a funeral as a wedding. It is a gesture of despair, more desperate because it is shown only as a gesture, never truly believed in, and so as one which can never succeed since the funeral remains precisely as a funeral. Another dramatic scene, that on the beach in section nine, where the fish and the flowers are seen together, is of the same kind. One might argue here that this shows the external life forces as now mingled with, eventually to conquer, the art/flower form of life, but one would be getting perilously close to nonsense if one said that since that is not how it reads. The image is surrealist, as indeed the ones previously mentioned had been; its function is to bring these objects together so that they negate each other and produce a world without meaning.

Art as a form of escape is what is stressed in this work: why should a funeral not be a wedding? This reduces art to the level of telling comforting lies, which is not its function. The truest poetry may well be the most feigning but it can hardly be the most lying. It is as if Yokomitsu wants to make sense of a reality too dreadful to permit sense to be made out of it, although not primarily to make sense out of it as to escape from it. Thus his whole effort to transform material so close to him begins to appear as a mistaken idea about the kind of transformation art achieves, particularly the symbolist kind he was aiming at. Here the case of Mallarmé is again instructive.

In 1879, when Mallarmé was thirty-seven years old, his eight-year-old son, Anatole, died. He made various notes at the time, preparatory studies for a work which would celebrate this death, but the work itself was never written. The notes, however, remain; two-hundred-and-twelve small sheets of paper (13 x 7½ cm.), which rarely permitted more than twenty words to a page, and which were published in 1961.[31] M. Richard's introduction shows (not deliberately, of course) the close similarity of what Mallarmé was attempting in this work to what Yokomitsu attempted in his.

L'objet de ces notes est moins en effet de s'attacher au fait matériel d'une mort tragique qu'aux mouvements de toute espèce par lesquels celle-ci pourra être dépassée et niée.*[32]

He points out that it was not Mallarmé's habit to evoke the facts of his private life, and that what he had attempted to do in this work was to write a "generalization," a "consolation" in which the people appearing in it would be only types, and in which every event would be shown as only the cause of a moral and spiritual significance which would surpass that event.[33]

A few quotations from these notes should make their nature clear, as well as indicate why the work eventually could not be written.

mort, il n'est que des consolations, pensées—baume: mais ce que est fait est fait—on ne peut pas revenir sur l'absolu contenu en mort—†

---

*The objective of these notes is not so much the grasping of the material fact of a tragic death as a seeking after all those various modifications whereby it may be surpassed and denied.
†dead, there are only consolations, thoughts—balms: but what is done is done—you can not go back upon the absolute contained in death—

Je ne peux pas croire à tout ce qui s'est passé—Le recommencer en esprit
au delà—l'ensevelissement etc—*

ô terre—tu n'as pas une plante—à quoi bon—moi qui t'honore—
bouquets, vaine beauté†

que veux-tu, douce vision adorée—qui viens souvent vers moi, te
pencher—comme écouter secret (de mes larmes)—savoir que tu es
mort—ce que tu ignores—non je ne te le dirai pas—car alors tu disparaîtrais—et je resterais seul pleurant, toi, moi, mêlé, toi te pleurant
enfant en moi l'homme future que tu ne serais pas, et qui reste sans vie
ne joie.‡

non—je ne laisserai pas le néant—père—je sens le néant m'envahir

et si au moins—esprit—je n'ai pas donné sang suffisant—que ma pensée
lui fasse une vie plus belle—plus pure.§

Quoi, ce que je dis est vrai—ce n'est pas seulement musique‖.34

Here one can see how very close the experience reflected in
these notes is to that which Yokomitsu set in his completed
work. "Je ne peux pas croire à tout ce qui s'est passé" is the
center upon which the whole work turns (or would have turned),
as is Yokomitsu's questioning of the truth of his own lived experience. Where the two writers profoundly differ, however, is in
that Yokomitsu writes his *tombeau* but Mallarmé does not write
his, implying that there were, for him, certain realities too close
to the writer to be transmuted into the world of symbolist literature. This is not to imply that symbolism is limited in some fatal
way, for Mallarmé's poetry has considerable scope, from tender

---

*I can not believe in all that has taken place—must begin it all over again in my
mind from there—the burial etc—
†On earth—you have not one plant—for what use are they—yet I honor you—
bouquets, vain beauty.
‡What do you want, sweet adored vision—who often come to me, to lean—as if
listening in secret (of my tears)—to know that you are dead—since you do not
know—no I shall not tell you—for then you would disappear—and I should be
left alone weeping, you, me, mingled together, you weeping the child in me the
future man whom you will never be, and who stays here without life or joy.
§no, I shall not let be this nothingness—father—I feel it invade me
and if I feel at least—in mind—I never gave him blood that would suffice—
then let my thought create for him a life more beautiful—more pure,
‖Look, what I say is true—it is not only music

love poetry ("O si chère de loin et proche et b.anche") to "social-problem" literature ("Pauvre Enfant Pale") which says more real things about human suffering than most self-gratifying protest literature can achieve. What is limited in symbolism is a matter of tone, a striving to create a perfected form which is obliged to keep things out. It is a form of literature that, in each individual work, needs to achieve a dangerous sense of balance, of disturbing elements not being there. One can see this in the "Tombeau" on Verlaine already quoted. Why is the lovely, simple, line, "Verlaine? Il est caché parmi l'herbe, Verlaine," so moving? Is it because, in a stodge of symbolist pretentiousness, at last the human voice speaks out? Surely it is not. Reflections upon death are finally given human, concrete shape in that line, and thus the concluding image of drinking from a stream is led into by such concreteness, and also allowed the weight of symbolic reference which has been created in the main body of the poem. But the line itself is a cold line; if it were not so it would set the poem off balance, perhaps even destroy it.

How different it is in tone from this really moving passage from the notes on Anatole's death (this time given as in the Richard text).

que veux-tu, douce
vision adorée—
qui viens souvent
vers moi, te
pencher—comme
écouter secret [de
mes larmes]—
savoir que tu es
mort
—ce que tu ignores?
—non je ne
te le dirai
pas—car alors tu
disparaîtrais—
et je resterais seul
pleurant, toi, moi,
mêlé, toi te pleurant
       enfant

What do you want, sweet
adored vision—
who often come
to me, to
lean on me—as
if to hear in secret
(tears of mine)—
to learn that you are
dead
—which you don't know?
—no I will not tell
you—for then you
would disappear—
and I would stay alone
weeping, you, me,
mingled together, you weeping for yourself
       the child

| en moi | in me |
|--------|-------|
| l'homme | the future |
| futur que tu ne seras | man you will not be, |
| pas, et qui reste | and who stays here |
| sans vie ni joie. | with neither life nor joy. |

In the context of the other notes with their continual sense of striving to understand and to transform, the feeling of letting go here, of giving in to the terrible truth of this death, is heartbreaking. The lovely use of the word "pencher" with the pause after it; surely it must be a very odd reader who is not deeply moved by this? But Mallarmé is not "making" anything (at least not in the sense that he made his poems); he is, as it were, weeping through his pen (the word "larmes" soon appears, and the end of the passage with its repetition of the word "pleurant" is given over to the profound dignity of ordinary language and emotions). To be able to write like this is certainly the mark of greatness in a man, since in what other terms could one write directly about the death of a child? And yet writing of this kind would destroy any one of his created works if it should appear there, since Mallarmé's is not that kind of literature. There are experiences in the personal life which are too close to be shaped into the form they essentially are; the act of shaping would be an indignity towards them. They must stay in the realm of the formless, of what is not to be grasped. This does not mean that Anatole's death does not find its way into his literature, since it may well have been formative for that literature; but it was not formative in its own form. In an even greater writer the death of eleven-year-old Hamnet may be somehow present in the indeterminately aged Hamlet, but not in its own shape. Shakespeare's favorite daughter may move through his last plays, but hardly as herself.

Is this to imply that Yokomitsu has failed in this work by doing what art should not attempt to do? To answer in the affirmative would be to imply definite ideas about what art (all art) is and can do, which I do not have. What can be said is that Yokomitsu's writing does not become symbolist literature, although it may strive in that direction, and that is one, perhaps the strongest, reason why the literature is unsatisfying. "Ideas of a Flower Garden" is a profoundly moving work, but it does not move one in the way that "Il est caché parmi l'herbe, Verlaine" moves, but rather as "l'homme futur que tu ne seras pas" does. Does this then mean that Yokomitsu gets all his strength from the confessional "I-Novel" tradition, and that the rest of the work is "a stodge of symbolist pretentiousness" from which "at last the human voice speaks out?" One must answer again in the negative, and in doing so the achievement and failure of the literature may perhaps become clear.

The aim of symbolist art is to give shape to ideas, states of mind, feelings that escape us, and so fix the ungraspable as object. It is a form of literature at which only a considerable, and tormented, intellect would aim. "Combien de temps faudra-t-il à la nature pour refaire uncerveau pareil?"* was Rodin's question after Mallarmé's funeral, a question one would not apply to Yokomitsu. Criticism directed at Yokomitsu in the early postwar years called him quite openly an imbecile, totally incapable of understanding writers like Valéry or Gide, and even friendly critics rarely stress his intellectual brilliance. Nearly everyone recognizes the confusion of his critical writings. Yokomitsu's mind was not brilliant, but it was honest and not superficial. Yokomitsu had the honest, unpretentious depth one associates with Oriental wisdom, the quality that makes a *haiku* poet.[35] Some Western readers at times may have felt tempted to dismiss the *Analects* as a collection of platitudes or the remarks of Zen masters as bluff, but such temptation shows that they are looking for the wrong things, and so they find nothing.

In the case of Yokomitsu (and here he becomes representative of most modern Japanese writers), he was perhaps looking for "wrong things" himself. It is in this sense that Western influence has a meaning. Yokomitsu's notions about literature were formed from Western sources, a fact that is true of nearly all the Japanese writers of his time and since.[36] However, the word "notions" is used advisedly, and it needs to be stressed. What really forms a writer is the culture he grows in, that culture reflected in

*How much time would Nature require to recreate a similar brain?

his everyday acts and experiences. That is why the early experiences in a writer's life are so decisive. The reason Western literature is not, as it were, taken over by Japanese writers is that literature works from deep sources which make this impossible. The concept of misunderstanding is of slender validity when applied to this process. By Yokomitsu's time Western literature, as a conceptualized form of literary aims and objectives, existed as a kind of guilty conscience. The desire toward experimentalism was nurtured by this, a sense that making it new, or making it different, was the required thing. The true reasons for experiment did not exist, but only these misguided ones, rather as the actual motive behind the writing of the weird "Heads and Bellies" seems to have been a concealed apology to Kikuchi Kan rather than any proper literary one. However, in the case of Yokomitsu, the events of his personal life created a set of literary needs which the prevailing literary mainstream, the "I-Novel," did not satisfy, because a literature aiming at a harmonious state of mind, at an acceptance of the world, could never have meant anything to him. He took in European modernism in terms of its basic literary tradition, which is a symbolist one, and tried to write symbolist stories, a form of fiction in which he never succeeded (one in which, it should be added, few writers elsewhere have been successful, because the symbolist tradition is basically a poetic one). This does not mean that Yokomitsu tried to follow Western literature (this idea has already been rejected), and he was not well enough acquainted with that literature to attempt such an unlikely and profitless task. However, because Western literature existed, a style full of dislocated sentences, cold and detached images, with the world shown as a jumble of alienated objects, became acceptable; became, indeed, the very thing to do. The literary world achieved in these works was still nothing like its Western counterparts, because a Japanese writer apprehends Japanese realities. This is not a pessimistic statement, any more than calling William Blake an English writer would imply that he was cut off from other cultures, or that his works had no meaning outside his own culture. It is simply a statement of what literature is, something made out of a language which has a national meaning. The Japanese reality Yokomitsu records is that the central meaning of life is a great emptiness, something not to be grasped with the mind. The cold images reflect this fact, this "nothingness"; they are not an apprehension or understanding of that meaning, since there is nothing to be understood. Mallarmé's black rock, dove, star, stream, are efforts to give shape to death and what it means; they arise from a feeling that life is to be understood. Yokomitsu records this only as an emptiness; the basic truth of life being that it is not to be rendered in ideas. The child-like simplicity of the *haiku* and *kōan* are an expression of this same basic attitude toward life.

The argument has now returned to where it was in the previous chapter and there seems little to be said for pushing these ideas further. The conclusion to be drawn is that if the world is seen as something not to be grasped except as an emptiness, then the idea of structure has no place in the description of that world. Japanese art concentrates on the moment, a fact particularly true of poetry and the drama. Admittedly Japanese culture, like any culture, is full of stories, but they either stress moral injunctions and thus accept established social norms as the truth, or they are a series of incidents (*Chūshingura,* for example) or a single incident, as in *Kanjinchō,* which acquires its full meaning in a story seen only as a background. The comparison, for example of *à la recherche du temps perdus* and *Genji,* which sees these two works as fairly similar, is surely a misreading of both. Proust's structure truly moves forward, since its hero is creating an understanding of what life means. *Genji* progresses because time does and for no other reason. The meaning of getting old in *Genji* is that one gets old, although I should be the last to claim that this is a superficial grasp of life, since in fact I believe the opposite; but it is one with which Western writers, particularly from the Romantic period, have not been satisfied. Whether one can then judge either culture because of that seems an irrelevant question (outside the foolish world of national prestige), since it is difficult to see why one should want to do so.

"Ideas of a Flower Garden" has no real structure because it also grasps at no meanings. The literary attempt may seem to be trying to do so but, in effect, it becomes only an attempt to escape from the truth which has always been there, namely, that death is death, a blank darkness, and only that. The cold images, the main bulk of the story indeed, become not the meaning of the work but its meaningless background. It is against this background that what really matters to the writer, not what the experience means but just the experience itself, is recorded. It is in this sense that the literature works, for the frigid detachment makes the emotional scenes shine out like stars in darkness. The moving ending, for example, moves one in the way that autobiography does, but its power comes because so much of what is cold and dead has been created before.

This very success, however, underlines where the story has gone wrong. If a darkness has been created, it is certainly not an emptiness, being full of things, perhaps irrelevant things. Traditional Japanese art has always used emptiness, such as the blank spaces in ink painting or the gaps between the flowers in a flower arrangement. It is as if Yokomitsu had filled all this in with violent, even if only background, colors, although essentially his view of life is no different. Finally, all the symbolism about fish and flowers and eyes and fountains, although each scene or image may work well enough in itself, gives an accumulative sense of junk, like a Japanese room full of Western things, all of which may be good in themselves but which become oppressively irrelevant in their new context, and whose best function seems to be to stress the repose which is still there in the garden, although it has been destroyed in the room.

Ce qui m'empêche de me prendre au sérieux, quoique j'aie l'esprit assez grave, c'est que je me trouve très ridicule, non pas de ce ridicule relatif qui est le comique théâtral, mais de ce ridicule intrinsèque à la vie humaine elle-même, et qui ressort de l'action ou du geste le plus ordinaire. Jamais, par exemple, je ne fais la barbe sans rire, tout ça me parait bête.

Flaubert*[1]

# Chapter Six: Defeat

There was the sound of clogs running over the stones in the garden; they stumbled once, even seemed to fall. Then my brother-in-law appeared, red faced beneath the persimmon tree, and said:

"The war's over. The war's over. Total acceptance of the Potsdam Declaration."

"Is that right?"

"Yes. They just said so on the radio."

I felt I was going to collapse and rested one hand on the floor and looked at the steep garden slope. The hanging cliff of swarming summer chrysanthemums burned the color of flame.

Yokomitsu[2]

THE DEATH OF Akutagawa Ryūnosuke in 1927 left the literary world without a dominating talent. Shiga Naoya had been living in the Kansai area for some years, producing almost no literary work. Tanizaki Jun'ichirō had also moved to Kansai immediately after the earthquake. Nagai Kafū was living in Tokyo, but avoiding literary connections. This period also marked a creative low for him from which he did not begin to emerge until 1931. Satō Haruo, a figure

* What stops me from taking myself seriously, although I have a grave enough temperament, is that I find myself very ridiculous, although not in that relative sense which gives birth to the comedy of the stage, but rather in terms of that ridiculousness which is intrinsic to human life itself, and which occurs in the most ordinary action or gesture. I can never, for example, shave myself without laughing, since the whole business seems to me so stupid.

of importance a few years earlier, was writing long novels of low quality for newspaper serialization. Into this vacuum came Yokomitsu Riichi.

The late 1920s saw the literary world breaking up into two factions ("proletarian" versus "artistic" writers), but, more importantly, they saw the disappearance of the old, closed-in literary world in which writers had formed a real society, where they had been known to one another and wrote for a comparatively small and receptive audience. Now they began to face the fact that they could become rich and successful in terms unknown to previous generations. The feeling that literature as a way of life (rather than as a trade) was played out was a common one during these years, and perhaps the true significance of Yokomitsu's writings from this point on is that they illustrate the movement of serious ("pure") literature toward the new mass audience.

This period also saw a publishing revolution in Japan, first in the "one-yen volumes," and then in paperbacks. The significant years were 1926 and 1927 with the publication of a 63-volume *Collection of Modern Japanese Literature* from Kaizōsha, a *Collection of World Literature* from Shinchōsha, and the creation of Iwanami Bunko, the first paperback library. The reading audience for books widened, magazines aimed at this audience appeared, and the newspaper audience widened and altered in the same way. The opportunity to become affluent was particularly open to the young writer who, as an opponent of the established literary world, was at one with the publishing revolution. The fact that he was young and new fitted in with this revolution in which the packaging began to be important in the selling of a product. Thus one finds such a project as the publication of *Sekai Daitokai Sentan Jazu Bungaku* ("World Metropolis Vanguard Jazz Literature," which means the latest in Jazz literature from the great cities of the world, if that can be said to mean anything), the first volume of which, *Modan Tokio Enbukyoku* (Modern Tokyo Waltz, "Tokio" being written so in the original, not in characters), included young writers as serious as Kawabata Yasunari and Hori Tatsuo, neither of whose writings could be considered adequately described as vanguard jazz literature, or even as a jazzed-up oriental waltz. Here all the vulgarity of modern publicity can be seen as early as 1930.

The year 1927, the year of the publication of "Ideas of a Flower Garden" in January and of his second marriage in February, saw little creative production by Yokomitsu. Clearly "Ideas of a Flower Garden" marked the end of one form of literature, and the direction his literature should now take became a problem never truly resolved throughout the rest of his life. By mid 1928, however, he was embarked upon his first long novel, *Shanghai*, the first portion of which was published towards the end of that year, implying that some form of solution had been found. In fact, 1927 was occupied by his marriage, the building of a new house, and his transformation into a powerful literary figure, even though his publications during this year were so desultory, consisting of a few poems, a play, various articles, and an aggressively Shinkankaku short story, "Nanakai no Undō" (Movements on the Seventh Floor), which shows that type of literature in a form so extreme as to read like a parody of itself. Yokomitsu was apparently trying to retain a belief in this literature during this year by writing critical articles about it in order to persuade himself that it was still important, since he was no longer able to write that kind of literature convincingly. With the writing of the novel *Shanghai* there is a definite attempt to maintain that style through a long novel. As he wrote the novel the need to write such articles disappeared, since, with the progress of the work, the Shinkankaku style was gradually dropped, and the problem became one to be worked out in its own way, and no manifesto statements were required.

Yokomitsu went to Shanghai in April of 1928, apparently intending to make a tour of China, although in fact he remained in that city for just one month. On his return to Japan he began his long novel about the city, using a group of characters who would normally belong in the pages of a sensational popular novel (a dancing girl, a Turkish-bath attendant become prostitute, a beautiful Chinese woman revolutionary, a Japanese Asian nationalist who trades in corpses, a nihilist out-of-work bank clerk, an opium-addicted Chinese capitalist whose Japanese wife runs the

Turkish bath, a Russian prostitute called Olga), and it centers on the kind of event, the 30th of May Movement, which would be a natural subject for a proletarian novel. Yokomitsu's novel can thus be seen as a challenge to proletarian and mass literature, an intended demonstration that only a true literary treatment of such material could arrive at its truth. As he began publication of this novel, he also became involved in a literary controversy with the proletarian critics, a debate which ended in a fairly substantial defeat for Yokomitsu's party, resulting in the breakup of the party; and *Shanghai* as a novel is not a success either. It is the last word in his concern with Shinkankakushugi, a demonstration of its failure to mean anything more to him, and his farewell to it.

Although the novel was not published in book form until 1932, most of it appeared in the magazine *Kaizō* within the space of about one year, from November 1928 to December 1929, under a series of eccentric Shinkankaku titles; "Bath and Bank," "Legs and Justice," "Doubts of the Dregs," "Hemorrhoids and Bullets," and "Concerning the Harbor." These represent the novel as such. Two additional chapters, published in 1931, are more properly thought of as a second volume, one never completed. The following year, 1930, was a year of change in his literature, an attempt to escape from the stylistic dead end which *Shanghai* turned out to be. The following is one critic's account of that change.

In 1930 Yokomitsu Riichi suddenly changed. This was *Kikai* ['The Machine'] which appeared in the September issue of *Kaizō*. A translation of *Ulysses* was appearing at the same time, and there is unmistakably the influence of Proust who had been published in *Bungaku*. I had just bought the magazine and started to read "The Machine" as I was walking along the main street in Ushigome, and the impression it made was such that it took my breath away. He had suddenly dropped the jumpy, impressionistic *Shinkankaku* method he had followed right up to *Shanghai*, and was now approaching a style that was flexible, in the phrase of Tanigawa Tetsuzō an "arabesque-like" associationist method of writing, in which the language went forward without intermission and the printed text had hardly an indentation in it, the type literally crammed on the page. Quite honestly it seemed that what Hori [Tatsuo] and I had been trying to do although we didn't have the power to bring it off, was here being performed in the only shape it could take in Japanese by this stolid senior of ours. The literary world was astonished; it was called a

masterpiece; and Kawabata Yasunari and Kobayashi Hideo wrote excited articles about it. However, one very odd thing was that one saw no
criticism which referred to the influence of the new French and English
literature that had been appearing in *Shi to Shiron* [Poetry and Poetics]
over the previous two years.[3]

The generally accepted position (that taken by the author of
the above, Itō Sei, and others) is that with the publication of the
quarterly magazine *Poetry and Poetics* from September 1928 on,
modern postwar European literature was introduced with a detail
and scope quite new in the Japanese literary world. Instead of the
haphazardness of a few years earlier with its misplaced emphases
upon such writers as Paul Morand, the mainstream of European
modernism—Cocteau, Breton, Aragon, Éluard, Valéry, Proust,
Gide, Joyce, Eliot, Lawrence—was presented to Japanese readers.
The magazine was run by young, virtually unknown writers, and
the fact that Yokomitsu contributed to it when the columns of the
big magazines were open to him indicates his interest. This interest appears nowhere in his writing for the year 1928, and the
resurgence of a concern with modernist European literature in
the following year (in place of literary disputes with Marxists) is
a fact not to be overlooked.[4] It is necessary to point out, however,
if one is concerned with not overlooking things, that this interest
is not particularly profound, as an incompetent essay of his on
Max Jacob shows quite clearly, if compared with those of other
Japanese writers of the time, such as Hori Tatsuo or Itō Sei. In
October of 1929 another magazine, a monthly called *Bungaku* (Literature), began to appear. Both Yokomitsu and Kawabata were
on its editorial board, although its presiding spirit was Hori Tatsuo, whose illness brought about the early demise of the magazine. A translation of *Du côté de chez Swann* began to appear with
the first number, and in February 1930 some selections from
*Ulysses* appeared, although a complete translation began to come
out only with the publication of *Shi: Genjitsu* (Poetry: Reality) in
June of the same year. One of the translators was Itō Sei, which
may account for his over-zealous concern with such influences.
Thus in 1930 Yokomitsu's style changed, and here we see what
some critics claim are the basic causes.

Not all critics accept this accepted position, as an example of which I give the following:

It is claimed that the writing of *The Machine* was modelled on that of Proust, and presumably the impact of the long sentence in that work on its readers may have called Proust to mind, but the idea that *The Machine* and *À la recherche* . . . are a similar kind of literature is an absolute joke, since it is quite impossible to discover anything like a resemblance between Yokomitsu and Proust.[5]

Even a brief, superficial comparison of Yokomitsu's "Machine"[6] and Proust will show that Hinuma is right, although it is still a fact that the style did change. The main foreign influence came from reading Valéry, rather than an interest in Proust, and will be taken up below. Indeed, the only interest in comparing Proust with Yokomitsu would be to show how completely different they are. Yokomitsu's new involved style was a way of laying hold of nothing (in contrast to the richness of implication one finds in any page of Proust), and in this sense it is more like a return to the style of *The Price of Unhappiness* than a move in any forward direction. The one profound difference between the present and the earlier styles is in the change of attitude toward what it is describing, being now subtle, light, and humorous rather than heavy and sentimental, but the obsessive sense of worrying over something which finally cannot be understood is there in both. One of the interests of this change of style (and here the evidence comes so pat the reader may well have doubts about the thesis it supports) is that it first appears, not in "The Machine" but in yet another rewriting of the material of *The Price of Unhappiness*, in a story published in February 1930 (seven months before "The Machine" and in the same month as the first appearance of *Ulysses*, so that particular influence will have to go) called "Tori" (The Bird).

This story tells of the same competition between friends over one girl, the girl being attracted by accident to the narrator, although his friend is his superior as a person, particularly excelling in those scientific studies they both pursue, although he himself will shortly be overshadowed by someone else. The girl starts to shuttle back and forth between the two friends, marries the narrator through the generosity of the friend. The marriage lasts for two years or so; but because the friend is now outshone in his studies the narrator wishes to do something for him, and one of the things he does is to present him with the girl. However, he gradually discovers that everything he does for the friend is truly being done only for himself, and the story turns into a mass of contradictions and misunderstood motives and actions, a feature it shares with "The Machine" and "Time." The style may be involved and comic (Yokomitsu's Japanese of this period is much funnier than English renderings manage to make clear), but the underlying meaning of this work (and the others written in this year) could hardly be called so, since it implies that the confusion of life is insoluble, a truth which can be tolerated only if one does not take it seriously; if one becomes, in fact, a fool. In this story all is finally resolved when the narrator and the girl take a ride in an airplane, thus turning their marriage into the free existence of a bird. As the airplane flies through a world of perpetual rainbows formed by the drops of moisture on its wings they feel newly remarried. It is a straightforward escapist image, but not one subjected to irony, for it is only such innocent stupidity that can make any sense out of life, since such sense is not, in reality, to be found. As a fine ironic comment on how such sense was not indeed to be found in reality, when Yokomitsu flew with other literary men to Manchuria later that year he was sick on the plane both ways.

Where this story most contrasts with *The Price of Unhappiness* and other versions of the same material is not so much in a change of style as in an altered attitude toward the external world. Certainly it is related to the change of style, which had been nowhere near as abrupt as Itō Sei suggests, since it had been taking place throughout the writing of *Shanghai,* but the style does reflect this changed attitude and can not be said to have brought it about. It is as extreme as what happened in *The Sun in Heaven,* and has similar implications. If the attempt of *The Sun in Heaven* had been to see the world without moral imperatives, then this is an effort to see it with just one simple one, which is that the world can be tolerable only if one is foolish to the point of being totally innocent. The final injunction of the hero in *Shanghai* had been to stop thinking, and this is what the narrator of "The Bird" puts into practice. In the same way the narrators of both "The Machine" and "Time" are people whose foolishness is shown as a consistent, even if unreal, way of organizing the world, and in the story "Basha" (The Carriage)[7] the narrator is an intellectual suffering from a nervous breakdown, who literally stops thinking on doctor's orders.

These stories may reveal Yokomitsu at his most brilliantly talented, but they have an incompleteness about them which prevents them from being his best work; some ideological obsession seems to lie behind them. The most famous critique of "The Machine," that by Kobayashi Hideo, published in the month after the story appeared,[8] concentrates on this ideological aspect rather than on any evaluation of the work; in fact, it is not at all clear whether he thought "The Machine" any good or not.

Kobayashi's emphasis is upon innocence, which I have referred to as foolishness or stupidity. Kobayashi's choice of "innocence" indicates how positive a value he is prepared to accord to it, although the tone of "The Machine" itself and Yokomitsu's inability to go on writing this kind of literature make it difficult to believe that this positive value is really there. "The Machine" is rather a gesture of despair about the form living takes, and in particular about the form it takes in literature, an interpretation which his subsequent literary career supports. This last outpouring of serious writing soon led to the writing of popular novels for the daily press, albeit those novels attempted to remain under the guise of the real thing. That the despair one finds in the literature was also present in the life of the writer (at least in his mental life) can be shown.

In 1929, the year in which the bulk of *Shanghai* was written, Yokomitsu came across Valéry's *L'Introduction à la méthode de Léonard de Vinci*, which excited him enough to make him try to learn French.[9] Discovering that so great a man existed, he felt like throwing away his own pen. Reading this work, which he saw as a *sutra* or even as the Devil's Bible, he felt he had suddenly advanced five years. His letter breaks off at this point, but is taken

up ten days later, his enthusiasm now even stronger. He sees
what is new in Valéry as a nihilism placed at the center of the individual consciousness, a nihilism which Valéry grasped in
terms of physical laws.[10] All writers up to now had died unaware
of this truth and so had been living in a dream. His own eyes
were now open, at the age of thirty-two (thirty-one by Western
reckoning), although it was an awakening with no sense of exhil-
aration. The road that Valéry opened for him was one that could
lead only to madness, and what he most felt like doing was going
back to the countryside and writing nothing, simply spending
his time amusing his child. Is he an idiot? Is he going to fall into
that state of mind, into the vanity of seeing himself as a fool and
being contented with that? He doesn't know, and yet surely he is
a fool. The letter ends by saying there remains nothing else but
to descend into Marxism.[11]

    In the month after this letter (in October 1929) the magazine
*Bungaku* brought out its first number, that in which the translation of Proust began to appear. In February of the next year,
1930, the short story "The Bird" was published. In May he went
into the hospital with hemorrhoids and in the same month wrote
a letter in which he said he believed himself to be a Marxist, so
far as the study of man was concerned, although he still felt the
ideologies behind Marxism and literature were opposed to each
other. However, the attractions of Marxism were growing
stronger and stronger. A letter of uncertain date of the same year
says he is no longer young and all he is really fit for is playing the
fool in front of his young son (three-years-old in November),
since his own stupidity is getting stronger and stronger.[12] In
August 1930, he did in fact go to the country, to a hot spring on
the Japan Sea coast (in a village connected with his wife's family), but he did not throw away his pen (or brush), but used it to
write "The Machine," which was published the next month. November and December saw the first newspaper serialization of a
novel of his, and during the next year he had two novels serialized, one in a newspaper and the other in a ladies' journal. Thus,
to put it briefly, an earlier concern with stupidity as a positive (it
appears even in his earliest stories) was brought to life by the

reading of Valéry in 1929 and was written out in serious short stories during 1930. By 1931 he was a confirmed popular novelist. The process was not quite as total as that suggests ("The Carriage" was published in January 1932, for example), but the general movement was definite enough.

In a letter written in May 1931 this praise of folly had become a belief, one which he then associated with what he felt the Japanese tradition to be:

I've been reading Saikaku for three or four days now. As far as I can tell from my limited reading Saikaku was a man who thought about nothing. People from Kansai have never liked thinking very much, it's the local character. You can see the virtue of that way of not thinking in Saikaku's works. There's a great power in not taking thought. The reason Saikaku can astound people is because, in fact, he's a fool. I think Bashō went the same way. So I've stopped writing . . . And then Tanizaki Jun'ichirō is a man who doesn't like thinking. Thinking leads to one's ruin. The Japanese are a weird race. After all, Dialectical Materialism, isn't that for us just a form of not thinking?[13]

In another letter dated the same month he wrote:

Thinking about *Le Bal du Comte d'Orgel*, well I've been getting through the days with things like that, but the rain keeps falling so I stop thinking about these exotic Western things, and I get out the *ukiyo zōshi*, I imagine because the rain and the *ukiyo* prints go so well together.[14]

At this period in his literary life, and possibly some time before, Yokomitsu had gone back to using the brush as the result of a bout of rheumatism which made it difficult to hold a pen. He continued the practice because the brush seemed to him the right tool for writing psychological descriptions; and it is at least likely that this decision had more influence upon his style than any amount of Proust or Joyce or Radiguet. The influence of Valéry, however, is certainly there (although in no direct stylistic sense of course) and one quotation from the work in question will show what that influence was. The experience of struggling with the French may be of particular value for the reader here, since, especially if at times it leads to real incomprehension, it may help to demonstrate what Yokomitsu's own response to the book was.[15]

L'homme que l'exigence de l'infatigable esprit conduit à ce contact
de ténèbres éveillées, et à ce point de présence pure, se perçoit comme
nu et dépouillé, et réduit à la suprême pauvreté de la puissance sans
objet; victime, chef-d'œuvre, accomplissement de la simplification et de
l'ordre dialectique; comparable à cet état où parvient la plus riche pensée
quand elle s'est assimilée à elle-même, et reconnue, et consommée en un
petit groupe de caractères et de symboles. Le même travail que nous
faisons sur un objet de réflexions, il l'a dépensé sur le sujet qui réfléchit.
　　Le voici sans instincts, presque sans images; et il n'a plus de but. Il
n'a pas de semblables. Je dis: *homme*, et je dis: *il* par analogie et par
manque de mots.
　　Il ne s'agit plus de choisir, ni de créer; et pas plus de se conserver
que de s'accroître. Rien n'est a surmonter, et il ne peut pas même être
question de se détruire.
　　Tout ≪génie≫ est maintenant consumé, ne peut plus servir de rien.
Ce ne fut qu'un moyen pour atteindre à la dernière simplicité. Il n'y a
pas d'acte du génie qui ne soit *moindre* que l'acte d'être. Une loi mag-
nifique habite et fonde l'imbécile; l'esprit le plus fort ne trouve pas
mieux en soi-même.* [16]

Such a quotation probably gives the impact of the work
upon Yokomitsu's mind more truly than any explication or ex-
position of the ideas themselves would, since it is doubtful that
Yokomitsu understood those ideas as a form of argument. Nowhere does he give coherent or extended account of what Valéry's ideas meant to him. It seems reasonable to say, as some of

*That man who has been brought to this contact with awakened shadows
through the unceasing demands of his mind, to this point of pure presence,
becomes aware of himself as naked and despoiled, reduced to that supreme
wretchedness of power which lacks an object; the victim and yet the perfected
achievement of simplification and dialectical order; much like that state to which
the richest thought attains when it is assimilated to itself, and recognizes and is
consumed in a small group of characters and symbols. That same effort which we
use upon the object of our reflections it has expended upon the subject which
reflects.
　　See him now without instincts, almost without images; and he no longer has
a goal. There is no one who is like him. I use the word *man* and *he* only by anal-
ogy and because I lack the proper ones.
　　There is no longer any question of choice for him, nor of creation; he does
not conserve himself nor does he grow. There is nothing to be overcome, and
there is not even any chance that he might destroy himself.
　　All genius has now been exhausted, for it could serve no further purpose. It
was only a means for attaining this final simplicity. Any act of genius must be *less*
than the act of being. The idiot's existence is founded upon a magnificent law
which also dwells within him; the most powerful of minds will find nothing superior within itself.

his Japanese critics have, that he was incapable of understanding them. If one considers the kind of literature he wrote in 1930, however, one can see how some of the phrases from the passage given above (in their Japanese forms) echoed in his mind, creating not that "desperate clarity" in which Valéry was interested but a desperate confusion from which the uncomplex and now unreal past with its fixed simplifications (people from Kansai don't like thinking, so all problems can be dismissed in that phrase) offered a way out. That this was hardly satisfactory the desperate tone of the literature shows, but it did at least suggest there was a road one could take. What it suggested was, in fact, that one should simply stop trying, for Yokomitsu was ceasing to believe that literary modes of apprehension could get at the truth, a process which can be seen fully worked out in his second long novel *Shin-en* (The Garden of Sleep).

The first half of this was serialized in a newspaper, the *Ōsaka Mainichi Shinbun,* in November and December of 1930; then, after a break of sixteen months, the second half appeared in the literary monthly *Bungei Shunjū* from April to December 1932. During the intervening year of 1931 another novel, *Hanabana* (Flowers) was serialized in *Fujin no Tomo* (The Ladies Companion) from April to December, and another, *Gaka* (Song of Songs) in a newspaper, the *Hōchi Shinbun,* during August and September. The transformation into high-grade popular writer is complete, and the success he had now achieved can be seen by the number of editions of his works which appeared in 1932 when he was still only thirty-four.[17]

Despite the reservations one might have about the short stories written in 1930 they are still a literature of very considerable interest and value, whereas *Shin-en* comes as a real disappointment. The story is one which was to become almost a norm in his long novels, and which has obvious connections with his earlier literature, being that of two men and one woman; although in this case the men are ideological ciphers representing two opposed ways of life. This was the pattern he was to maintain from here on. The woman, Nanae, is married to Niwa, although she had been in love with Kaji before her marriage, and her dissatisfaction with her husband renews her interest in him, an interest that had, in fact, never disappeared. Niwa is shown as boring and insensitive, but he is "good" and represents the positive the novel wishes to emphasize. Although he is not dominant throughout the work, it is with an image of him on which the novel ends. Kaji is a representative of the "self-conscious" modern intellectual whose life lacks the solid foundation of the other. This is not that clearly stated in this work, but the constant repetition of the same theme in later novels seems to show that this interpretation is right. The "Garden of Sleep" is referred to only once in the book, being the mausoleum of a Chinese Emperor, but the title is also meant to imply the unconscious mind and, according to Kawabata Yasunari, the true theme of the work is that while Nanae consciously aims at Kaji she is unconsciously seeking her estranged husband. That is an interesting account of a novel, although unfortunately not of the novel that Yokomitsu wrote. It is true there are signs that might support that interpretation, but as one reads the book it is clear that all we have is a commonplace love triangle, and any profundity of interpretation could be supported only by careful editing of fragments of it, never by the work as a whole, and must consequently be judged as false.

Niwa is a great shooting enthusiast, and the central incident of the plot is a hunting accident. Nanae shoots her husband while apparently trying to save him from a rampaging wild boar. The motive is made complex by the fact that immediately before firing at Niwa an image of Kaji had come into her mind. However, the question of motive, which appears as if it were going to occupy the center of the novel, is dealt with in a very perfunctory way, and the level of psychological insight never rises above that of a commonplace popular novel, a fact that contrasts strikingly with the wonderfully assured grasp of the complexity of human motive seen in so much of his previous writing. Of course, the modern Japanese novel is not remarkable for psychological analyses, nor is there any reason why it should be, since such analyses are not essential to the novelist's purposes. Does the novel work through images, then, through hints and undertones, in the way that Kawabata's *Snow Country* appears to do? One has to reply that it does not, but works, rather, by spinning itself out in a number of conversations and happenings that indicate how little interest Yokomitsu has in what he is doing. When the novel does, as it were, remind itself that what is involved is an undertaking of importance, the main impression it gives is one of incompetence, or of not even wishing to be competent, which is something new in Yokomitsu's literature. All his earlier writing gives a deep sense of the author's involvement, even in those cases when it perhaps fails to come off. The novel opens, for example, in a mist in the mountain resort of Karuizawa with all the characters looking for, and failing to find each other. The slightly sick feeling the reader may experience at the thought that a symbol is being lumbered into position will soon be dispelled by the novel itself, since nothing is written about in a way which would allow such an interpretation. Uninteresting people walk about in a mist and have tedious conversations. To find any symbolical meaning would be pure generosity on the reader's part, based on an assumption that the openings of novels do often have symbolic overtones, or that mist might symbolize something, or that, since what is read is so dull, it must be "deep" in some way. But symbol implies insight, and no insight is shown here, as no connections with what follows are worked out. There is nothing in fact.

In a shorter episode further on in the work such meanings seem to be pointed at, but in a way that leads to no sense of clarification. This occurs when Kaji, who is going bankrupt, has had money sent to him by Nanae, but sent to him impersonally through the agency of Niwa, with only a very formal accompanying letter. Kaji is irritated by this and decides to return the money with a curt letter of thanks. Having written the letter but not posted it, he goes out for a walk, and his complex feelings towards Nanae are fairly skillfully related to speculations about the amount of money involved, since he had been too proud to look. The passage is then completed with an image, and since this image is that from which the book takes its title one is justified in thinking that this passage is of importance, even of central importance. Kaji has come out by the river bank and notices how the mist flows over the river but not with it. The writing has here reached a distinguished level, and various meanings seem to be tentatively pointed at. It continues:

Then something suddenly snapped in his mind and a sense of desolate emptiness began to rise and swell within him. As he squatted on the bank staring at one solitary, cold-looking stake poking up out of the water, a scene quite different from this before him drifted into his head, a Garden of Sleep seen while travelling in some foreign country. Then he remembered something seen before that, the thick scales of a marble sculpted Chinese dragon, by which it was said only one angel might ascend to heaven, and how he had cockily clambered across it; and all the splendid momentary dreams of that time came to him, and he compared it to what life was now and saw the useless emptiness of it all.[18]

In this passage the symbol does not act as a statement that resolves what has gone before by giving it concrete shape (as does Virginia Woolf's lighthouse or Proust's spires of Martinville), but is only an image that gets rid of what it should actually summarize by condemning it to transience and finally to nothingness. Nothing of what has been felt and thought about Nanae is expressed here, since what is finally expressed is a world that has no place for her nor for anything else. This is not a way of grasping the real world but only of rejecting it: the world is a background to insight, but the insight is not into that world but into a value over and beyond it. This is "Oriental Nothingness," the silence which is the final truth about the world, the emptiness. In a "psychological novel" it has no place, since the sleeping garden of the mind is not empty but full, waiting to be roused, not merely excavated to reveal that life is no longer, nor indeed ever had been, there.

"The New Psychological Novel" is the label applied to Yokomitsu's writings (and those of others) of this period, and it is true that he does show some interest in revealing human nature by way of inner mental processes rather than through purely external images. Yet this results in ambivalences of a kind whereby the depiction of a state of mind is little indication of what the human mind is like, but is perilously close to the vulgar shorthand of the cheap novelist eager to get on with the story. Nor was he writing a novel which explored the subconscious depths of the human mind, since Yokomitsu never believed that human life could be got hold of in that way. His early literature shows a definite turning away from the attempt to portray the actual workings of human motive, that being the nightmare of *The Price of Unhappiness* from which he had wished to awaken. His return to such involvements was an effort to show them in such a light whereby they would no longer matter, yet that only led to the even deeper darkness of "The Machine" and of "Time." How deep this darkness was, how indeed it was the only thing that truly interested him, can be seen in an illuminating, if misguided, comment on *Ulysses*.

The dark side of reality—of course reality does presumably have a dark side. However, what we refer to as this dark side is something that absolutely cannot be expressed in words. The achievement of *Ulysses* is not in having portrayed the dark side of human psychology, but in his having gone further and more dangerously than anyone else in investigating this dark side to show it as a very blankness which escapes the written word.[19]

This is not very good on Joyce, but it certainly reveals the truth about Yokomitsu. Since he feels this way how, then, is he to write what he has admitted cannot be written? "Human psychology cannot be written about, but a writer must write it since only by attempting the impossible can he ascertain the limits of his powers."[20]

This is the journalistic, inflated image of the writer as the great explorer which is handed out to people who have no interest in literature itself, and are incapable of understanding what the truly exploratory nature of a new literature might be. One can see how easily Yokomitsu has slipped into this mass media world, one from which he was to begin to emerge only with the disasters of 1945. His literary career from now to then is that of an established figure whose output is of little other than sociological interest. There is the occasional short story in which the deep and moving strength of his earlier writing remains, and the long novels often have good things in them, since Yokomitsu had

considerable literary talent and a mind creative enough to produce passages of interest and distinction in all his work. However, these novels have little to do with his real importance as a
writer.

The Garden of Sleep ends with the image of Niwa (now the
rejected husband, since by this time Nanae has run off, although
it is not quite clear to where and for how long), the moral positive who is to be stressed throughout the novels after this.

A rifle shot rang out, and Aiko gave a start remembering Nanae and all
that had happened, and she automatically glanced at Niwa's face. One
could not be sure if he had heard the shot or not, for the shadow of
unease which had sometimes darkened his face in the past was completely gone, as he stood, his eyes narrowed, gazing at one portion of
the sky, beaming graciously like some huge buddha.[21]

The word hotoke (buddha) can also mean a "fool," and here
we have Niwa's foolishness given divine shape. Besides demon-
strating the author's moral preoccupations, it also gives an
image, slightly and unfairly preposterous perhaps, of Yokomitsu
himself. The hero has been off in the mountains hunting
dangerously real game, which he fails, despite all his skill, to
shoot, and, in the process, is almost fatally injured by his wife.
His recovery is long and slow, but the story will end in the celebration of that recovery which his club will give him, because he
is its most important member, its crack shot. The club members
wear a new uniform designed for them by Niwa [the New Psychological Novel], one which he himself puts on for the occasion.
A relative (Aiko, an ambiguous successor to Nanae) arrives with
the news that his wife (the muse, the god Hercules) has left him,
but the tale ends with this not yet divulged to the hero who is
still in complete command of himself. Now he will go on being
the club's finest shot, will score any number of bull's eyes (if
popular acclaim and accomplices in the butts can be considered
true indications of marksmanship), but the targets are not real,
only clay pigeons. The wild boar still roam the mountains
beyond.

In 1934 Yokomitsu's second son was born and this seems to
have removed him even further from his past with its unequivo-

cal devotion to literature. In an article that year he said that he had come to despise the idea of writing a masterpiece and then dying young, for he no longer liked literature, although he had not yet arrived at that age or degree of experience by which he would be able to say he quite positively disliked it. What he most wished to say was that it was a dislike of literature which particularly made him wish to write it, and he felt that people who could say without reservation that they liked literature were very fortunate. "Ten years ago I wrote easily with the pleasure that comes quite naturally out of a complete absorption in what one is doing, but things do not work out like that now." [22]

In the same year, 1934, he published perhaps the most ambitious of his completed long novels, *Monshō* (The Family Crest), whose principal interest is in the two heroes, who represent contrasting styles of life which begin to take on clear cultural overtones as representatives of native and imported civilization, a theme which was to become predominant in *Ryoshū* (Travel Sadness), work on which was begun three years later in 1937. The quarrel with the "I-Novel" upon which his literature is based was then stated clearly at the opening of a critical article published in 1935, his "Junsui Shōsetsuron" (A Theory of the Pure Novel). Here he maintained that modern Japanese literature had reached an impasse in that the basic elements of the novel as fiction had been relegated to the world of the popular novel, whereas serious literature (*junbungaku*) had concerned itself with realism, with what was "real" in the author's experience, what "really" happened to him, and had thus been condemned to becoming a mere species of diary literature. Yokomitsu begins the article [23] by stating that unless serious literature is to popularize itself it can have no future. If one looks at the productions of the past ten years what in fact is there of interest? If one wanted to show a foreigner what could be interesting in contemporary Japanese literature, would not one show him a popular writer, like Kikuchi Kan for example? This situation can be remedied only by admitting that the role of fiction is to create possible worlds, and by permitting such elements of the popular novel as accident and sentimentality, to be brought back into the novel proper, as in Dostoevsky. Since Yokomitsu is not really clear about what he is arguing for, the logic of the essay does not permit one to present it as anything other than a few simple ideas, a few of which sometimes stand out from the defensive qualifications which try to hedge them in (Hirano Ken's comment that the essay is "pathetic confusion" is only a slight overstatement).[24] Its principal impact on the literary world seemed to be an attempt to show the conversion of the hero of *junbungaku* to the popular camp. That this process had been going on for some time has already been argued, and the "Junsui Shōsetsuron" reads in some sense like a notebook on Yokomitsu's writings from *Shanghai* on, a point he made himself in the same article.[25]

In making that remark Yokomitsu had André Gide and the Notebook to *Les Faux Monnayeurs* in mind. It is true that the similarities are so slight as to be nearly non-existent, and yet the remark has a certain relevance, since there can be little doubt that Yokomitsu was coming to see himself as the Japanese Gide. The *junsui shōsetsu* is Gide's "roman pur" (although Yokomitsu seems to have lost most of what Gide wished to imply by that term), and one notices that Kobayashi Hideo in his extremely influential essay on the "I-Novel" (*Shishōsetsuron*) moves automatically from a brisk consideration of Yokomitsu's ideas to a much lengthier discussion of Gide, on the assumption, no doubt, that what Yokomitsu was trying to say the French author had more properly said.[26] Kobayashi is fairly indulgent towards Yokomitsu, although the occasional tart remark shows that this period meant the parting of the ways for the two of them. He puts him quite firmly in his place over the idea (which has little to do with Gide) that Dostoevsky employed the "accidental" and "sentimental" in his novels like any popular Japanese novelist. Kobayashi properly objects to imprecisely used terminology of that kind, pointing out that the "accidental" in a Japanese popular novelist is merely a series of devices for keeping the plot machinery in motion, whereas in Dostoevsky it is an attempt to bring that everyday consciousness into question. He also feels that talking about "popular" and "serious" in the context of *Crime and Punishment* has no real meaning, since the only category it truly fits into is that of a very fine novel; the fact that one can extract characteristics from it that might be termed "popular" is another and not really relevant question, as also is the fact that Yokomitsu might wish to talk in this way because present-day *junbungaku* had become so uninteresting. This is the one part of the essay where Kobayashi is clearly irritated with Yokomitsu, although he softens his annoyance by saying he had forced himself into such contradictions through having chosen Gide as his master. This last statement is by no means true, but it at least allows him to avoid having to say anything really damaging.[27]

Yokomitsu's concern with Gide was a constant one. Gide was often the subject of the baffling lectures he was in the habit of giving during the latter years of his life, and yet it is difficult to see the concern as any more serious than the ponderous absurdities with which he would bemuse his audiences, such as "the accidental is the necessary" and "the works of Kataoka are a straight line of decision."[28] Such remarks (and he was not in the habit of expanding them) are bluff, a form of bluff which seems to have taken in the speaker as well as the audience. Yokomitsu's use of Gide in the essay under consideration is a similar kind of bluff, since it is not a way of investigating various ideas but merely makes use of them, producing them as the occasion requires. If one looks, for example, at the various remarks on the novel scattered throughout *Les Faux Monnayeurs*, some fit in with what Yokomitsu has to say and some do not; and the ones which do fit interact only at a very simple level. When, for instance, in part 2, chapter 3, Edouard gives his ideas on the novel, he certainly attacks the realist tradition of the modern novel "si craintivement cramponné à la réalité,"* as also the naturalist obsession with its "tranche de vie."†[29] But this realist tradition is not much like the Japanese one Yokomitsu was writing against, and Edouard's belief that only a withdrawal from life permitted the creation of a style, an art form as true to life and yet as distanced from reality as seventeenth-century French drama, is nowhere in the Yokomitsu of this period (although something like it can perhaps be seen in some of his earlier writings), and his long

---

*so timidly clinging on to reality
†slice of life

novels are about as distant from that belief as they could possibly be. Edouard's desire to write a novel without a subject is far removed from Yokomitsu's abstract moral problems, and the idea of "purity" as a casting out of all elements from the novel which do not essentially belong there (exterior happenings, accidents, traumatisms) seems to be quite the opposite of Yokomitsu's wish to put all that popular contrivance back in again. It is true that Gide does employ "accident" in the novel itself (Bernard gets possession of Edouard's journal by way of a dropped luggage ticket, which it just so happens . . .),[30] but this seems to be a willful attempt on the part of the author to make the plot machinery unmistakably creak, an aristocratic joke of the *"tant pis pour le lecteur paresseux"* * variety. The truth is that Yokomitsu used Gide for his own personal reasons, principally to retain his up-to-date image, and showed little sign of trying to understand him.

To give an example of use without understanding, Yokomitsu used the phrase *"chaban shōsetsu"* (*"chaban"* is a kind of farce) about one of his novels, *Kazoku Kaigi* (The Family Conference). This term is normally taken by Japanese people (although not by scholars of French literature) as derogatory, implying a novel written to amuse people and make money. Judging by the context in which Yokomitsu used the word, it seems fairly certain that he too interpreted the word in that way.[31] However, *"chaban shōsetsu"* is the Gidean term *"sotie,"* a word he applied to such works as *Le Prométhée mal enchaîné* or *Les Caves du Vatican,* since those works were a mixture of the fantastic and the preposterous, like a medieval farce. The word is a piece of "brilliance," a triumphant discovery of *le mot juste,* and is meant to be descriptively apt. It can by no means be considered as any form of modest self deprecation concerning the value of the works in question. It is most doubtful that Yokomitsu could have grasped that; he used the word because it would puzzle people, and then really stump them when they discovered it was a recent fashion in Paris. Still, that kind of behavior hardly allows one to approach a writer in the spirit, and it is symbolically apt that Yoko-

* bad luck for the lazy reader

mitsu should never have met Gide in the flesh, although they did, by pure chance, travel on the same train from Berlin to Moscow. But they never actually meet, and the caption beneath a snapshot of Yokomitsu taken in Moscow explains rather lamely that Gide had been there just before it was taken (presumably an attempt was made to get him into the picture without his knowledge or consent), but he had, unfortunately, moved away at the vital moment. This was perhaps as near as Yokomitsu was ever to get to most of his European "influences," since they are rarely in the picture when it is actually taken.

However, people attended Yokomitsu's lectures on Gide and they bought his novels, and the significance of his works during this period is that they did reach a wide audience, although not one normally associated with the popular novel. In his "Shishōsetsuron" Kobayashi Hideo wondered what kind of people read a novel like Yokomitsu's *Flowers* with its, in his opinion, time-wasting and slightly dull romantic involvements; he also wondered who read the translation of *La Porte étroite*, which seemed to sell better than any popular novel ever did.[32] Kobayashi did not answer his own questions, although it would have been easy to do so since the answer to both was the same. This was a new middle-class audience (or an audience which wished to belong to that class), whose tastes had been Westernized to the point where the old popular novel with its historical setting and conflicts between duty and human feelings had ceased to be of interest, or at least had ceased to be of interest all the time. What gives a continuity to the novels Yokomitsu wrote at this time even more than their abstract theme is their milieux of leisured upper-middle-class people doing smart things: Westernized things for the young, Japanese things for the old, and a mixture of the two for the middle-aged. It is remarkably like the world of the present-day television commercial. It is a world which makes its appearance in *The Garden of Sleep* and never disappears from these long novels after that. People are very rich (even if they are poor they have just stopped being rich), and the tragedy of the Westernized intellectual is that of having nothing to do, an attractive tragedy for people who have to work hard. The novels are full of descriptions of expensive clothes, of people with expensive tastes who spend a lot of time in hotels eating exotic foods, and it is all slightly reminiscent of the dropping of brand names in the James Bond novels. The novels invite the reader into a fantasy world (*La Porte étroite* and *Ouvert la nuit* could present the same kind of invitation for a Japanese reader), and the cipher-like nature of the heroes and heroines, in particular the hopeless Westernized intellectuals, makes the acceptance of this invitation easy. These are the classic traits of the popular novel. They are a form of passing the time, a function taken over to a considerable extent in modern Japan by television drama, which consists of period drama or drama of common life or drama of the emotional involvements of the well-to-do; a pattern identical to the form the popular novel took in the 1930s, the period drama having dominated up to that time. It would be useless to object to this, since the desire to have a fantasy life and pass the time pleasantly when one is tired is a human trait I have no desire to condemn since I share it myself; but it would also be wrong to pretend it is other than it is. Again, no genre condemns any example of it to conformity to what the genre essentially is; many of the masterpieces of nineteenth-century English fiction were best-sellers, and there is nothing to prevent television drama from making as serious demands upon its audience as does Flaubert. However, the norm does not do that, and neither do these long novels by Yokomitsu. He had grasped (how consciously one cannot say, but perhaps not very) that a new kind of popular novel for a new mass audience was required, and he wrote it. That it masqueraded as something else simply indicates what sort of popular novel it was, and tells one something about the pretensions of its audience.

I repeat that I do not wish to give an impression of unrelieved badness in these novels. Yokomitsu always remained a reasonably competent professional and there are good things in the novels even if they do represent (the point I am trying to make) a loss of faith in literature as a way of arriving at the truth of human life, becoming instead a way of conveying simple beliefs in a form which never tried to question those beliefs, or else was merely a profitable way of keeping oneself occupied. They represent such a steep falling off from the true seriousness of his earlier writing that some such interpretation seems called for.

Yokomitsu's six-month voyage to Europe in 1936 (officially to cover the Berlin Olympic Games for a newspaper, although in effect it meant going through the endurance test of "Western Life," which was felt at that time, as now, to be a necessity for distinguished literary figures) provided the motive force for the long work which was to occupy him on and off for the ten years until his death, at which time it was still incomplete. The novel *Ryoshū* (Travel Sadness) makes the ideological concerns of his previous novels even more clear, and it represents an open conflict between Oriental and Western ideas, dramatized through the persons of Japanese living in Paris and their responses to the society about them. It fails in the same way as the other novels, although there are some passages of real quality which underline how considerable a talent had gone to waste. Dealing with it would entail only a repetition of what has already been said. Although immediately after the war it was condemned for its "fascist ideas," that charge now looks so childish that it can be safely ignored, as can its position in the history of Japanese thought since it is such a marginal one. It is true that Yokomitsu supported the war effort, as almost all Japanese writers and intellectuals did, but since there seems nothing to be surprised at in that it requires little comment. Indeed the novel is perhaps more remarkable, considering that so much of it was written during the war years on such a sensitive subject, by the lack of any kind of spitefulness directed at his country's enemies. It thus seems an example of that honesty towards experience and moral decency which goes directly against the totalitarian ideologies which have dominated so much of our times. Presumably it was this honesty which prevented him from performing the sudden *volte-face* required at the end of the war, as so many others so readily did, and he was genuinely heartbroken by the defeat. The privations brought about by this period (apparently he thought that the Black Market was the name of an actual shop he was always unable to locate) made him ill, and his faith in old-fashioned Oriental health cures meant that by the time Kawabata persuaded him to see a real doctor it was already too late. He died on the thirtieth of December 1947, in his fiftieth year.

According to Nakayama who visited the house the morning after the death, Yokomitsu's face was contorted with pain, with his teeth clenched together. It was as if he were saying, "I don't want to die. If I die now like this I'll be dying like a dog."[33] Yokomitsu's last recorded words, however, are a complete contrast to these imagined ones: "I want to ride in an airplane."

Yokomitsu's literary reputation has fallen since his death, but he is still accorded a relatively important place in literary history. There are even indications of a movement towards revaluation of his work as a writer, although it seems unlikely that the esteem in which he was held in the 1930s will ever return. Also this revaluation, if it does occur, will almost certainly be aimed at the long novels, for the modernism of the Shinkankakuha has long since been placed by Japanese critics, and I would not be rash enough to argue that their judgments are wrong even if they do not accord with mine, which is that Yokomitsu's writings during the mid 1920s is the only modernism in Japanese prose of the period still readable and, consequently, of genuine literary importance.

Modernism in Japanese literature has established a tradition (*the* tradition, in fact,) in poetry, but has affected few prose writers, and when it has done so it has only been for a brief period of time. One sees this in the reappearance of the experimental novel in about 1960, in the early writings of Ōe Kenzaburō and Kurahashi Yumiko which show a desire to write a heavily foreign influenced, experimental prose, although this desire does not persist for long. The novels of Abe Kōbō have never been modernist in this sense, since they show no real assault upon language as such, being anti-rational structures written in what is essentially a rational form of prose. Thus the most accessible Japanese literary modernism remains these early writings of

Yokomitsu, for poetry is never properly available in translation, and postwar modernist prose has been too conscious of what has gone before to give other than a distorted image of what Japanese modernism had to be.

Yokomitsu is, of course, only one example of such modernism, and the reader will understand that Japanese modernism is much more than Yokomitsu's writings, and his writings are much more than the aspects which I have stressed. In chapter 3 I gave an account of what is only a lunatic fringe of modern Japanese poetry. I did so because I wished readers to have an account of the kind of disastrous effect an attempt at rapid Westernization could have upon that literature, so that they might then be able to evaluate the things that Yokomitsu was writing in this same period as highly as I believe they deserve. However, it would be unfortunate if readers were led to believe that modernism in Japanese poetry produced nothing more, for it did indeed see the first volumes of Miyoshi Tatsuji and Anzai Fuyue, and the lengthier achievement of Nishiwaki Junzaburō. Poetry of that quality could hardly be given the cavalier treatment meted out to the poets I dealt with. Also, modernism has now been assimilated into the Japanese poetic tradition, to the extent that the thesis I have put forward no longer fully applies to it. I have wanted to look at the question in as pure a form as possible, and the early writings of Yokomitsu allowed me to do so. They extended over a short period of time only, and were an experiment which was abandoned. It is thus easier to draw conclusions from them than from other Japanese modernist writings, for Japanese modernism has been altered and assimilated into forms other than those with which it began. With something as living, complex, and happily impure as literature, this very stress upon purity means that the whole truth will not be told, as it surely has not been told here.

However, if this study were to be other than a recital of the facts of literary history, plus a few guarded or over-cheerful value judgments, its aims needed to be limited in this way, and it will be as well to state them again here. In this work modernism is seen as providing the most extreme instance of Western influence upon Japanese literature, the purest form available in writing of what such influence has been, and allows conclusions to be drawn which could apply to areas other than those of literature alone. Earlier literary movements were more of a general assimilation of the West, but by the 1920s this assimilation had been completed (to the extent that such a thing could ever be complete), and for a brief period of time we had the almost contemporaneous taking in of something in Europe which extended over almost the same period of time. I have argued that such modernism in Japan had to fail, since the symbolist tradition from which European modernism got its life did not exist in Japan. One needs only to alter the terms of the argument to see this as a pattern existing in other areas of Japanese life in this century. I have not gone into such areas because I wanted to keep this literary study as pure as possible, and also because the general idea is so commonplace.

Everyone knows that one aspect of a culture can not be imposed upon another which does not share the same past, and yet there are few studies of this commonplace; so few one might even start to doubt its truth. My aim has not been to question this generalization, only to see what it could mean in a particular case, hoping it would be elucidatory and suggestive, not just a useless piece of dogma. My use of the word "abstraction" when writing of the nature of this influence was meant to be a way of holding together a number of facts and insights: no one in his right mind can believe a whole culture can be pinned down with a word, and the aim of this work with its limited objectives was to give life, to give real concrete existence, to a generalization of that kind. The generalization was to be considered as a microscope placed (and only occasionally placed, certainly not all the time) upon an object to allow it to come into focus, and implying that the same act of focussing might be applicable to other objects. It was not to be a wide-ranging telescope clapped firmly over one's blind eye. Also the goal of this work was not the generalization itself but the giving of reality to it; it was a question of trying to see how the particular methods of literary criticism could help an abstraction such as "influence" to take shape, "influence" being presumably the key word to what modern Japan is. Like most literary criticism, however, the principal aim was not so much to define the generalization as to unravel what it implied; not only to give life to the generalization but also to prevent it taking life away from what it purports to describe. What I most wanted, in fact, was that the generalizations we use when talking about foreign cultures should take on the shape of things which truly exist, in this case that of works which had been written and of the living man writing them. One reason for the existence of this work has been a belief in Yokomitsu's representative status, but I hope to have gone beyond that to show the writings, for all their defects, as of unique and true value, and the act of writing them as a genuine, even heroic one.

# Appendix:
# Yokomitsu Riichi
# 1898–1947

This book has given only an edited account of Yokomitsu and his writings, and so in order that the
reader may not be misled, a more inclusive, even if
considerably briefer, account of his life and literature as a whole is added here.

Yokomitsu Riichi was born on March 17, 1898,
at a small hot spring called Higashiyama in the Aizu
District of Fukushima Prefecture. This was not his
home, and it is arguable that Yokomitsu never had a
home, for homelessness and the constant search for
something which could be called one's own is a
dominant theme in his literature. His father was
thirty-one years old at the time, a civil works engi-
neering contractor engaged in the building of rail-
ways, whose life consisted of a series of moves to
places where there was work, including three long
periods in Korea, where he eventually died. He was
from the north of Kyushu, and, while engaged in
constructing one of the tunnels which were his spe-
ciality, he married the daughter of the house where
he was lodging, at Tsuge in Mie Prefecture. She was
four years his younger, of the Matsuo family, and it
has been claimed that she may be a direct descen-
dant of the great *haiku* poet, Matsuo Bashō, since

his family belonged to these parts (Ueno); but there is no conclusive evidence, so it must remain a supposition.

Yokomitsu's early life was spent in a sequence of different houses, either those of relatives or rented houses in Tokyo, Kure (near Hiroshima), and Ōtsu (east of Kyoto on the shores of Lake Biwa) where the family moved when the period of work was long enough to justify so doing. Since his father was not actually employed by the Public Works Department but received only a number of limited subcontracts from them, the family situation varied financially from being well-off to near poverty. Yokomitsu and his father seem to have remained virtual strangers (as one can see in an early story of his, "Chichi" [Father]), and after his death, his father came to represent a form of life which Yokomitsu felt obliged to combat, the enlightenment tradition stemming from the writings of Fukuzawa Yukichi.

He was a person who had accepted the teachings of Fukuzawa Yukichi in his youth and never went beyond that Europeanism. And so ignorant of Europe he had stayed true to what he had learned from Fukuzawa of beating the foreigners at their own game, and confidently believed that by working away digging tunnels through mountains that those very tunnels themselves would actually produce the required "culture." (*Ryoshū, Kawade Collected*, 8:295)

In her reminiscences of her brother, Yokomitsu's sister writes: "Father used to spend most of his time out. When he was at home he would be absorbed in *go* and would hardly talk to Riichi. Sometimes he would ask mother, How's the lad getting on?" (*Bungei Yokomitsu Riichi Tokuhon*, May 1955, p. 55).

Yokomitsu's relationship with his mother was much closer, but in stories concerned with the death of his father there is a strong, underlying sense of criticism of her, and the possessive love he felt for her (that possessiveness he was so skilled at describing in all human relationships) seems to have sprung from some sense of betrayal. It is not possible to say with any certainty why this should have been so, since there is no reliable evidence. Still, there is a short story (written in 1919) which seems very clear about this, although how much it can be considered as based upon any kind of biographical reality must remain a matter for conjecture only. What one can say is that there are other biographical writings of this period, and the form of writing is unlike that of those other stories, having an unevenness in both structure and style which suggests it may have been written under strain.

The story ("Hi" Fire) concerns a boy and his mother and the mother's involvements with the man next door and with the embroidery teacher (also a man), both of whom she sleeps with. The center of the story is the child's sense of desertion, which leads him to write on the village walls, "Last night Mr. Kane and mummy," and then not be able to write any more. His father is away in America (an interesting alteration of reality, Korea being a country for which the Japanese have a distate), and he is also so ill that the family is short of money. The story ends with the child being sent upstairs while the mother entertains the teacher who is to stay the night. The child falls asleep with the lantern lit, knocks it over, and would normally have been burnt to death, except that his mother senses that something is wrong, comes upstairs, and the fire is safely put out. Thus the story has a harmonious ending.

It is no doubt fictionalized reality, and the event from which the story takes its title may be purely imaginary, creating a harmony which did not exist in real life. However, the background and tone of the story, the realism of the description of the relationship of child and mother, make it seem to be an attempt to write close to actual experience. The story was not published during his mother's lifetime.

The sense of uncertainty with regard to his mother would have been increased by the periods he had to spend away from her. The beautiful recollections of him written by his sister make the solitude of his early life quite painfully clear.

My brother would have been nine-years-old, I think, in his third year at school, and father was away in Korea working on the construction of a railway line for the army, and mother had to leave home and go to the hospital in Yokkaichi for an operation on her stomach, and the two of us were left behind. Two of my mother's sisters looked after us, but we children were very lonely. We used to go to sleep in each other's arms in

one of the upstairs rooms in the empty house. Then there was an out-
break of trachoma at school, and we both caught it, on top of which my
brother caught mumps as well, and I can remember him with his face all
covered in bandages and holding his hand and taking him to the doctor's up on the hill. Aunt used to pass by at night on her way back from
the fish shop and make sure we'd got all the doors and windows closed
and were being careful not to start a fire. Then our relations had a family
meeting and decided that since I still had to go to the doctor's sometimes
I should stay behind, but my brother should go to the temple of another
aunt who had married a priest, and so uncle took him away there. I
remember uncle told me Riichi was like some stray kitten sitting there
silent and lost in a corner of the enormous room in which he left him,
and how I cried when I heard it. Every morning he had to get up early to
ring the temple bell and put the offerings ready in front of the Buddha
before going to school. (*Bungei Yokomitsu Riichi Tokuhon*, pp. 8:53–54)

Perhaps even more than the loneliness, what emerges most
clearly from the above is the dependence upon his sister, who
then married early, in 1911 when she was seventeen and Yokomitsu was only thirteen. His sister conditioned Yokomitsu's
sense of what a woman should be, but as a woman always not
available to him. In the stories about his childhood she is mentioned, but always as being away somewhere else, although it is
clear from what she has written that this is an alteration of reality. When she finally appears in stories about his student days
she is married. The remarkable purity of his image of what a
relationship between a man and a woman should be, and the
despair at finding that life was not like that, seems to have arisen
from this childhood dependence, for she was all he had to rely
upon emotionally. Nearly all that is deeply personal in his early
stories centers on her, and what is not personal is very much detached from what he describes, being written about with an almost inhuman objectivity. This frigid treatment of the outside
world has been noted by almost everybody who has written
about his literature, and to understand its cause one has only to
think of a small boy asleep in his sister's arms in a deserted
house, or being taken to the doctor's smothered in bandages.
This sister was to marry four years later. These are the experiences which decide a writer's fate.

This suggests a tragic, crippled figure, and yet Yokomitsu at school seemed to be nothing like that, but rather the opposite. He was the school's star baseball player, a member of the judo club, an adept at public speaking, but with little aptitude for literature; that did not appear until late in his school life. This cheerful image is then contradicted by his first year at the university. He went to Waseda University in Tokyo in April of 1916, then suddenly returned home in November of the same year for reasons already suggested in the main text, and did not return for almost a year and a half, in April 1918. Yokomitsu now had a home to return to, if only for a short period, at Yamashina to the east of Kyoto. His sister was within walking distance at Ōtsu just over the hills. It was during this period at home that he began to write in earnest.

Yokomitsu had lived in Tokyo for a time when he was very small, and has left some pleasantly rural reminiscences of it (*Kawade Collected*, 10:342–43); but returning was different.

I left Tokyo when I was six and didn't return until I was eighteen. At that time Tokyo was like a home town I had not seen, a place I was almost desperate to revisit. When finally I was able to visit this home town it was horribly changed from that which had held my thoughts for so long, a monotonously flat town with almost nothing of beauty.

This was in 1916 when he entered the preparatory course at Waseda University. When he returned in 1918 he became a first-year student in the English Department of the same university. Waseda seems to have been quite lacking in any kind of intellectual stimulation at the time, and he attended classes rarely, being now totally committed to writing.

There was one student who stood out. He wore a black cloak over Japanese dress. His hair was extraordinarily long, cut just above his shoulders. He was of an unpleasantly unhealthy pale complexion, with only his lips red. His nose was rather snub, his eyebrows of a profound upward slant, his eyes narrow, with a large mouth drawn in one straight line. You could see at a glance that he was "different" and yet even more conspicuous was his arrogant bearing, totally ignoring everything about him with an expressionless look on his face. He would come into the classroom, plump down on a chair all alone right in the middle of the room without bothering to remove his cloak, then, with one large movement of his head reminiscent of the lion dance in *Kabuki*, he would shake back his great mane of hair, glare all about him, then raise his right hand and start to scratch his head. Quite clearly he was aware that he was a different order of being, and quite consciously he was out to show other people that he knew it. That was Yokomitsu Riichi. (Muramatsu Shofū, *Kindai Sakkaden*, 2 vols., Tokyo, Sōgensha, 1:179–80)

The year 1918 marked the beginning of the Rice Riots, a sign that the period of economic well-being created in particular by World War I was coming to an end. It was from this year that his literary friendships with Nakayama Gishū and Kojima Tsutomu began. His love affair with the sister of the latter probably started in the next year, 1919, when he was twenty-one and she was only thirteen. The date is uncertain, but even the latest possible date makes her only fourteen when he was definitely in love with her, and a letter written in 1922 states that he had been in love with her for four years, which would put her age down to twelve. The writing of *The Price of Unhappiness* can be dated about this time, with 1920 perhaps a more likely date than 1919, for, as his letters indicate, the love affair was causing him acute misery in 1920.

Yokomitsu's apprentice writings were otherwise all short stories, as are most of the works of his early years (excluding the plays) until the writing of *Shanghai* at the age of thirty. The stories can be divided into two kinds; those which are a form of autobiographical writing, or which, at least, make use of material close to the author, and those of a cold, objective realism about village life. One example of the latter is called "Teki" (The Enemy), about the rivalry between two men who work at the same country railway station. Owing to the machinations of one, plus various pieces of bad luck, it takes the other many more years than his rival to qualify for promotion from one grade to the next. When at the age of forty-three he finally reaches the next grade and returns in triumph to his home station (one of his pieces of bad luck had been a transfer elsewhere) in order to show his new uniform to his rival, the man is understandably not impressed. All that rivalry is dead, in the past, forgotten about. However, the failure does have the satisfaction of seeing his rival put on *his* cap by mistake, but that is all the satisfaction there is for him. As he tastes this petty triumph he begins to wonder what he had been doing with his life and starts to weep.

Another story of a similar kind is "Nanboku" (North and South), about a long family feud (one branch in the north of the village and one in the south), and of the arrival of a distant relative who is shuttled back and forth, from one house to the other, for a variety of subtly described motives. Eventually the village council decide to build a hut for this wanderer, but almost as soon as he is installed there he dies. The coffin causes more family dissension, and the story ends, as it had begun, with a brawl, this time over a dead body. The descriptions always maintain the same sense of distance, and those of the dead body have a stylistic ornateness, a rendering of everything in cold images, which would be employed more fully later in *Nichirin* (The Sun in Heaven).

Both stories are real achievements, having something of that frigid perfection one finds in Joyce's *Dubliners,* and at the same time suggest that the writer will not be content to write that sort of thing for long. A fact of interest is that almost every story of this period (and not only of this period) is about people who are obsessed to the point where their behavior starts to lose meaning as it takes on the repetitive nature of the machine. The stories which use personal material do not differ much in this respect, as one can see in "Kanashimeru Kao" (A Face to Sorrow Over), written in 1917–18.

A twenty-year-old student is back from Tokyo staying in the country with his sister and brother-in-law. He is perpetually worried about his face. His sister teases him about letters she claims come every day (in fact they do not) from a particularly ugly girl who, like himself, has a face "like a ladle" (*shakushigao*). He goes to the public bath and notices a young girl there, but he lacks the courage to look straight at her. When he finally manages to do so she has been transformed into an old lady. He goes to the movies with his sister and the baby Mie. Mie behaves very badly and this embarrasses him. He notices a girl looking at him and wonders if this is love at first sight, and if it is the same girl he half saw in the bath. He imagines a variety of ways of getting

messages to her. Mie has now gone to sleep so they decide to
leave, or rather he suggests this to his sister, but she has now
become absorbed in the big, sentimental, unrequited love picture that has just started. People all over the cinema are weeping.
His sister, who has deposited the baby somewhere, is gazing in
rapt attention at the screen. He realizes that this is all wrong, but
he is also aware that if he looks directly at his sister (enthralled
by the perfect masculine profile on the screen) and beckons to her
with his face, his own face will be seen in the worst possible
light by the girl. There is the crash and tinkle of a bottle falling.
Mie bursts out crying. His sister tells him that a splinter of glass
has damaged the child's eye. He runs for the doctor; he runs for
his brother-in-law. He returns home and wonders if the child is
scarred for life. He goes to his room and looks at his own face in
the mirror. He decides to marry Mie but wonders if he can wait
twenty years. It would be best to scar his own face too. He attempts to slash it with a knife, but cannot. He weeps.

The comic descriptions in this story are remarkably assured
(the scene in the cinema, for example), and the humor is warm;
thus the desire for a tragic end seems almost weird, for the balance of the story is upset by this attempt to impose a meaning, a
moralistic meaning, upon material unable to bear the weight of
such an interpretation. The masterpiece of these early stories,
"Onmi" (translated as the title piece of *Love*), is about a similar
obsession of a student with his sister's baby over a period of two
to three years. In it Yokomitsu succeeds in making a meaningful
statement not only about the involvement of a man with a child
but about all the confusions in the emotional world that men
create for themselves. One imagines that this is because he used
this situation (as he had also used another) to transfer to the
stories the feelings which his relationship with Kimiko had
aroused within him. It can also be seen as a parable of the artist's
life as his aesthetic obsession is degraded by the real world about
him into a form of slavery. This theme is, much more openly,
that of another work of this period, "Warawareta Ko" (The Child
Who Was Laughed At, also translated in *Love*), about the son of a
farming family whose skill at carving masks results in his becom-

ing a clog maker. The story ends with the moronic hero realizing that the mask he had made was responsible for the life he now leads. He smashes the mask in two, and then, seeing how the two fragments would make a fine pair of clogs, returns to his former vacancy. This story was based upon one of Yokomitsu's uncles, but the sense of personal relevance seems to be strong here. The hero, as a child, had had a nightmare about the face in the lion dance, and the mask he makes of that face so impresses his father that he decides the boy can be a clog maker. Here the artist's attempt to create objects of a transcendental beauty which can contain and conquer one's deepest fears is seen as ending in a failure which turns those objects into the ones most degrading (in Japanese culture, the clog). Yokomitsu's symbolist concerns were clearly present even in his pre-modernist writings.

The period from 1922 to 1927 has already been dealt with in detail, and a few facts only need be repeated here. The year of the little magazine, *The Tower*, 1922, is also that of his father's death in August at the age of fifty-five. His literary debut came in 1923 with *The Sun in Heaven*, the year of the Great Kanto Earthquake in September. By this time Yokomitsu had established some kind of stable relationship with Kimiko, although one can not say when they actually married since the marriage was not officially recorded until after her death. Kimiko's brother, Tsutomu, objected to the match, as did Yokomitsu's mother. A letter as late as May 1924 says that Kimiko is living with him although her relatives have not come round. Since it was common at the time to leave official registration until the first son was born, or the first child was on the way, none of this suggests that they were "living in sin." Some form of ceremony would probably have been gone through, some time in 1924, the year which also saw fairly regular publication of his writings in magazines, his first volume, *Onmi*, in May, and another selection of his stories in August. *Bungei Jidai* was brought out in October 1924, but 1925–26 was occupied with his wife's illness. After her death in June there was a renewal of creative activity and his place in the literary world (which had been endangered by the Shinkankakuha controversy) became assured, as the publication of a three-volume *Works* in October indicates. Another volume of short stories, *Haru wa Basha ni Notte,* appeared in January of the next year, 1927, and that April saw his second marriage, a son being born in November.

April of the next year was the month of his trip to Shanghai; he was now thirty years old. In a letter to Kawabata Yasunari he wrote: "My cabin steward knows my name and treats me with deference, which does not please me, particularly as I had used a false name which was soon seen through. When I think how famous I've become it all seems rather ridiculous" (*Kawade Collected,* 12:310).

This year also saw the publication of a volume of his plays, and a fairly comprehensive Selected Works consisting of fifty-five stories in one volume. This was the great period for proletarian literature, and most writers were affected by leftist tendencies in some way, including Yokomitsu, although he continued writing an occasional article in support of "Formalism" against the Marxist variety. However, his letters indicate more truly than his literary polemics what he really felt:

> As far as the study of Man is concerned, then I believe myself to be a Marxist. Of course, this isn't what a Marxist would call Marxism since, as far as I'm concerned, the ideologies of Marxism and of literature are opposed to each other. This is what my basic attitude in my critical articles is.
>
> However, I shall stop writing things like that. The attraction for me of Marxism is gradually getting stronger and stronger. (*Kawade Collected,* 12:318)

This letter is postmarked May 13, 1929, during the period when he was writing his first long novel, *Shanghai.* It seems clear that the novel was written as a Shinkankakuha reply to proletarian literature, and the style (particularly as it first appeared in magazine serialization; later editions see it considerably revised) is the sharp, impressionistic one analyzed in the main text, and often of considerable brilliance. The novel's descriptions of the city of Shanghai, particularly of crowds in movement or in riot, have an energy which still makes the book very readable (there is an Italian translation by Fratelli Fabbri, Milan). But the relationships

between people remain unreal, probably because of the limitations of the style, which may be the main reason that the style
gradually changes as the novel progresses. One of the interesting
oddities of the book lies in the fact that the conservative and
traditional ideas it tries to put forward seem irrelevant to the still
revolutionary prose and nihilistic stance of its hero. The hero,
Sanki, who is dismissed from his job at a bank because he is
ironically insolent to the manager, gets another job in a factory
run by the brother of the married woman he is in love with; a
woman who never once shows up in the novel, her function presumably being to give the hero something to be desperate about.
Since Sanki is continually shown in nihilistic terms, it is surprising to hear him say (quite early in the novel):

"My life is my duty towards my parents. My body is my parents' body,
my parents'. What do I know about anything?" (*Selected,* p. 157)

Nothing in Sanki's behavior, however, reflects this belief,
since his acts are mainly, and deliberately, empty of positive
meaning. Presumably, if his behavior were to be consistent with
this belief, he would hold on to his job, or get a better one, make
good, and despatch considerable sums of money home. He does
nothing of the sort. Yet neither does his behavior lead him to
discard this belief, which remains a mindless positive held on to
in a life of equally mindless negatives. These three short sentences might well stand as the central meaning of the book, implying that nothing is real except what has been handed down to
one, and the questioning of such beliefs, which the hero's life
style implies, then becomes only a kind of sport. Sufficient stress
has already been given to the amount of playing at alienation in
the Japanese modernism of this period, and the political ideas
that could lead to are a major part of Japanese intellectual history
in the 1930s.

This mindless traditionalism, which nothing in Sanki's life
connects to and yet which it does not deny, can be seen in another incident fairly early in the novel. A girl attendant at the
Turkish bath has been thrown out of her job by the manageress
out of jealousy because Sanki shows some preference for her. She

goes to Sanki's flat and waits for him, but he does not return until the next morning. Instead his friend Kotani comes and, during the night, rapes her. Since Sanki is back by the time she wakes up, she cannot be sure which of them has done this thing. Sanki's attitude towards her is absolutely correct: if he touches her, he must marry her. His life style, however, not only ensures that she be raped by his friend, but also that she eventually becomes a prostitute for lack of anywhere to live or any means to do so. His "correctness," his "morality," is a form of self-indulgence, a way of being on moral speaking terms with himself. That this incident is yet another version of that dealt with in chapter 2 (the lower-class girl who waits for him and trusts him, the moral purity on his part, the rape by the friend, the arrival too late) is something that need not be argued.

One reason for this constant set of contradictions is that Yokomitsu was writing a novel which had a political object. Yet the political ideas reflected in the novel seem to be more a rejection of those of the proletarian writers, mainly to avoid their form of literature, rather than to show any interest in political ideas for their own sake. The novel deals with the disturbances in China in 1925 known as the May 30th Movement (the same described by Malraux in *Les Conquérants*, although Malraux chose the politically significant happenings in Canton), but Yokomitsu's main concern is with the disruption of the lives in the foreign (mainly Japanese) community. In an essay written in 1937 (*Kawade Collected*, 12:161–66), and so some years after the event, he explained that he was interested in writing about Shanghai because it represented the city of the future, with all cultural traditions gone and life lived on its simplest and most basic terms: money, politics, sex, and food. In such a situation concepts of morality would not apply; if a wife is beautiful, then she is good; if a man has money and muscles, then he has happiness in his hands. Art and philosophy become useless irrelevances; morality is a question of the cut of one's clothes, of one's manner of drinking or of borrowing money.

The novel gives one the impression that what it is really about is a sense of not being at home, and the strong feeling of personal identity that homelessness can give. Yokomitsu's interest in Asia and politics is of this kind, as something not to do with him that yet confirms what he is; a justification, indeed, of the nihilism of its hero, just as the reading of Valéry in 1929 seemed a confirmation of his own nihilism, although in this case the sense of emptiness extended to the act of writing itself. The stylistic transformation of the year 1930 is thus an extension of this and not at all as dramatic as has been claimed, although "The Machine" is so much a *tour de force* that it drew sudden attention to what had happened.

By mid 1931 ("Time" was published in April of that year) the creative energy he had devoted to this new style seems to have left him; his second novel for newspaper serialization appeared in July and August, and another novel was serialized in magazine form from April to December. This latter novel, *Hanabana* (Flowers) is an even slighter work than the *Garden of Sleep* (published in the previous year), describing the involvements of its hero with a maid whom he gets pregnant; and the relevance of its theme to earlier obsessions is obvious. Despite the skill with which the nihilistic hero is drawn and some interesting accounts of everyday life and scenes, the book is lacking in energy, presumably because it is so consciously aimed at the audience of the ladies' journal for which it was written. The newspaper novel, *Gaka* (Song of Songs), describes the love affairs of two couples and the great difficulties they have in achieving union. By the title, with its Biblical reference, Yokomitsu seems to have been thinking in terms of a "healthy relationship" between man and woman, although such a relationship is never actually achieved. It is a very slight work, but its labored attempts to describe psychological processes in detail could be seen as something new, and so of historical importance in the Japanese novel. However, the powerful resemblance of its main characters to those who had appeared in the three previous works suggest that the writer's creative energies were at a very low pitch. Still, this year and the next (1933) saw the publication of a number of fine short stories. "The Carriage" appeared in January of 1932 and "Yukige" (The Thaw) in 1933, "The Carriage" being the last successful attempt to maintain the convoluted style of "The Machine" (both translated in *Love*), and "The Thaw" being a very fine "I-novel" about the death of a girl he had known at school. This contrast suggests that essentially Yokomitsu had given up experimentalism, although one of the most ambitious of his long novels, *Monshō* (The Family Crest) appeared in the next year. A great many of his books were now being reprinted, and, with the destruction of the proletarian movement now fully accomplished, this being a great year for "conversions," Yokomitsu was the leading Japanese novelist.

The *Family Crest* is a serious attempt to write a long novel dealing with important themes for a wide public, and since it covers a wide area of Japanese intellectual life at that time it still has considerable interest. The two heroes, who represent contrasting ways of life, begin to take on clear cultural overtones as representatives of native and imported culture, a theme which was to become dominant in his final novel, *Ryoshū* (Travel Sadness). The main hero, Karigane, is the heir to a prominent family name, although financially the house has been reduced to something near poverty by the dynamics of the new Western-style economy. To restore these fortunes he engages in scientific research, a quest for new, practical discoveries. The research is stimulated by the spiral of rising prices in the capitalist economy, and shares something of the same mania, being of a slightly crazy kind, extracting soy sauce from potatoes or alcohol from banana skins. His "innocence" is betrayed by the corrupt commercial world in which he moves, and even when he finally succeeds in extracting soy sauce from fish, he is smeared as an imposter in a newspaper campaign engineered by his rival. The son of this rival is the other hero, a representative Westernized intellectual who has no idea what to do with himself. Their conflict is made concrete through the wife of the latter. The theme of the novel is that of the innocent, Don Quixotic hero who is betrayed by the world he is in and takes no revenge upon that world except by remaining indifferent to it and aloof from it. His research reduces him to near insanity (as in "The Machine," for he is an extension of the hero of that work), but his innocence remains, and, although he stays poor, he is dedicated to the road of discovery and more discovery.

A good case could be made for the importance of this novel, but it would be hard to make one for the next, *Tokei* (The Clock), which appeared in the same year, in the *Ladies Companion*. The main characters of *The Garden of Sleep* reappear under various disguises in a plot very like that of *Song of Songs*. The only real difference is in the amount of natural description, at which Yokomitsu was very accomplished, although it has little function in a novel which is only a set of repetitions aimed at its not very demanding audience. In 1934 his second son was born.

In 1935 he became a lecturer at Meiji University, *The Family Crest* was awarded a literary prize, and his essay on "The Pure Novel" was published. Three new novels, which could be seen as attempts to put the theory of his essay into practice, also appeared.

The first of these, *Seisō* (Gorgeous Attire) takes its title from the wedding garments the heroine will wear once she has made up her mind which of two men she will marry. The image of casting off disguises is also implied in the title, particularly in the relationships of the heroine with the people who surround her elegant, refined, and slightly devilish brother (the form into which the Westernized intellectual has here been transformed). There is also a character like Karigane in *The Family Crest*, and it may well be that the novel has too many themes to be other than light, slightly confusing reading. Another, *Tenshi* (Angel), is the one of the three not serialized, so it is not clear when it was written, but since it lays such heavy stress upon the "accidental" one may assume it was written in support of his "Theory of the Pure Novel" and thus at about the same time. It is remarkable for the number of good people who appear in it, presumably another concession on his part to popular mores, although, as seems inevitably the case in Yokomitsu's literature, their "goodness" results only in trouble for themselves and for others. The last of these three, *Kazoku Kaigi* (The Family Council) is, in contrast to the other two, one of the most interesting of his long novels, and still very readable today. The theme of the rivalry between the

stock exchanges in Osaka and in Tokyo is something quite new
in Japanese literature, and Yokomitsu (as seen in *Shanghai*) is
wonderfully skilled at describing the hysteria of people running
after money as a form of profession. As far as the question of
money and its values was concerned, Yokomitsu had Gide in
mind, although the deeper meaning of Gide's (not, admittedly,
very profound) novel seems to have escaped him. However, the
characters in Yokomitsu's novel are well described, and alive, so
that it seems doubly unfortunate that so much space is devoted
to dull romantic involvements in which it is difficult to believe he
had any real interest. When he gets back to what he is really concerned with, as when the hero finds all his shares falling on the
Tokyo market, he writes quite brilliantly.

Yokomitsu's traditionalism had now taken the form of a
growing interest in the literature of Saikaku and the practice of
writing *haiku*, which meant he was in a reactionary attitude towards the culture of contemporary Europe when he made his six-
month trip there in 1936, at the age of thirty-eight. He was now
at the peak of his literary career and an ignorant bystander, astonished at the hordes of people who had come to see Yokomitsu
off, was told that this was "Japan's top novelist." It was no overstatement. While he was away he wrote a journal, which was
published in monthly installments. It gives a very honest account
of what experience of a foreign country can be like, admittedly of
a negative, gloomy kind, but nonetheless true. However, the
principal fruit of this trip was his novel *Ryoshū* (Travel Sadness),
which occupied him on and off for the final ten years of his life,
and was incomplete at his death. The first installment, published
in 1937 and broken off apparently because of the beginnings of
open hostilities in China, is perhaps the best section, the description of the relationship between the hero and heroine during their stay in the Alps being one of the finest things in the
whole of his writing. Unfortunately, the ideology of the earlier
novels gradually becomes more oppressive, and the main characters turn into ciphers needed to express this not very brilliant
debate about the Westernization of Japan. It is clear from the one
portion of the manuscript still remaining, that of the 1937 news-

paper installment, that Yokomitsu (from the number of deletions) was having to push himself hard in the writing of these "ideological" sections, and it is unfortunate that he felt the need to do so.

After breaking off *Travel Sadness* in 1937 he wrote another novel, this time for the *Housewives' Companion* called *Haruzono* (Spring Garden), an almost fairy-tale story about an illegitimate daughter abandonned by her father, but educated by her teacher into a model young lady. Here Yokomitsu describes a very Westernized household (that of the father in a house surrounded by a large garden) in critical terms as an example of the corruption of the Japanese spirit. Fortunately, Yokomitsu had a complex mind, and the attitude the novel takes is similarly ambiguous, for the garden isolates people from the realities around it, and it is not clear just how bad, or even good, that may be. The young lady also redeems the household. This kind of happy ending is reminiscent of that at the end of the short story, "The Bird," a cheerful answer to an unanswerable question. There are also ambitious stylistic features in the work, including an attempt to work *haiku* into the prose, although not on the same scale as in *Travel Sadness*. In 1938 there came another novel about a similar heroine, *Mi imada Juku sezu* (The Fruit Is Yet Unripe). This time she is entangled with two young men, and the general tone of the narrative suggests that the readers of the young ladies' journal for which it was written must have been very young indeed.

In 1939 came another installment of *Travel Sadness,* and another section was added to *The Family Crest* in 1940. In 1941 his final long novel (if one sets aside the continuation of *Travel Sadness*) *Keien* (Chicken Farm), about two separated couples, has the same theme as the previous two, and contrives to be less interesting than they. The war years saw little production except the occasional pieces of *Travel Sadness,* and since so much of Yokomitsu's reputation rests upon this work perhaps some more should be said about it. The question at issue here is whether one of the two heroes will marry the heroine, who is a Christian and represents an intolerant foreign importation which the Japanese spirit, that is, the hero, is not certain that he can accept. The other hero is, again, the Westernized intellectual, and there is a great deal of talk between the two about cultural problems. The main failing of the novel is that these discussions never get properly linked to the romantic entanglements which are supposed to symbolize the debate. It is also noticeable that the Westernized hero is as dogged by worries about filial piety as his counterpart in *Shanghai*, an indication of how little Yokomitsu's ideas about things changed. His nationalism was not mere opportunism, but a true indication of his belief. The novel's main interest now is as a part of intellectual history, since it was widely read in the final years of the war and the early ones of defeat, but as a literary achievement it would be difficult to praise it.

In 1945 he sent his family to the home of his wife's parents in Tsuruoka on the Japan Sea coast, where he joined them in June. By that time even a smallish city in the provinces was being bombed, so Yokomitsu, his wife, and two sons moved into the real countryside, renting one small room in a farmer's house. There were no mats on the floor, just bare boards, and the place was jumping with fleas. They remained until the late autumn of the same year, and while there he wrote a journal, *Yoru no Kutsu* (Night Shoes), concerned with the unbroken and unchanging life of the farmers, something to be held onto in the confusion and destruction of the defeat. It is a very fine piece of work in which the apparently casual form of the journal is held together by a series of empty sounds which echo through it from the sound of clogs at the beginning to the whistle of the train as it drives through the early winter wind at the end. The tone of the work is one of elegy, as is that of the few writings he accomplished in his final two years.

The privations of his life in the country, and then back in Tokyo, made Yokomitsu as physically ill as he was spiritually hurt, and the coldness of the literary world chose him as a victim. Outwardly, however, he seemed cheerful enough, waiting for the time when he could make a literary comeback. In fact, his books were being reprinted, as many as fifteen in 1947. Then in early summer of 1946 he suddenly vomited blood, collapsed, and took to his bed, his body seemingly half paralyzed. He imagined it was some form of consumption brought on by his hard months in the country. The doctor told him it was a slight attack of cerebral anemia, a mistaken diagnosis as it turned out, but one which made no difference because Yokomitsu put all his trust in such homely cures as massage, moxa, and the "bee treatment," which consisted of being stung by bees until there was a rush of bleeding to the throat, and this ensured that the blood would not get to the head and so one would be cured. He wrote a poem about the heaps of little black corpses that he thought were giving him life.

By 1947 he was getting no better and was still having fainting fits. Remembering that both of his parents had died of cerebral anemia caused him anxiety and he spent many days brooding alone. In September Kawabata finally persuaded him to see a real doctor at Tokyo University. On learning that he did not have cerebral anemia he cheered up and started work again, this time on the short story "Bishō" (Smile).

This story tells of a young mathematician who has apparently invented a death ray which will end the war. The narrator (Yokomitsu himself) is enthralled by the unlikeliness of this, and when he meets the genius it is his brilliant smile which convinces him that the impossible may be true. The way the young man talks has the same effect, for, although all his tales seem close enough to lies to be called by that name, it is the same brilliant impossibility about them which makes the narrator wish to believe. Even when he hears from the Military Police that the young man is mad, he holds on to his belief which has, in effect, already been taken away from him. A dinner with the genius, where he describes a meeting with the Emperor and experiments with his death ray of a similar marvelous improbability, goes on against a background of news of defeat on all fronts. In their final meeting the narrator attends a celebratory meeting for the genius who has apparently been awarded his doctorate, although the narrator can no longer accept this. However, the meeting, one based upon an illusion, upon nothing, is a success, although as the narrator looks at the sleeping figure of the genius all he can see in him now is the fear of death. As an account of the meaning of Japan's involvement in an improbable war and of Yokomitsu's own intellectual development as he tried to come to terms with the deep emptiness he felt within him, it is of profound importance, and a story of such brilliance that it seems fitting that it should have been the last work he completed before he died. (There is a translation in *Love*.)

He was working on an essay of childhood reminiscences when on December 14, 1947, he had another fainting fit. After dinner the next day he complained of violent pains in his stomach and lost consciousness for a time. The doctor diagnosed a stomach ulcer. Yokomitsu was put to bed and visitors were forbidden. The illness worsened, a hole opened in the peritoneum, which turned into acute peritonitis and he died on December 30. The funeral took place on January 3, 1948, and the funeral oration, a very moving one, was given by Kawabata Yasunari.

# Notes

## Chapter One: Situation

1. Written in 1928. "Mazu nagasa o," *Kaizō Collected,* 22:146.

2. Gustave Flaubert, *Correspondance,* R. Dumesnil, J. Pommier, and C. Digeon, eds., 9 vols. (Paris: Conard, 1926), 8:517.

3. See Michel Raimond, *La Crise du roman* (Paris: Librairie José Corti, 1967), pp. 93–94.

4. Tayama Katai, *Tōkyō no Sanjūnen* (Tokyo: Kadokawa Bunko, 1955), p. 160.

5. Tayama, *Tōkyō no Sanjūnen,* p. 193.

6. Tayama, *Tōkyō no Sanjūnen,* p. 237.

7. Usui Yoshimi, *Taishō Bungakushi* (Tokyo: Chikuma Sōsho, 1963), p. 241.

8. Emile Zola, "Le Roman expérimental," in H. S. Gershman and K. B. Whitworth, eds., *Anthology of Critical Prefaces to the Nineteenth Century French Novel,* University of Missouri Studies 37 (Columbia, Mo.: University of Missouri Press, 1969), p. 172.

9. Angus Wilson, *Emile Zola* (2d ed.; London: Secker and Warburg, 1964), p. 39.

10. Pierre Martino, *Le Naturalisme français* (Paris: Armand Colin, 1969), p. 62.

11. Arima Tatsuo, *The Failure of Freedom* (Cambridge, Mass.: Harvard University Press, 1969), p. 71.

12. F. R. Leavis, *D. H. Lawrence, Novelist* (Harmondsworth: Penguin, 1964), p. 18.

13. "Kindai Bungei no Kenkyū: jo ni kaete, Jinseikanjō no Shizenshugi o Ronzu," in Nakamura Mitsuo, ed., *Bungaku no Shisō* (Tokyo: Chikuma Shobō, 1965), pp. 182–83, 185–86, and 186–87.

14. Richard Storry, *A History of Modern Japan* (Harmondsworth: Penguin, 1960), pp. 147–48.

15. *Nihon no Rekishi, 22, DaiNihon Teikoku no Shiren* (Tokyo: Chūōkōronsha, 1966), pp. 430–32.

16. All three quotations can be found in Usui Yoshimi, *Taishō Bungakushi* pp. 14, 12, and 52 respectively.

17. Nakano Yoshio, ed., *Gendai no Sakka* (Tokyo: Iwanami Shinsho, 1955), pp. 58–59.

18. Arima, *The Failure of Freedom*, p. 61.

19. *Fukuda Tsuneari Hyōronshū, Sakkaron* (Tokyo: Shinchōsha, 1966), 3:45.

20. See my English translation in *Japan Quarterly* (April-June 1975), 22:2.

21. Flaubert, *Correspondance*, 4:61–62.

22. See Hirano Ken, et al., eds., *Gendai Nihon Bungaku Ronsōshi* (3 vols.; Tokyo; Miraisha, 1956), 1:108–14, 132–34.

23. *Ibid.*, 1:139–60.

24. Both quotations in Usui Yoshimi, *Taishō Bungakushi*, pp. 202 and 203.

25. "Waga kokoro o kataru," in *Nihon Gendai Bungaku Zenshū 58* (Tokyo: Kōdansha, 1964), p. 198.

## Chapter Two: The Sun in Heaven

1. Letter to Louise Colet, Nov. 29, 1853. *Correspondance*, 3:389.

2. Letter to Satō Kazuhide, Sept. 7, 1920. *Kawade Collected*, 12:280.

3. See Jun Eto, "An Undercurrent in Modern Japanese Literature," *Journal of Asian Studies* (May 1964), 18:433–55.

4. Examples are "Love" and "The Child Who Was Laughed At," in *Love*, pp. 3–27.

5. Muramatsu Shofū, *Kindai Sakka Den* (2 vols.; Tokyo: Sōgensha, 1951), 1:183.

6. Nakayama Gishū, *Daijō no Tsuki* (Tokyo: Shinchōsha, 1963), pp. 10–13.

7. *Love*, pp. 31–68.

8. *Kanashimi no Daika*, in *Selected*, pp. 45–46.

9. *Selected*, pp. 45–46.

10. I.e., Kimiko. The name "Kimiko" does in fact appear in the story as the name of a friend of his country sweetheart. This attachment of the important name to an unimportant personage is a common device in dreams, and supports the contention that this is lived fantasy.

11. *Selected*, pp. 43–44.

12. *Selected*, pp. 508–09.

13. See Hoshō Masao, *Yokomitsu Riichi* (Tokyo: Meiji Shoin, 1966), pp. 75–76.

14. Ikuta Chōkō, trans., *Saramubō—Kindai Seiyō Bungaku Sōsho 2* (Tokyo: Hakubunkan, 1913).

15. *Selected* pp. 76–77.

16. Gustave Flaubert, *Salammbô* (Berlin: Internationale Bibliothek, 1922), p. 239.

17. Edmond and Jules de Goncourt, L. Ricatte, ed., *Journal, Mémoires de la vie littéraire* (4 vols.; Paris: Fasquelle/Flammarion, 1956), 1:912–13.

18. C. A. Sainte-Beuve, *Nouveaux Lundis iv.* (Paris: Calmann Lévy, 1897), pp. 31–95, especially pp. 86–89.

19. Georg Lukács, *The Historical Novel* (Harmondsworth: Penguin, 1969), pp. 218–29.

20. *Correspondance*, 2:345.

21. *Ibid.*, 1:225.

22. *Salammbô*, pp. 125–26.
23. *Salammbô*, p. 2.
24. *Selected*, p. 116. Note how the images in Yokomitsu stay apart from each other, like a *haiku*, and how those of Flaubert flow into each other as in a *symboliste* poem.
25. *Selected*, p. 93.
26. *Ibid*, p. 103.
27. *Salammbô*, p. 5.
28. *Ibid*, p. 119.
29. *Salammbô*, p. 274.
30. *Selected*, p. 110.
31. See Lukács, *The Historical Novel*, pp. 221–22.
32. English version in *Love*, pp. 31–68.
33. *Selected*, p. 9 and 336–37; *Love*, pp. 35–36; *Kaizō Collected*, 2:12–13.
34. *Kaizō Collected*, 2:66; *Love*, p. 68.
35. *Kaizō Collected*, 2:66; *Love*, p. 51.

## Chapter Three: Shinkankakuha—Background and Theory

1. Quoted in "Pour Dada," André Breton, *Les Pas perdus* (Paris: Gallimard, 1969), pp. 80–81.
2. "Deux Manifestes Dada," in Breton, pp. 64 and 66.
3. Written on the cover of the poetry magazine *Aka to Kuro* (Red and Black).
4. André Breton, *Manifestes du Surréalisme* (Paris: Gallimard, 1969), p. 78.
5. "Dynamo electric *(deinamō erekutorikku)*" in the original.
6. Given in French in the original.
7. See Kikuchi Yasuo, *Gendaishi no Taidōki* (Tokyo: Genbunsha, 1967), pp. 152–53.
8. See Onchi Terutake, *Gendai Nihonshi Shi* (Tokyo: Shōrinsha, 1958), p. 12.
9. Quoted in Onchi, p. 13; also in Kikuchi, pp. 187–88.
10. Quoted in Onchi, pp. 36–37.
11. *Jun Eto, Journal of Asian Studies*, 18:441.
12. Kikuchi, p. 210.
13. *Ibid.*, p. 229.
14. Quoted in *Les Pas perdus*, p. 74.
15. "Memoirs of Dadaism," by Tristan Tzara: Appendix II of Edmund Wilson, *Axel's Castle* (London: Fontana Library, 1961), pp. 239 and 242–43.
16. Onchi, pp. 298–99.
17. *Kōkakurui Kenchiku;* see Onchi, p. 297.
18. Taken from the editorial statement for the first number of *Aka to Kuro* (Red and Black); Onchi, pp. 276–77.
19. Onchi, p. 280.
20. *Gendai Nihon Bungaku Taikei 67* (Tokyo: Chikuma Shobō, 1973), pp. 167–68.
21. See *Raskolnikov*, in Kono and Fukuda, eds., *An Anthology of Modern Japanese Poetry* (Tokyo: Kenkyusha, 1962), pp. 16–17.
22. *Aru otoko to michi o arukinagara*, note 20, pp. 185–86.

23. "Zetsubō o ataeru mono" ("What Makes One Despair"), *Shinchō* (New Tide, the leading literary magazine of the day), July 1923.

24. "Atarashiki seikatsu to atarashiki bungaku" ("New Literature and a New Way of Life"), *Gendai Nihon Bungaku Kōza* (Tokyo: Sanseidō, 1962), p. 345.

25. *Gendai Nihon Bungaku Ronsōshi*, 1:197.

26. *Gendai Nihon Bungaku Ronsōshi*, 1:204.

27. *Ibid*, 1:198.

28. *Ibid*, 1:205–07.

29. Gaëtan Picon, *Panorama de la nouvelle littérature française* (Paris: Gallimard, 1949), p. 34.

30. *Situations II*, (Paris: Gallimard, 1948), pp. 226–27.

31. *Ouvert la nuit* (Paris: Gallimard, 1968), p. 8.

32. *Ibid*, pp. 30–31.

33. *Gendai Nihon Bungaku Ronsōshi*, 1:217.

34. *Ibid*, 1:218.

35. *Ouvert la nuit*, p. 271.

36. *Gendai Nihon Bungaku Ronsōshi*, 1:219.

37. *Ibid.*, 1:221.

38. Noma Hiroshi, *Bungakuron* (Tokyo: Gōdō Shuppan, 1967), p. 68.

39. *Gendai Nihon Bungaku Ronsōshi*, 1:238–39.

40. *Ibid.*, 1:242–43.

41. "New Sensation Theory." The original title was "Sensation Behavior: A Paradox for the Attacks upon Sensation Behavior and Sensationalist Creations."

42. Hoshō, *Yokomitsu Riichi*, p. 102.

43. "Kankaku to Shinkankaku." Available in *Bungaku no Shisō*, pp. 340–41.

44. *Ibid.*, p. 342.

45. *Ibid.*, pp. 345–46.

46. *Ibid.*, p. 344.

47. *Ibid.*, pp. 344–45.

48. August Strindberg, *Inferno*, trans. Sandbach (London: Hutchinson, 1962), p. 163.

49. Hirano Ken, *Gendai no Sakka* (Tokyo: Aoki Shoten, 1956), p. 46.

50. Written in 1941. *Kawade Collected*, 12:232–33.

51. Quoted in Sasaki Kiichi, "Shinkankakuha oyobi sore igo," *Iwanami Kōza Nihon Bungakushi* (Tokyo: Iwanami Shoten, 1959), 25:10.

## Chapter Four: Shinkankakuha—Practice

1. *Chūbō Nikki* (1936). *Kawade Collected*, 6:328.

2. *Correspondance*, 2:361.

3. Sasaki, *Iwanami Kōza Nihon Bungakushi*, p. 23.

4. *Ibid.*, p. 27.

5. *Ibid.*, p. 29.

6. *Naval Battle;* J. M. Ritchie, trans., *Vision and Aftermath: Four Expressionist War Plays* (London: 1969).

7. Sasaki, *Iwanami Kōza Nihon Bungakushi*, p. 3. Also Nakamura Mitsuo, *Fūzoku Shōsetsuron* (Tokyo: Shinchō Bunko, 1970), pp. 154–55.

8. See Noma Hiroshi, *Bungakuron* (Tokyo: Gōdō Shuppan, 1967), pp. 41–54 and 57–71.

9. Takami Jun, *Shōwa Bungaku Seisuishi* (Tokyo: Kōdansha, 1965), p. 20.

10. Sasaki, *Iwanami Kōza Nihon Bungakushi*, p. 15.

11. Odagiri Susumu, *Shōwa Bungaku no Seiritsu* (Tokyo: Keisō Shobō, 1965), p. 83.

12. All these points made in Odagiri, pp. 83 ff.

13. This story, like the other four mentioned, can be found in *Nihon Gendai Bungaku Zenshū 67, Shinkankakuha Bungakushū* (Tokyo: Kōdansha, 1968). This quotation is on p. 273.

14. *Nakagawa Yoichi Zenshū*, 12 vols. (Tokyo: Kadokawa Shoten, 1967), 1:31–49 and 155–67.

15. *Shinkankakuha Bungakushū*, pp. 21–25.

16. *Ibid.*, p. 314.

17. Odagiri, *Shōwa Bungaku no Seiritsu*, pp. 80–81, 104–6, 120–23.

18. *Ibid.*, pp. 106–7.

19. "Heads and Bellies" is about an express train stopped for no apparent reason at a small station. Everyone gets out except an idiot country boy who goes on singing his songs. The others all rush about protesting. They are then transferred to another train going in a very roundabout way to their destination. As that train leaves, the original express, with only the idiot left aboard, mysteriously sets off as before. The aim of the story seems to be that of showing human beings behaving in a way similar to machines.

20. *Tabi:* she is wearing Japanese dress.

21. The woman is talking. This is unmistakable in the original, but perhaps not so in this translation.

22. *Kawade Collected*, 2:145. One page of a fourteen-page story.

23. These are headlines he had previously read in the newspaper.

24. *Kawade Collected*, 2:151–52.

25. *Kawade Collected*, 2:158–59.

26. See John Bester's translation, *Time and Others* (Tokyo: Hara Shobō, 1965), pp. 70–102.

27. *Kawade Collected*, 2:236.

28. Here is a passage describing two crows: " 'Look!' she said laughing. Joseph and Mary were fighting. Anyhow they all went up again, and the air was shoved aside by their black wings and cut into exquisite scimitar shapes. The movement of the wings beating out, out, out—she could never describe it accurately enough to please herself—was one of the loveliest of all to her. Look at that she said to Rose, hoping that Rose would see it more clearly than she would. For one's children so often gave one's own perceptions a little thrust forward." Virginia Woolf, *To the Lighthouse* (London: Hogarth Press, 1930), p. 126.

29. *Daijō no Tsuki*, p. 38.

30. *Kawade Collected*, 12:108–09.

31. *Kawade Collected*, 2:237–38.

32. "Ryokōki" (Travelogue), *Bungei Jidai*, November 1924; "Aoi Ishi o hirotte kara" (After Picking Up a Blue Stone), *Kuroshio*, January 1925; "Aoii Taii" (The

Pale Captain), *Kuroshio,* January 1927 (the official date, but evidence shows it was written, and published, during 1925).

33. "Machi no Soko" (The Depths of the Town), *Bungei Jidai,* August 1925.

34. A kind of carrot which means Korea to the Japanese in the way that spaghetti or garlic would mean Italy to the British.

35. *Kaizō Collected,* 22:35–37.

36. *Daijō no Tsuki,* p. 26.

37. *Love,* pp. 71–114.

38. *Kaizō Collected,* 4:217; *Love,* p. 99.

39. *Kawade Collected,* 2:199–200; *Love,* p. 71.

40. *Kawade Collected,* 2:201–2; *Love,* pp. 73–74.

41. *Kaizō Collected,* 4:219; *Love,* p. 99.

42. *Kaizō Collected,* 4:217–18; *Love,* p. 99.

43. *Kawade Collected,* 2:244–47; *Love,* pp. 111–14.

44. Japanese armor is made of slatted pieces of brown wood, thus the image may certainly be *recherché* but, at least visually, it is not impossible.

45. "Naimen to Gaimen ni tsuite" ("On the Internal and External"), *Bungei Jidai,* January 1926.

46. *Love,* pp. 23–27.

47. *Kaizō Collected,* 22:84–85.


## Chapter Five: The Death of a Wife

1. Stéphane Mallarmé, *Pour un Tombeau d'Anatole,* J. Richard, ed. (Paris: Editions du Seuil, 1961), p. 177.

2. Nakamura Shizuko, "Otōto Yokomitsu Riichi," recollections of him by his sister in *Yokomitsu Riichi Tokuhon, Bungei* (Tokyo: 1955), p. 55.

3. *Daijō no Tsuki,* pp. 48–50.

4. *Ibid.,* pp. 58–60.

5. *Kawade Collected,* 2:233–35, which misdates this as April.

6. *Kawade Collected,* 12:296.

7. *Kaizō Collected,* 22:77–78 and 2:329–35.

8. "Mujō no Kaze," *Kaizō Collected,* 22:73–76.

9. *Kawade Collected,* 12:308–09.

10. *Bungei Yokomitsu Riichi Tokuhon,* p. 64.

11. The same point is made by Hinuma Rintarō, *Bungakkai,* 17:132–33.

12. *Bungei Yokomitsu Riichi Tokuhon,* p. 64.

13. *Nihon Bungaku Zenshū 33,* Takii Kōsaku, Ozaki Kazuo, Kambayashi Akatsuki (Tokyo: Shinchōsha, 1963), pp. 387–415.

14. *Selected,* p. 130; *Love,* p. 117.

15. *Nihon Bungaku Zenshū 33,* pp. 395–96.

16. *Selected,* p. 131; *Love,* pp. 118–19.

17. Odagiri Susumu, *Shōwa Bungaku no Seiritsu* (Tokyo: Keisō Shobō, 1965), p. 125.

18. *Selected,* pp. 131–32; *Love,* p. 119.

19. *Selected,* pp. 134–35; *Love,* pp. 123 ff.

20. *Selected,* pp. 138 ff.; *Love,* pp. 126 ff.

21. *Selected*, pp. 141–55; *Love*, pp. 133–49.
22. *Selected*, p. 141; *Love*, p. 133.
23. *Selected*, pp. 148–49; *Love*, p. 142.
24. *Selected*, p. 150; *Love*, p. 144.
25. *Selected*, p. 151; *Love*, p. 145.
26. *Selected*, pp. 154–55; *Love*, pp. 148–49.
27. Yura Kimiyoshi, "Kyokō to Yōshiki Gengo—Yokomitsu Riichi no Baai" (Fiction and Formal Language: The Case of Yokomitsu Riichi), *Bungaku*, 39:385–407, 674–91.
28. *Ibid.*, p. 392.
29. Yura, p. 691, notes a thematic resemblance to Keats's "Ode on a Grecian Urn." This is a valid remark, although it also underlines how very different the organization of the two works is, and thus how they make their meanings in different ways.
30. Stéphane Mallarmé, *The Penguin Poets—Mallarmé*, A. Hartley, ed. (Harmondsworth: Penguin, 1965), p. 92. The translation given here is mine.
31. See epigraph and n. 1 at the beginning of this chapter.
32. *Ibid.*, p. 31.
33. *Ibid.*, pp. 31–32.
34. *Ibid.*, pp. 179, 185, 245, 247–48, 288–89, 290.
35. On these points see an essay by Kuwabara Takeo, "Yokomitsu Riichi Shi no Aki no Hi," *Kuwabara Takeo Zenshū*, 7 vols. (Tokyo, 1968), 3:101–7.
36. See Nakano Yoshio, ed., *Gendai no Sakka* (Tokyo: Iwanami Shinsho, 1955), *passim*.

## Chapter Six: Defeat

1. *Correspondance*, 1:262.
2. *Yoru no Kutsu, Kaizō Collected*, 20:3.
3. A widely-quoted recollection made after the Pacific War. See Hirano, *Shōwa Bungakushi*, p. 87; Odagiri, *Shōwa Bungaku no Seiritsu*, pp. 249 ff.
4. Hoshō, *Yokomitsu Riichi*, p. 111.
5. Hinuma Rintarō, *Bungakkai*, 17:131.
6. *Kikai* is available as "The Machine" in *Love*, pp. 153–80, and in Edward Seidensticker's translation, "Machine" in Ivan Morris, ed., *Modern Japanese Stories* (Rutland, Vt., and Tokyo: Tuttle, 1962). A translation of *Jikan*, "Time" is available in Donald Keene's anthology, *Modern Japanese Literature* (New York: Grove, 1956).
7. *Love*, pp. 183–225.
8. Kobayashi Hideo, *Sakka no Kao* (Tokyo: Kadokawa Bunko, 1969), pp. 153–64. An essay on this most distinguished of Japanese critics by Edward Seidensticker appears in Donald H. Shively, ed., *Tradition and Modernization in Japanese Cutlure* (Princeton: Princeton University Press, 1971), pp. 419–61.
9. A letter postmarked Sept. 11, 1929; *Kawade Collected*, 12:314 f.
10. *Ibid.*, 12:316.
11. *Kawade Collected*, 12:316 f.
12. *Ibid.*, 12:318–19.

13. *Kawade Collected*, 12:321. Yokomitsu himself was from Kansai, and spoke with the local accent, which when spoken by a man, is usually considered slightly moronic by people from Tokyo.

14. *Ibid.*, 12:322.

15. English translation in Paul Valéry, *Collected Works*, Vol. 8, *Leonardo Poe Mallarmé* (London: 1972), pp. 95–96.

16. Paul Valéry, *Morceaux Choisis* (Paris: 1953), pp. 72–73.

17. A Selected Works, editions of *Kikai, Shanghai, Shin-en, Gaka,* and a collection of essays, thus six books in all, published within the space of one year.

18. *Selected*, p. 428.

19. "Genjitsu Kaiwai" ("The Vicinity of the Real"), 1932, *Kawade Collected*, 12:19.

20. *Ibid.*, 12:20.

21. *Selected*, p. 452.

22. *Kawade Collected*, 12:80–81.

23. *Kawade Collected*, 12:91–102.

24. "Mijime na konran." *Gendai Nihon Bungaku Ronsōshi*, 3:301.

25. *Kawade Collected*, 12:101.

26. Kobayashi, Hideo, *Samazama naru Ishō, X e no Tegami* (Tokyo: Kadokawa Bunko, 1968), pp. 67–98, 83–89.

27. *Ibid.*, pp. 89–91.

28. 'Gūzen to wa hitsuzen de ari," "Kataoka no sakuhin wa ketsuron no chokusen de aru."

29. André Gide, *Les Faux Monnayeurs* (Paris: Gallimard, 1967), pp. 230–32.

30. *Ibid.*, pp. 232, 93, and 97–105.

31. *Kawade Collected*, 12:159. Iwakami Jun'ichi, *Yokomitsu Riichi* (Tokyo: Tōkyō Raifusha 1956), assumes that Yokomitsu is using the word in this meaning, and he makes no mention of Gide (p. 135).

32. Kobayashi, pp. 95–96.

33. *Daijō no Tsuki*, p. 272.

# Bibliographical Note

The fullest bibliography of writings in Japanese on Yokomitsu can be found in Inoue Ken, *Yokomitsu Riichi: Kindai Bungaku Shiryō* 7, Tokyo: Ōfūsha, 1974, brought up to date in a Selected Bibliography in the same writer's edited, *Yokomitsu Riichi: Sōsho, Gendai Sakka no Sekai 1*, Bunsendō Shuppan, July 1978. Inoue's *Hyōden: Yokomitsu Riichi*, Ōfūsha, 1975, is the definitive biography.

Critical works I have found useful are: Shinoda Hajime, *Dentō to Bungaku*, Tokyo: Chikuma Shobō, 1964, and *Nihon no Kindai Shōsetsu*, Tokyo: Shūeisha, 1973, both of which have long sections on Yokomitsu. Also three articles by Hinuma Rintarō, "Yokomitsu Riichi Ron" in *Bungakkai*, 17(11): 132–41, 17(12): 124–33, and 18(1): 213–21. Most Japanese critics have articles on Yokomitsu, but few are worth reading, although Hirano Ken's essay in his *Gendai no Sakka*, Tokyo: Aoki Shoten, 1956, and Nakamura Mitsuo in *Fūzoku Shōsetsu Ron* have interesting things in them. Hoshō Masao, *Yokomitsu Riichi*, Tokyo: Meiji Shoin, 1966; Kikuchi Yasuo, *Gendaishi no Taidōki*, Tokyo: Genbunsha, 1967; Nakayama Gishū, *Daijō no Tsuki*, Tokyo: Shinchōsha, 1963; and Odagiri Susumu, *Shōwa Bungaku no Seiritsu*, Tokyo: Keisō Shobō, 1965, provide much useful information in an intelligent fashion.

A selected list of the few translations available in English can be found in my *"Love" and Other Stories*, which also suggests a few works for background reading. I also give the titles of some of my articles which supplement this work, but which have appeared so obscurely I fear the reader will find them difficult to come by.

"Looking at a Foreign Country: Yokomitsu and Malraux," in *Studies on Japanese Culture*, Tokyo: Japan P.E.N. Club, 1973.

"The Shinkankakuha: A Japanese Literary Movement of the 1920's," in *Transactions of the International Conference of Orientalists in Japan*, Tokyo: Tōhō Gakkai, 1971.

"Flaubert and Yokomitsu: Does Stylistic Influence Take Place?" in the same journal for 1972.

"Portrait of a Thought Criminal: Yokomitsu Riichi and *'Ryoshū'*," in *Journal (Kiyō)*, Literary Department, Japan Women's University, 1974.

A new, definitive *Collected Works* in 16 volumes will begin publication in the spring of 1980 from Kawade Shobō Shinsha.

# Index

## Modern Asian Literature Series

## Neo-Confucian Studies

# Translations From the Oriental Classics

## Studies in Oriental Culture

## Companions to Asian Studies

*Approaches to Asian Civilizations,* ed. Wm. Theodore de
  Bary and Ainslie T. Embree                                    1964
*The Classic Chinese Novel: A Critical Introduction,* by C. T.
  Hsia. Also in paperback ed.                                   1968
*Chinese Lyricism: Shih Poetry from the Second to the Twelfth
  Century,* tr. Burton Watson. Also in paperback ed.           1971
*A Syllabus of Indian Civilization,* by Leonard A. Gordon
  and Barbara Stoler Miller                                     1971
*Twentieth-Century Chinese Stories,* ed. C. T. Hsia and Jo-
  seph S. M. Lau. Also in paperback ed.                        1971
*A Syllabus of Chinese Civilization,* by J. Mason Gentzler, 2d
  ed.                                                           1972
*A Syllabus of Japanese Civilization,* by H. Paul Varley, 2d
  ed.                                                           1972
*An Introduction to Chinese Civilization,* ed. John Meskill,
  with the assistance of J. Mason Gentzler                      1973
*An Introduction to Japanese Civilization,* ed. Arthur E. Tie-
  demann                                                        1974
*A Guide to Oriental Classics,* ed. Wm. Theodore de Bary
  and Ainslie T. Embree, 2d ed. Also in paperback ed.          1975

# Introduction to Oriental Civilizations
Wm. Theodore de Bary, Editor

| | | | | |
|---|---|---|---|---|
| *Sources of Japanese Tradition* | 1958 | Paperback ed., 2 vols. | 1964 |
| *Sources of Indian Tradition* | 1958 | Paperback ed., 2 vols. | 1964 |
| *Sources of Chinese Tradition* | 1960 | Paperback ed., 2 vols. | 1964 |